The Analytic Patient and the Developing Child

The Analytic Patient and the Developing Child

The Selected Papers of Manuel Furer

Edited by Herbert M. Wyman, MD

IPBOOKS.net
Infinite Possibilities

International Psychoanalytic Books (IPBooks)
New York • http://www.IPBooks.net

The Analytic Patient and the Developing Child: The Selected Papers of Manuel Furer

Published by IPBooks, Queens, NY
Online at: www.IPBooks.net

ISBN 978-1-956864-31-1

This volume of her husband's papers is dedicated to

Vivian Furer 1927–2021

Who edited, transcribed and organized
Every single one of them.

IN MEMORIAM

Andrew Furer 1961–2010

Rachel Furer 1955–2020

Acknowledgments

The Editor wishes to thank Jessica Furer for her
Indispensable support and tireless work in the
Preparation of this volume.

Also helpful have been Nellie Thompson, Archivist
And Sharon Weller, Administrative Director, both of
The New York Psychoanalytic Society and Institute

Contents

Editor's Introduction

"There is an aspect of psychoanalytic thinking...that should now be made explicit: The era of the domination of American ego psychology, which found its culmination in the ideas of Heinz Hartmann, is over" (Furer 1999).

With these words Dr Manuel Furer marked the transition of psychoanalysis from the field into which he entered as a candidate in the 1950's to the field in which he had emerged as an important leader throughout the subsequent half century.

The transition is ongoing and has not been easy. The first two sections of this volume depict Furer's efforts realistically to integrate this transition, to separate out new ideas from old, to criticize some new theories and to support others, all the while striving to preserve what he held to be the fundamental clinical techniques of psychoanalysis.

The first part of this volume "Psychoanalytic Technique in the World of Pluralism" contains papers devoted to the discussion of various theoreticians and their influence toward the progression or retrogression of the field. The second part of this volume "Psychoanalytic Training" extends this discussion into the field of education, and conveys Furer's dedication as a teacher, supervisor, and administrator.

Readers may well recognize Manuel Furer more readily from the third part of this volume "Psychoanalysis and the Developing Child" Here will be found his most important contributions toward the study of the emotional disorders of early childhood, and also his work on Separation/Individuation with Margaret Mahler. As was well known to every child who met him, and every adult who worked with him, Manny Furer had special gifts of warmth and empathy. His signature concept of "emotional refueling" conveys these gifts.

The introductions to the Freud lectures and to the Furer Symposium offer biographical portraits of one of our generation's most multitalented psychoanalysts.

Herbert M Wyman, MD
August 2021

Part One: Psychoanalytic Technique in a World of Pluralism

CHAPTER 1

Introduction to Manuel Furer's Freud Lecture (April 1, 1995)

by Martin Stein

I am very pleased to be given the opportunity to introduce a dear friend and admired colleague, Dr. Manuel Furer. I have known him since 1954, when I was a youngish teacher and he was one of the most gifted in an exceptional group of candidates at the New York Psychoanalytic Institute. He was recognized then as a person of promise as a scholar and clinician. That hope has been splendidly fulfilled, which is why he is giving the Freud Memorial Lecture this evening.

It is customary in these introductions to describe at length the career and scholarly accomplishments of the speaker, and I shall do so. But I assume you are interested less in what Manny has done in the past than what he has to say in the present. shall therefore condense the substance of a distinguished career as well as I can, and add a few observations based on a long and close personal and collegial friendship.

A precocious youth, he received his BA from Cornell at the age of 19, and his MD from the same University four years later. He conducted and published the results of research in the psychophysiology of pain perception, then received clinical training in internal medicine and pediatrics, all of which contributed to the broad and perceptive view that has characterized his approach to psychiatry and psychoanalysis.

His interest in psychoanalysis was evident in medical school, and in 1948 he began his personal analysis. After a spell as a psychiatrist in a Naval Hospital, he worked at Hillside Hospital (in the good old days), as resident in child psychiatry with Dr. Loretta Bender, becoming her junior in 1954. That same year he entered The New York Psychoanalytic Institute, as a candidate, graduating four years later (which not everyone did). He completed his training in child analysis in 1962. So much for his formal training.

The following year, he joined Dr. Margaret Mahler as coprincipal investigator on the NIMH project on symbiotic child psychosis, a study that resulted in a vast increase in interest and understanding of a poorly understood field of psychopathology, and more important perhaps, cast a new light on the vicissitudes of normal child development. For six years he was director of a treatment program for preschool psychotic children at the Master's Children's Center. This experience led to a group of eight papers, some with Dr. Mahler, on the subjects of child psychosis, others on normal development and the separation-individuation phase. These publications, well balanced in their approach, have had a profound influence on modern thinking in the field of child psychiatry. This work was followed by a series of important publications on the superego concept and moral values, on construction and reconstruction in clinical work, and in 1977 by a paper on Kleinian theory that was the outcome of two debates with Hannah Siegal. Here, as elsewhere, we become aware of an enviable combination of sympathetic understanding and incisive critical analysis.

Since then, he has participated in many panels under the aegis of the American Psychoanalytic Association, and discussed many papers at both the American and the New York Institute, dealing with every aspect of the field including child analysis, clinical technique and theory. One of the latest was a contribution to a symposium on the clinical value of conflict and compromise formation recently published in the *Journal of Clinical Psychoanalysis* (Nov. 1994).

In the late sixties and early seventies, I had the privilege of working with Manny on a study of training analysis sponsored by the American Psychoanalytic Association. His friendly, understanding manner, that accompanied, but did not conceal his intelligent curiosity, contributed a great deal to the frankness and depth of our discussions with groups of training analysts and recent graduates—His insights were also of the greatest value, as our Study Group evaluated the content of our meetings, that we later related to COPE and to the Board on Professional Standards-The observations he made in the course of this research became the impetus for his Brill Lecture in 1985, which he examined the questions of how much and what analysts recall of their own experiences in training analysis. He pointed out that they, that is, we, tend to forget a good deal and distort even more, just like ordinary citizens, I am amused to add that Manny himself has forgotten the title of his own Brill Lecture! Make of that what you will, Manny became a Training and Supervising Analyst In 1967, and has been active in both capacities ever since. As an active and successful teacher from the early sixties to the present, he has taught everything from Phobias to Advanced Technique, a course he is currently giving. Understandably, he is in demand as a consultant as well as a clinical analyst and supervisor.

But Manny's contributions have not been confined to analyzing, writing and teaching. Having served at various times with distinction as chairman of the Curriculum Committee, the Admissions Committee and the Faculty, he has done something very few others have done. He served as Chairman of the Educational Committee, not only once, but again, occupying this post at the present time. It is a job that demands

3

an enormous devotion to one's organization and to colleagues and to students. It bespeaks not only a high degree of administrative skill, but also energy and tact as well as the quality of survivorship, whatever that consists of. Here and as Fellow of the BoPS of APsaA, he has fought hard, for the maintenance of high standards in the profession at a time when powerful forces have been mustered to compromise them. He has done so with effectiveness and a lack of rancor, an ability that sets him apart from most of us who have been involved in that issue.

He has made his contribution in still another context; for thirty-two years he has been an active and valued member of Group Two of the Center for Advanced Psychoanalytic Studies, an organization that brings together analysts from all over the country to meet twice a year in Princeton for the purpose of sharing clinical experiences and theoretical challenges

So much for his professional accomplishments, a recital that may make him sound like a very serious, intelligent, but not very interesting fellow, the stereotypical "good analyst." He is much more than that, and his interests and activities are much wider. For one thing, under his benign and amiable exterior, there lives a wide-ranging and a rebellious spirit, that informs, but does not impair his professional interests. He knows a great deal about politics, with a scholarly interest in revolutionary movements. He counts among his friends many people in the academic community; and if you know Manny well, you will detect more than a trace of the university professor, acute but with an endearing and quite misleading hint of absent-mindedness.

He has the capacity of being able to get along with most people, including some notoriously difficult ones. This has made it possible for him to function very successfully in the field of psychoanalytic institutional life, which is not altogether free of internal conflict surprising as that may seem. As Chairman of the Educational

Committee, and Fellow of the Board on Professional Standards of the American, he demonstrated an unerring sense of how matters stood at any time, and was quick to step in and propose solutions that made sense, even if they didn't satisfy everyone. Manny always accepted the dictum that politics is the art of the possible, at the same time, never giving up his devotion to maintaining the best possible psychoanalytic education. His sureness of action, combined with a lack of arrogance and dogmatism account for much of his success in getting his ideas across.

A very careful professional man, proper in behavior and speech, withal a bit impish in manner, there is a side to him that only his friends and family may be aware of. An enthusiastic and skillful sailor and swimmer, he has also taken up the sport of wind-surfing, liking nothing better than making his way out into open water, accompanied by the anxiety of his wife and whoever else may be around on shore, wondering whether he'll ever make it. back. I haven't recently had the pleasure of driving with him, but I suspect it might be thrilling.

I should add something critical, just to balance things and avoid hagiography. it's hard to think of some grievous faults. He does have an almost illegible handwriting, but I'm hardly in a position to make that point. He's not always prompt in getting out written replies or answering telephone calls but I can't say that he's much worse than most of his colleagues whose compulsiveness takes other forms; I should add that he's modest, but not to a fault, and he doesn't boast about it.

His lecture tonight is entitled "Changes in Psychoanalytic Technique: Retrogressive or Progressive." I leave it to him to tell you about it.

CHAPTER 2

Changes in Psychoanalytic Technique, Progressive or Retrogressive

(1998). *Journal of Clinical Psychoanalysis,* 7(2):209–235

In this paper I will consider psychoanalytic technique in new and old dress, and a remarkable congruence in the technical writings of Sandor Ferenczi with those present-day revisionists of what we call standard technique. The title of the paper, "Changes in Psychoanalytic Technique, Progressive or Retrogressive," is adapted from a paper by Ferenczi delivered in 1929 as "Progress in Technique" and published in 1930 as "The Principle of Relaxation and Neocatharsis" (Ferenczi, 1930). Perhaps, Ferenczi said, the term *progress* is a misnomer; perhaps the tide should be "retrogressive or reactionary." But, as he said, backward can be forward. Ferenczi advocated a return to Freud's early theory when the pathogenesis of neurosis was thought to be the traumatic impact on the child of seduction by the adult, and the remedy was recovery of memory, catharsis, and the use of the personality of the analyst to influence the patient. On this position, "unjustly neglected" (Ferenczi, 1933, p. 156), Ferenczi constructed an alteration of the early technique with emphasis, enhancement, and expansion of the role of the analyst that would bring about not only a reliving of the trauma but in addition, a corrective experience, and thus a "neocatharsis" that would heal in a way that other techniques had failed to do.

Ferenczi's new technique of 1930 was also a significant alteration of what was at that time already very close to the standard technique of today. The role of transference had by 1930 almost reached its current preeminence (Strachey, 1934), and a greater understanding of transference and countertransference was available. Ferenczi added to the trauma of sexual seduction, the powerful, malevolent force of the hypocrisy of the parent as the major pathogenic agent and of the hypocrisy of the analyst as the obstacle to cure.

I am indicating, as is evident in my tide, that the current technical changes as recommended and practiced, are retrogressive in the sense of returning to an earlier tradition, namely Ferenczi's technical procedures of the early 1930s, excluding the more radical experiments of the dying Ferenczi disclosed in the *Clinical Diary* (Ferenczi, 1988).

In tracing the influence of ideas one can point to a direct connection between Ferenczi and the school of Sullivanian psychiatry in that many of his pupils and analysands gravitated to this interpersonal theory and method, and several became influential teachers. In the writing of the adherents of this school then and now, what is considered pathogenic is the continuation of maladaptive solutions to the child's conflict with the external world of caretakers, without, however, a focus on sexuality. In this school, as with Ferenczi, cure lies in the interaction between patient and analyst; the behavior of the analyst is paramount. For many decades the beliefs and practices of the Sullivanian school seemed to remain encapsulated, that is, not integrated into conflict theory.

There does not seem to be the same acknowledged intellectual heritage by other schools of revisionist thought, but there is a sense of a shared culture. However, in the spectrum of Freudian analysts, that is, those for whom intrapsychic conflict remains basic for pathogenesis, the source for this retrogressive movement is even less clear. There now seems to be a spillage or seepage from the one school to the other (Mitchell, 1993; Greenberg, 1995). However, like Ferenczi, all share the belief that in the here-and-now of the analytic experience, all psychic manifestations of the analyst in interaction with the patient have the major part in determining the content of the psychoanalytic process. This interaction is not only considered a more accurate observation of what happens, but like Ferenczi, a coming together of technique and a theory of cure.

My interest in this paper is on what I believe to be Ferenczi's influence on contemporary revisionist thought. I will not address most of the contributions to what is a very wide-ranging debate over data and procedure, but instead I will choose what seems to be most useful to illustrate that influence. As a practicing analyst, of course, I cannot avoid joining the debate.

Both for Ferenczi in his day, and for his contemporary heirs, what is considered to be new is a more sophisticated understanding of the analytic relationship. Ultimately, the source of these additions to standard technique rests on Freud's discovery in 1914 that transference is the past alive in the present: "The patient does not remember anything of what he has forgotten, but acts it out; he reproduces it not as memory, but as an action; he repeats it without of course knowing he is repeating it. We must treat his illness as a present-day force" (Freud, 1914, p. 151). We have only to add that what set Freud on this road was his discovery that the wishes and desires of this "force" are directed at the analyst, making for a complex and formidable detour in the Freudian psychoanalytic endeavor to recover the past.

In the papers on technique, the analyst was an objective observer, unless countertransference resulted in a blind spot. Freud did not articulate the existence of a constant interaction as Ferenczi did. To me, that continuous interaction is part of any human relationship that is of any intensity. I agree with Brenner (1976) and Loewenstein (Arlow, 1982) that there is no model in life for the relationship in the psychoanalytic situation in that in the mind of the analyst, and increasingly one hopes, in the mind of the patient, the purpose is to understand the operation of the patient's mind both within the analytic situation and outside it in life.

Ferenczi's Contributions

I turn now to those precepts of Ferenczi's that reveal the therapeutic capacities for which Freud had commended him, and that are still in use in our contemporary standard technique. The intensity and persistence with which Ferenczi sought a better therapy leads one to recall that he was often referred patients who had failed with other analysts (Ferenczi, 1988, p. xix). He emphasized, as in much of contemporary writing, the need for a sensitivity by the analyst to himself at work, to his countertransference and to his subjectivity. He wrote in 1919, "The doctor is always a human being, and as such liable to moods, sympathies and antipathies, as well as impulses— without such susceptibilities he would of course have no understanding for the patient's psychic conflicts" (Ferenczi, 1919, pp. 186–187).

In contrast to Freud, he thought "it used to be held that an excessive degree of 'antipathy' was an indication against undertaking an analysis, but deeper insight into the relationship has caused us to regard such a thing as unacceptable in principle ... the unconscious aim of intolerable behaviour is often to be sent away" (Ferenczi, 1928, p. 95). In our time this would be described as an actualization, as for example by Boesky (1990), or as the role thrust on the analyst as

Sandler (1976) described it. To me, as to Ferenczi, the response can be potential and not inevitably interactive.

The following composite quote from Ferenczi anticipates Ernst Kris' (1952, pp. 243–264; 303–320) conceptualization that he termed, "creative thinking" and included Hartmann's (1939) construct of autonomous functioning of the ego, emphasizing what Freud called "the small quiet voice of the intellect" (Freud, 1927, p. 53).

[On the one hand analytic therapy requires of the analyst a free play of association and fantasy, with full indulgence of his own unconscious. We know from Freud that only in this way is it possible to grasp intuitively the expressions of the patient's unconscious that are concealed in the manifest material and in manner of speech and behavior. On the other hand, the doctor must subject the material submitted to him by the patient to a logical scrutiny and may only let himself be guided by the result of this mental effort. This constant alteration between the free play of fantasy and critical scrutiny, presupposes a freedom, an uninhibited motility of psychic excitation on the doctor's part [1919]. However, not for one moment must we relax the vigilance and criticism made necessary by our own subjective trends [1928].

In 1930, as we shall see, Ferenczi found that certain subjective trends in the analyst supplied both traumatic and corrective experiences that would become particularly useful in cure. Earlier he described the development of the countertransference in the career of the analyst, as a simple straightforward evolution. In the first stage, the new analyst, having very recently been a patient himself, unconsciously identifies with his patients, becomes their champion, and wants their wishes fulfilled. Subsequently he resists this attitude, represses it, and enters the second stage of counterresistance; overcoming the earlier identifications by setting up the contrary attitudes of overdetachment and losing thereby the intimate contact with his patient's unconscious.

Finally, he strikes a balance between these two polarities, a sublimated countertransference: The analyst identifies or detaches himself to the degree and in the manner required for his rational purposes (Lewin, 1946). The mature analyst is now able to "let himself go," that is, to give full indulgence to his own unconscious, but also to listen to his preconscious signals so as to know when to put his critical scrutiny into operation. It is this oscillation between the free play of fantasy and critical scrutiny that characterizes the experienced analyst. What has been added recently is that the patient's fantasies are meant by him to be responded to by the analyst, "actualized." That there is an aim and an object of these drive derivatives to me emphasizes the usual burden or as Freud called it, a temptation for countertransference (Freud and Jung, 1974). In current theories of technique these responses are thought to be particularly useful. I would emphasize the quantitative factors in both patient and analyst that result in variations in response as in variations of free play and critical scrutiny. This makes for differences among individual analysts and differences in the same analysis at different times. However, the idea that enactment or actualized responses by the analyst take precedence over the oscillation of free play and reflection and conscious judgment is what I must question.

The problem as seen by me, in discussion with various colleagues (Erle, 1996, Grossman, 1996 [personal communications]), is that these interactions, often more subtle in standard technique, foster a resistance to self-awareness. The work required of the patient is subverted in the acting out of infantile wishes; of course, with the analyst as object of these aims. To try to alter the analyst's response, or to try to establish one, is also sought by the resistance. The illusion that the transference wish is being partially fulfilled is inevitable as Boesky (1982) maintains, but as Nunberg (1951) and Tarachow (1962) pointed out, the closer that wish-fulfillment is to a reality in the patient's mind, the less likely it is that the patient can be analyzed.

Self-reflection and insight diminish the resistance and also those elements of repetition in the transference that are addressed. Without abstinence, that is, not fulfilling transference wishes, the need of the patient to understand is diminished. I should add that in practice the analyst on reflection may have to alter his behavior with certain patients when it is apparent that he is aiding the resistance; for example, Brian Bird (1972) found he had to speak less in order for his patient to recognize that it was his fantasy that the analyst was nagging him as his mother had.

To return to Ferenczi: The best explication of Freud's maxims about the surgeon and the mirror as understood at that time is contained in Ferenczi's admonition, "Before the physician decides to tell the patient something, he must temporarily withdraw his libido from the latter, and weigh the situation coolly; he must in no circumstances allow himself to be guided by his feelings alone" (Ferenczi, 1928, p. 90). The analyst like the surgeon must acquire the capacity for this temporary detachment; he does not come equipped with it. This is in contrast to some contemporary advocates of a technique that finds spontaneous emotional responses authentic, and hence especially useful (Levenson, 1988). For Ferenczi, understanding the patient is a function of the natural capacity for identification and it is the refinement of this capacity that he concluded is foremost in psychoanalytic technique. As in the countertransference of the third stage, despite sublimation or the receding of wishes, the latter remain unconsciously active.

Some contemporary analysts criticize the psychoanalytic technique of the 1950s, occasionally to the point of caricature, as authoritarian, arrogant, overconfident, and presumptuous in regard to the knowledge of the patient (Hoffman, 1996a). Some revisionist thinkers explain this harmful detachment as the unavoidable behavioral manifestations of the principles of abstinence and neutrality. Ferenczi, in his kinder way, cautions his colleagues:

Nothing is more harmful to the analysis than a school-masterish, or even an authoritative, attitude on the physician's part. Anything we say to the patient should be put to him in the form of a tentative suggestion and not a confidently held opinion, not only to avoid irritating him, but because there is always the possibility that we may be mistaken.

And later:

One must never be ashamed unreservedly to confess one's own mistakes. It must never be forgotten that analysis is no suggestive process, primarily dependent on the physician's reputation and infallibility. All that it calls for is confidence in the physician's frankness and honesty, which does not suffer from the frank confession of mistakes [Ferenczi, 1928, pp. 94–95].

Earlier in this cautionary lecture, Ferenczi also reminds his colleagues, "Every patient without exception notices the smallest peculiarities in the analyst's behaviour, external appearance, or way of speaking, but without prior encouragement not one of them will tell him about them, though failure to do so constitutes a crude infringement of the primary rule of analysis" (Ferenczi, 1928, p. 93). The patient's reluctance to make personal comments seems to have been rediscovered in the contemporary literature, but now, with the recommendation that the analyst ask the patient to focus his mind on what is assumed to be his correct observation, both to learn about ourselves and to foster interaction (Gill, 1994). Ferenczi advises that:

> [We] have no alternative but to detect ourselves from the patient's associations when we have offended his aesthetic feelings by an excessively loud sneeze or blowing of the nose, when he has taken offence at the shape of our face, or when he feels impelled to compare our appearance with that of others of more impressive physique [Ferenczi, 1928, p. 93].

One must contrast Ferenczi's ideas of continuous involvement and awareness of his own subjectivity with Freud's position and that of others who felt free to advise patients and to participate with them in what they felt to be harmless interactions (A. O. Kris, 1994). Perhaps, as Lipton (1977) suggested, Freud considered such action to be outside of technique and presumably a benign use of the knowledge of the patients. Overt self-disclosure as currently recommended is felt to be essential for equality and authenticity (Renik, 1995b). Then and now, such disclosure may not be harmless in distorting the transference or in influencing the life of the patient.

Another precept by Ferenczi is to the point here:

> A special form of this work of revision appears to occur however in every case; I mean the revision of the emotional experiences which happened in the course of the analyses. The analysis itself gradually becomes a piece of the patient's life

history, which he passes in review before bidding us farewell. In the course of this revision it is from a certain distance and with much greater objectivity that he looks at the experiences through which he went at the beginning of his acquaintanceship with us [Ferenczi, 1928, p. 97].

Ferenczi's Experimentation

I will be brief about his early experimentation that did not as yet bring to his recognition the meaning and effect of his behavior. His first experiment was called active therapy, when he tried to produce an accentuation of tension by forbidding covert discharge of libido in the analytic situation and sometimes outside, in order to concentrate the libido and focus it on discharge in associations and affective expression in the session (Ferenczi, 1919, 1920; Ferenczi and Rank, 1925). However, this method failed, and subsequently he followed Freud's character and ego analysis, which left him with the impression that the relation between physician and patient had become too much like that between teacher and pupil. At the same time, the patient did not dare rebel against this didactic attitude. Consequently he urged analysts to encourage the patients to give freer expression to their aggressive feelings. Nonetheless, he noted that his inflexibility about such matters as time, "produced a resistance which I felt to be excessive and a too literal repetition of traumatic incidents in the patient's childhood" (Ferenczi, 1950, p. 114). The use of this strictness by obsessional patients as resistance led him to "knock this weapon out of their hands by indulgence" (Ferenczi, 1950, p. 114). These exceptional cases became so numerous that it led him to propound a new principle, the principle of *indulgence*. He came to believe that in the standard analytic procedure there were two opposed elements: One produced a heightening of tension by the frustration it imposes, for example, immobility, and the other, relaxation, by the freedom it allows in speech and emotion. The patients resisted both. This, Ferenczi pointed out, corresponds to the training of children: tenderness and love, at the same time imposing the requirement to adapt to painful reality by renunciation. By giving in to the wishes and demands of his patients, he found that they developed a new confidence. They also developed hysterical symptoms that represented memories. What was special was that the reconstructed past had the feeling of reality and concreteness; recollections occurred in actions and affects. These reactions represented confirmation of unconscious childhood trauma, the memories of which following the "toilsome analytic work" recommended by Freud. Behind the structure of the neurosis as expressed in the transference was always a real psychic trauma resulting from conflict with the environment (Ferenczi, 1950).

At that time he still gave importance to the Oedipus complex, but found of much greater significance the repressed incestuous affection of the adults for children. The child, he said, wants even in his sexual life, play, and tenderness, not the passion brought to him by traumatic seductions.

Ferenczi reported, with relief and pleasure, Anna Freud's remark to him, "You really treat your patients as I treat the children whom I analyze" (Ferenczi, 1950, p. 122). He was referring in part to Anna Freud's preparatory period to win the patient's confidence, but in addition it was the activity of play by both participants that he felt was technically decisive (Ferenczi, 1931).

Ferenczi (1933) came to the conclusion that it was the similarity of the analytic procedure to the infantile situation that added to the compulsion to repeat and to the distortions by the patient. It was particularly the hypocrisy of the parent, who both seduced and projected the guilt of that seduction onto the child by denying their transgression and at the same time prohibited sexual behavior in the child, that was the ultimate pathogenic factor. The meaningful conflict, the original conflict, was between the individual and the outside world, and not within the individual.

In urging his patients to deeper relaxation and more complete surrender to impressions and emotions, he found the patients becoming more childlike in their speech and in other modes of expression, more nonverbal than verbal; expressive movement and visual ideas appeared as in children's play. The analyst's cool expectant silence, and his failure to manifest any reaction, had the effect of disturbing the freedom of association. The same manner might result in the disruption of the play of children in which the analyst is assigned a part. It is in the famous grandfather example that he illustrates this (Ferenczi, 1931, p. 129). The patient addressed the analyst as "grandpa," presumably half in belief and half in play. The analyst responded with the assigned role as though he was in fact the grandfather entering into the game akin to that reported in child analysis. As with certain children, at the intensification of the family play, Ferenczi was attacked for not taking the game seriously enough. This was the beginning of Ferenczi's final theory of pathogenesis and cure. The experience of the "hidden tendencies to act out" had to be relived fully in the present, but ultimately with the analyst outside the transference as a different or new object.

He concluded that the friendly, affectionate attitude of the patient was originally derived from the tender relations between mother and child. The fits of passion, naughtiness, and neurotic distortions were the later results of tactless treatment by those around the child.

18

Ferenczi now found that the patients were all too ready to express their aggression. In response he felt it was better to admit honestly that he found the patient's behavior unpleasant, interpreting, as well, the attempt to put the analyst in the role of the punishing parent. His final conclusion was that what is most traumatic is the insincerity and hypocrisy of the parents who profess to love the child unambiguously. The eventual purpose of his technique is the reconciliation between the new parent, the sincere analyst, and the mistreated child in this interpersonal theory: The patient knowing himself to be safe from the situation of his childhood allows him to repeat the painful past in affect and action.

Ferenczi observed that there is a split in the personality of the patient in which the child in him feels deserted and adopts the role of father or mother in relation to himself, undoing the fact of being deserted. The result under repression is the splitting of the self into a suffering, brutally destroyed, guilty part, and a part that knows everything but feels nothing. The latter is the analyst in the standard technique who is idealized by the patient in order to spare him.

A condensed summary of what is curative is as follows: After the analyst's interpretation and encouragement to the patient, the latter enacts more and more threatening behavior to compel the analyst to an act of punishment that the analyst delays. The child in the patient feels abandoned and must turn his aggression against himself, particularly if the adult's guilt is projected. The whole matter had been made worse because the adult had denied the existence of the child's experience, that is to say that nothing had hurt the child. To recover in the course of childhood is rare, because in addition to the mother having to be present with understanding and tenderness, she must also be completely sincere. The second part of this analytic work is the traumatic effect of the moment when the analyst finally puts an end to the unrestrained license. This reproduces the infantile situation, the helpless rage that requires tactful understanding, and a reconciliation with the analyst, instead of what Ferenczi called the lasting alienation in response to the situation in childhood.

Ferenczi also observed the patient's "exceedingly refined sensitivity for the wishes, tendencies, whims, sympathies and antipathies" (Ferenczi, 1933, p. 158) of his analyst, which were defensively repressed by their identification with him, abetted by the professional hypocrisy of standard analytic procedure.

Ferenczi's method, not acknowledged, was illustrated at a panel at the American (Panel, 1994). After the analyst's denial of his discomfort in telling the patient that his attack on the analyst was in order not to consider his inner reasons for deleting a session from his payments, the analyst honestly admitted to the concealing of his greed, not as a possibility, but as fact. This brought about an interaction with the analyst that activated the memory of the patient's defensive compliance with his father's deceptions. Ferenczi said, "It would almost seem to be of advantage occasionally to commit blunders in order to admit afterwards the fault to the patient. This advice is, however, quite superfluous; we commit blunders often enough" (Ferenczi, 1933, p. 159). At present such phenomena are explained as an interplay of transference and countertransference with a much greater complexity of motives, but the advice for this procedure is taking hold. For example, another hypocrisy presented at the panel is that the analyst seduces the patient to believe that he only and always wants to help him, when at times the analyst is competitive and resentful, to be disclosed as an actuality.

Ferenczi asks, "Can you really still apply the term 'psychoanalysis' to what goes on in these 'child-analyses' of grown-up people? ... What has become of the fine dissection ... of the reconstruction of the symptom-formation?" (Ferenczi, 1931). His answer was that his analyses too, "proceed on the level of the conflict between the intra-psychic forces" (p. 140) which may go on for years. Sooner or later, however, "a collapse of the intellectual superstructure" and of the distorting lens of intrapsychic conflict occurs, and the fundamental traumatic situation breaks through; the original conflict between child and his tactless caretaking environment.

To be complete about Ferenczi's theory of pathogenesis, he concludes that it is the precocious superimposition of the passionate, guilt-laden love of the adult on the immature guiltless child who craves tenderness that binds the child to the object, requiring a distortion of the self and a repression of this accurate knowledge of the adult. (See Laplanche, 1976 for a different opinion of the role of the adult's sexuality.) This past is relived by interaction with the analyst and is ultimately corrected by the analyst's authentic spontaneous responses.

Friend and foe alike agree that whatever the yield in delineating the human relationship in analysis, Ferenczi had spent his last years attempting to cure himself with only a partial understanding. He said, "In my case, infantile aggressiveness and a refusal of love toward my mother became displaced onto the patients. Instead of feeling with the heart, I feel with my head. Head and thought replace heart and libido" (Ferenczi, 1988, p. 86).

Contemporary Examples

Anton Kris found a problem similar to Ferenczi's in a group of narcissistic patients who had also had previous failures in analysis (A. O. Kris, 1990a). Their primitive unconscious self-criticism was projected onto the analyst who was then sadistically attacked: The syndrome was "A vicious cycle of self-deprivation and narcissistic entitlements." Interpretations alone were not sufficient and these patients required what Kris called support, an affirmative stance to prevent the return of the externalization of punishing criticism and thus to be able to continue to participate in the analytic process via free association that the patient was unable to do before. This seeming contradiction of the principle of neutrality (abstinence?) he calls "functional neutrality," as I understand it, not playing the role assigned to the analyst, that is, of the harsh superego.

In another paper A.O. Kris (1994) uses Freud's supportive efforts in treating Mrs. Riviere as an illustration of an intuitive response to what she needed. He points out the contrast between Freud's behavior and his insistence on objectivity and abstinence. Kris believes these principles arose from Freud's commitment to establish the scientific respectability of psychoanalysis and led to the minimalist austerity of classical technique. This impression of an ideal of a cold, detached, and silent observer is shared by many who were analyzed in the 1950s. James McLaughlin (1991) wrote a caricature of that analyst and Shelley Orgel (1995) gave a paper supporting that picture with the facts of his own experience in supervision.

The contemporary classical approach that I consider a reply to this criticism is given by Paul Gray (1994) who makes the point that the fantasy of the affectionate authority of the analyst provides a formidable resistance. He called this a "maternalistic" influence on resistance, superego permission as a defense, and quotes Ferenczi, "What such neurotics need is really to be adopted and to partake for the first time in their lives, of the advantages of a normal nursery" (Ferenczi, 1929, p. 124, cited in Gray, 1994, p. 139). According to Gray, the wider-scope patients, presumably Ferenczi's as well, cannot develop a capacity for relative autonomy and acceptance of reality, so that they require protective measures that preclude some of the anguish of the core psychoanalytic methodology. The patient is allowed to retain unconscious internalized superego defenses of a permissive approving form. This may also be the end result of Ferenczi's procedure, but in his method the patients could not be spared the anguish of reliving the painful past.

Other revisionist writers insist that some stance dictated by inter-subjectivity is inevitable (Renik, 1993a; Boesky, 1990). In this I tend to agree, but how it is experienced by the patient depends on his psychic reality, including the state of the transference at the time. In a paper on technique, Ernst Kris (1951) points out that the interpretation to the child that he was identifying with the aggression of the dentist as he breaks off tips of pencils, could be taken by the child patient as an interpretation of his feminine desire to be castrated and penetrated.

In regard to the analyst, these questions are raised by Ernst Kris' other example when, without being aware of it, he changed his words, in making an oft-repeated observation, saying to the patient, "your need for love" rather than "your demand for love" (E. Kris, 1951, p. 28). Was Kris' preconscious intuition at work as he claimed, or also countertransference, the giving of permission or the result of a response to a role thrust on the analyst to actively love?[1]

---

1 "An example that dates from the 1950s, from Kohut's first analysis of Mr. Z., offers a convenient point of departure.

"After about a year and a half, he rather abruptly became much calmer and his insistent assertion that his anger was justified because I did not understand him lessened conspicuously. When I remarked approvingly on the change and said the working through of his own narcissistic delusions was now bearing fruit, the patient rejected this explanation, but in a friendly and calm manner. He said that the change had taken place not primarily because of a change in him but because of something I had done. I had, he said, introduced one of my interpretations concerning his insatiable narcissistic demands with the phrase 'of course, it hurts when one is not given what one assumes to be one's due'

"Although the first analysis of Mr. Z. had been criticized as a caricature of analysis, because of the dogmatic manner in which Kohut applied Freud's theories, I believe that

Standard technique indicates that only subsequent associations will elucidate the matter. However, for revisionists where interaction is primary and corrective to past interpersonal maladaptive distortions, particularly in Sullivanian theory, it is not meaningful to ask for confirmation from the data of intrapsychic conflict as revealed by associations. There is a basic difference in the theory of how the mind works. For contemporary Sullivanians a relatively new epistemology that argues that there is no possible approach to objective truth either of the mind of the patient or of the analyst; only a cocreation of data (Hoffman, 1983, 1991a), shifts the issue entirely to the "analysand as a poem" and the analyst as a singular responsive reader (Eagleton, 1983; Mitchell, 1995).

Transference

Something odd has happened on the way to the Forum; the concept of the transference, the powerful conveyor of the patient's neurosis, but most simply, the putting of the analyst in the role of the parent and the analysand in the role of the child is now considered an authoritarian bias, inaccurate and misleading. Owen Renik states, "It is hard to see how that distinction, analyst and patient, can be made on the basis of either party's actual involvement, that is, the extent to which either one expresses emotional responses in action" (Renik, 1993a, p. 140). Since this is not yet the equality of mutual analysis, as in Ferenczi's

---

with regard to the analysis of 'insatiable narcissistic demands' Kohut's approach was not unusual in the 1950's. For example, Ernst **Kris** (**1951**), illustrating the operation of intuition in formulating interpretations, gave a remarkably similar account in which the attempt to analyze a patient's 'greed' became suddenly successful when he shifted from referring to the patient's 'demand for love' to his 'need for love'" (Kohut [**1979**, p. 5], cited in A. O. Kris [**1990a**, p. 612]).

very last experiment, the ground rules of the analytic construct that define it as a psychoanalysis of the patient, remains. However, we now no longer need to worry about the unequal power gradient in the analytic situation.

That the data of psychoanalysis are determined by mutual inter-action is confirmed, in the thinking of revisionists, it seems to me, by their observation that awareness of countertransference can only occur after its enactment. Dale Boesky, combining both ideas, states, "If the analyst does not get emotionally involved sooner or later in a manner that he had not intended, the analysis will not proceed to a successful conclusion" (Boesky, 1990, p. 573).

The power of the analyst as therapist seems to be ever present at the same time that his power as a transference figure is diminished, and furthermore can be disregarded so that responses become natural and beneficial. Dr. Renik, in a similar vein, says "many of the most useful things we do, we do for reasons of which we *cannot* be aware at the time" (1993a, p. 144).

These aspects of the analytic work may well be correct and should be carefully examined, as in the example of Ernst Kris' slip. However, if they are thought of, following Ferenczi, as in themselves curative because of the spontaneity and authenticity of a corrective experience, a great deal may be lost, particularly the patient's autonomous understanding of how his mind works.

For example, Renik states that his patient's therapeutic optimism reproduced a relationship he had with an aunt that activated the following fantasy in the analyst (Renik, 1993a, p. 148). Through transference and idealization he felt he could succeed with the patient where others had failed. There followed mutual disappointment and anger in the analyst, which put him back, he said, into the image of the patient's depressed mother. The patient's response to this unconscious but genuine competitive attack by the analyst as to whom would be pitied more, analyst or patient, led to the memory of the patient's guilt at his sadism toward his mother and his expectation of punishment. The argument given is that only the genuine emotional content of the countertransference, part of an interaction, led to the repetition and the correction of this childhood conflict. The final result, which seems to me to be based on the idea of a new experience with a new object, is, Renik states, "two imperfect people who care about each other can manage to sustain their relationship in the face of mutual disappointment" (Renik, 1993a, p. 151).

Renik speaks of the analytic conscience, putting the patients' welfare first, which akin to Ferenczi becomes crucial in the negotiation of a reconciliation in the present in contrast to the alienation in the past. Intrapsychic conflict is not diminished, but seems to me to become secondary. Ferenczi carries the goal of reconciliation perhaps a bit further, "The end result of the analysis of transference and countertransference may be the establishment of a kind, dispassionate atmosphere such as existed in pre-traumatic times" (Ferenczi, 1988, p. 27).

In pure interpersonalist technique, the analyst says, "What makes you think I would not be angry and want to hurt you?" with the intent of bringing the here-and-now experience, and eventually the reliving and correction of the past into the work (Levenson, 1988). Maintaining the autonomous observing function of the ego and enlarging it as a goal, as emphasized by Paul Gray (1973), would seem to me to be a daunting task after such procedures.

Reconciliation

Boesky argues that since the patient's mind is dealing with object representations, the assumption that the actual behavior of the analyst is perceived correctly is unlikely, and consequently, "The recent trend towards revelations of countertransference are deceptively honest" (Boesky, 1990, p. 569). This is not to say that the patient's correct perceptions of the analyst are irrelevant. The behavior of the analyst can override the transference, although as I have indicated I believe that this can happen, because the patient can include that behavior in his particular resistance. However, Boesky like Renik concludes that motor responses in the analyst are a clue that enactment has already taken place. However, that this means that the communication has reached the patient and has become significant in the analytic work, does not necessarily follow. I agree with Gitelson that it is persistent countertransference that has problematic effect, and that these "emergency responses" are easily dealt with (Gitelson, 1952). That resistances are created solely by the patient, Boesky believes, is a fiction; to me it is a useful fiction for the purpose of discourse. Analytic experience is of course more complex, but, fixed resistances, although strictly speaking compromise formations, do represent the patient's particular defensive organization. To say as Boesky does that "the true success is the understanding of the interaction between the failures" (1990, p. 575), in which both parties participate, to me is more properly understood as the collusion or interaction of resistances that can better be analyzed. Boesky's conclusion that resistances are negotiated between patient and analyst, I believe, like many statements of some contemporary Freudians, is probably meant to emphasize what they feel has been neglected; that is, Ferenczi's observation that interaction in the broadest sense as part of the human relationship is continuous in analysis.

The most crucial discovery by Freud for the practice of analysis is that transference consists, on the one hand, of the urge to repeat in action of any kind, silence, words, affects, motoric phenomena, etc., primarily to gratify or discharge unconscious instinctual wishes. On the other hand, it consists, from a technical point of view, of a resistance to remembering, the "substitution of enactments" as it is now called, for thought, reflection, memory, and conscious awareness. The ego psychology of the 1950s added the detailed consideration of the capacities and incapacities of the ego of the analysand in the process of psychoanalytic work. There is no difficulty, of course, in extending these same considerations to the mind of the analyst. However, when the distinction between introspection, reflection, self-awareness, and enactment is dissolved, that aspect of correction called insight is in danger of being lost. As Ferenczi asked, can the procedure he created in 1930 that is being revived today, obviously altered in regard to content and more sophisticated, elucidate the structure of the neurosis?

There is maturation and development from childhood of the capacity for self-observation and self-awareness. I agree with Paul Gray (1994) that they are inevitably involved in conflict, the analysis of which is an important part of our work. If this approach led to the cold detachment of the analyst, the pendulum at present has swung too far in the other direction. My knowledge of the analytic procedure of the decade of the 1950s when I was being trained, does not confirm this portrait of the analyst, although what is now called the subjectivity of the analyst and its effects on the patient were certainly not given the same scrutiny as they are today.

In the 1950s the understanding of the psychic reality of the patient was our exclusive concern, unless an obvious countertransference interfered; that countertransference considered in those days as only an obstacle to understanding and not an illumination (Stein, 1981). At the present, I should like to make a distinction between the recommendation to view interaction as an additional source of data about the patient and about the analyst and the injunction to put the emphasis on interaction as the data, and even more so from the recommendation for its use as therapy in psychoanalysis.

An illustration of these different orientations appeared at the American Psychoanalytic Association Panel on the Analyst's Influence in 1994.

Dr. McLaughlin reported that he was worried and perhaps exasperated; he burst out emotionally to his patient that her drug taking was self-destructive and that he was very concerned. In the discussion from the floor, Dr. Brenner asked why not ask her instead, what she thought about her own behavior, agreeing that it was self-destructive and should be pointed out, but why not return to the patient's psyche rather than pursue the interaction? Dr. McLaughlin replied that his spontaneous outburst had stimulated more material from the patient than had been forthcoming for some time in this somewhat stalemated period of her analysis and that he had addressed her psychic reality. Discussants on the panel made the argument that Dr. McLaughlin's procedure showed the proper respect for the equality of the participants, rather than the assumption of authority implicit in Dr. Brenner's question. Given the interaction having occurred, this one not of a subtle nature, I would prefer to observe carefully in her associations, either immediately or perhaps months later, the meaning and effect of the interaction both inside the analysis, that is, transference, as well as outside, where the effect is often displaced.

Proponents of the new technical ideal tend to caricature standard procedure. I summarize their position as follows, "the pursuit of maximal objectivity by limiting the influence of individual psychology departs entirely from the true nature of clinical events, just as the related efforts to be aware of personal motivations before acting on them can never be a successful strategy" (Boesky, 1995). The difference of this contemporary point of view to that of the 1950s is illustrated by Boesky's recommendation (1995) that we not restrict our passionate and irrational involvement in our clinical work and Hartmann's conclusion (1960) in a previous Freud lecture that analysis makes us more tolerant of the passions in ourselves. In the 1990s and for many years the awareness of our subjectivity and the effect it has in interaction has made analysis both more burdensome and more interesting, which scarcely alters the fact that the data of analysis remain the psychic reality of the patient.

Disagreement and Social Constructivism

There is another argument that ends up with similar recommendations based on the primacy of the analyst's subjectivity. It starts from what is thought to be contemporary epistemology, that objective truth cannot be obtained by an inevitably participating observer, if it exists at all—a postmodern set of ideas that has replaced the so-called naive positivism of Freud's day.

To paraphrase Terry Eagleton (1983), if thoroughgoing, this postmodern world view would cast grave doubt upon the classical notions of truth, reality, meaning, and knowledge, all of which could be exposed as resting on the naive representational theory of language. If reality is constructed by our discourse, rather than reflected by it, how could we ever know reality itself, rather than merely knowing our own discourse.

The less thoroughgoing derivative of postmodern thought, social constructivism, holds that reality is in the process of being constructed by the interacting parties, man and society or man and man from moment to moment. This epistemology introduced to social science in the 1960s by Berger and Lachman (1967) is promulgated by Irwin Hoffman, and was adopted, late in his life by Merton Gill, as follows: Hoffman writes, "Although the sense of the possible value of the relatively detached stance is retained, there is also a sense of uncertainty as to its meaning to oneself as well as to the patient at any given moment, along with recognition that other kinds of interaction might be possible and useful" (1992a, p. 291). "What is not possible in this point of view is the total transcendence by analytic therapists of their own subjectivity" (1992a, p. 292). Hoffman believes that the above contradicts the positivist paradigm of classical analysis as follows: "a view of the process in which analysts or psychoanalytic therapists are thought to be capable of standing outside the interaction with the patient so that they can generate rather confident hypotheses and judgments about the patient's history, dynamics and transference and about what they themselves should do from moment to moment" (1992a, p. 289). This criticism of analysts in the past seems to state that they were not only objectivists but also absolutists. The search for the ever-changing, incomplete, and imperfect truth by a participant observer is probably sufficient for unsophisticated investigators.

The new paradigm contends that the data from the analytic situation are cocreated by transference and resistance from both parties interacting. This being the case, the argument goes, the analyst is less bound by a priori theories, more open to the individuality of himself and the patient, and free to be spontaneous, emotional, and authentic. Particularly important is the assumption that the patient is actively interested in exploring the analyst's personal qualities, and is often accurate in his perceptions.

Curiosity, or I presume any other drive derivative, is said to be not only the expression of a forbidden or unrealistic wish, but also a relatively healthy search for meaningful contact with the analyst. In this interpersonal theory, curiosity is considered to be a basic tendency of human beings with its roots in the infant's interest in the subjectivity of the mother. It is a short step to a variation of Ferenczi's theory of the original conflict of the child with the inauthentic caretaker and the analyst as open and honest in undoing the trauma of tactlessness and hypocrisy.

The contradiction is apparent if we share the idea of the complexity and ambiguity of human responses that arise out of intrapsychic conflict. To ask for agreement on what is authentic becomes a very difficult question, if at all a meaningful example given by Hoffman of a purported absolutists position opposed to one of his own:

> The traditional idea that it is always better to explore the patient's wishes in this regard under conditions of abstinence and deprivation is another reflection of positivist thinking. The implication is that the "true" nature of the wish or need will be exposed if the analyst does not "contaminate" the field by yielding to the patient's pressures. In the constructivist model, whatever way the analyst responds is likely to affect what is then "found out" about the intensity and quality of the patient's desire [1991b, p. 89].

One further example will illustrate my disagreement with the direction of these trends: Renik (1993b) argues for the recognition of the irreducible subjectivity of the analyst, stating that it is liberating for both patient and analyst and also guards against the negative effect of making the analyst an ideal mother who understands perfectly. It seems to me that what is being downgraded is not only the power of the transference but also the validity of the analytic method. The analyst, I would maintain, cannot liberate the patient much less himself from idealization. This is a transference and a countertransference distortion, not an acceptance or rejection of the analyst's influence, of his blunders, or his correct interpretations. The subjectivity of the analyst can effect idealization or disillusionment, depending on the patient's fantasies that prevail, whatever the analyst's intentions, both conscious and unconscious.

The implied caricature of the traditional analyst may bring out some of our salient features, but what is even more striking are the prejudices coloring the caricatures. In the same vein, the patient is thought by the interpersonalist to know his parents, but does not attend to what he knows. To me, what he knows of his parents and of the analyst is a distortion through the lens of his drive-motivated intrapsychic conflict.

As far as I can tell, there is as yet no explicit theory of pathogenesis by many contemporary revisionists that corresponds to the purported new paradigm in technique. For others, the so-called new paradigm is made up of what has been the interpersonalist method of treatment, retaining the intrapsychic theory of pathogenesis of classical Freudian theory, a form of common ground neither possible nor scientifically productive. Another group has continued the Sullivanian tradition with acknowledgment of Ferenczi's influence. Some revisionist thinkers have added as an underpinning a recently fashionable epistemology to the essentially interpersonal theory.

One can understand and value the efforts of contemporary analytic thinkers to find a better way to heal. But I will conclude with a question: If we assume that our patient comes to the analyst, given that he has the belief, rooted in our culture, of the analyst's greater knowledge, and in that sense, greater authority, and what we know to be regressive transference that begins immediately; what would be the result of correcting this view at the outset? That is, indicating to the patient that there are different theories and different hypotheses, the analyst is not sure about any of them, certainly the analyst cannot be expected to have answers, and collaborative work of two equal partners is to be undertaken. Would that be a recommended enactment? Would it lead to a better understanding of the patient?

References

Abend, S.M. (1988). Intrapsychic versus interpersonal: The wrong dilemma. *Psychoanal. Inq.*, 8:497–504.

Alexander, F. (1933). On Ferenczi's relaxation principle. *Int. J. Psycho-Anal.*, 14:183–192.

Arlow, J.A. (1982). Introduction. In: *Practice and Precept in Psychoanalytic Technique*, R. M. Loewenstein. New Haven, CT: Yale University Press, pp. 1–15.

Aron, L. (1991). The patient's experience of the analyst's subjectivity. *Psychoanal. Dial.*, 1:29–51.

———— & Harris, A., Eds. (1993). *The Legacy of Sandor Ferenczi*. Hillsdale, NJ: Analytic Press.

Balint, M. (1965). *Primary Love and Psychoanalytic Technique*. London: Tavistock.

Berger, P., & Lachman, T. (1967). *The Social Construction of Reality.* Garden City, NY: Anchor Books.

Bird, B. (1972). Transference: Universal phenomenon, hardest part of analysis. *J. Amer. Psychoanal. Assn.*, 20:267–301.

Blum, H.P. (1994). The confusion of tongues and psychic trauma. *Int. J. Psycho-Anal.*, 75:871–882.

Boesky, D. (1982). Acting out: A reconsideration of the concept. *Int. J. Psycho-Anal.*, 63:39–56.

——— (1990). The psychoanalytic process and its components. *Psychoanal. Q.*, 59:550–584.

——— (1995). Countertransference and resistance: The impossible terms of the impossible profession. Lecture delivered to the New York Psychoanalytic Society.

Brenner, C. (1976). *Psychoanalytic Technique and Psychic Conflict.* New York: International Universities Press.

——— (1995). The nature of knowledge and the limits of authority in psychoanalysis. *Psychoanal. Q.*, 65:21–31.

Chused, J.F. (1991). The evocative power of enactments. *J. Amer. Psychoanal. Assn.*, 39:615–640.

——— (1992). The patient's perception of the analyst: The hidden transference. *Psychoanal. Q.*, 61:161–184.

Cooper, S.H. (1997). Modes of influence in psychoanalysis. *J. Amer. Psychoanal. Assn.*, 45:217–230.

De Forest, I. (1942). The therapeutic technique of Sandor Ferenczi. *Int. J. Psycho-Anal.*, 23:120-139.

——— (1954). *The Leaven of Love: A Development of the Psychoanalytic Theory and Technique of Sandor Ferenczi.* New York: Harper.

Dupont, J. (1994). Freud's analysis of Ferenczi as revealed by their correspondence. *Int. J. Psycho-Anal.*, 75:301–320.

Eagleton, T. (1983). *Literary Theory: An Introduction*. Minneapolis: University of Minnesota Press.

Ferenczi, S. (1919). On the technique of psycho–analysis. In: *Further Contributions to the Theory and Technique of Psycho-Analysis*, ed. M. Balint. New York: Basic Books, 1950, pp. 177–188.

—— (1920). The further development of an active therapy in psychoanalysis. In: *Further Contributions to the Theory and Technique of Psycho-Analysis: Selected Papers of Sandor Ferenczi*, ed. M. Balint. New York: Basic Books, pp. 198–217.

—— (1928). The elasticity of psycho-analytic technique. In: *Final Contributions to the Problems and Methods of Psycho-Analysis: Selected Papers of Sandor Ferenczi*, Vol. 3, ed. M. Balint. New York: Basic Books, 1955, pp. 87–101.

—— (1930). The principle of relaxation and neocatharsis. In: *Final Contributions to the Problems and Methods of Psycho-Analysis: Selected Papers of Sandor Ferenczi*, Vol. 3, ed. M. Balint. New York: Basic Books, 1955, pp. 108–124.

—— (1931). Child-analysis in the analysis of adults. In: *Final Contributions to the Problems and Methods of Psycho-Analysis: Selected Papers of Sandor Ferenczi*, ed. M. Balint. New York: Basic Books, 1955, pp. 126–142.

—— (1933). Confusion of tongues between adult and child. In: *Final Contributions to the Problems and Methods of Psycho-Analysis: Selected Papers of Sandor Ferenczi*, ed. M. Balint. New York: Basic Books, 1955, pp. 156–167.

—— (1950). *Further Contributions to the Theory and Technique of Psycho-Analysis: Selected Papers of Sandor Ferenczi*, ed. M. Balint. New York: Basic Books.

—— (1988). *The Clinical Diary of Sandor Ferenczi*, ed. J. Dupont. Cambridge, MA: Harvard University Press.

———— Rank, O. (1925). *The Development of Psychoanalysis*. Madison, CT: International Universities Press, 1986.

Frederickson, J. (1990). Hate in the countertransference as an empathic position. *Contemp. Psychoanal.*, 26:479–496.

Freud, S. (1914). Remembering, repeating and working through. *Standard Edition*, 12:145–156. London: Hogarth Press, 1958.

———— (1927). The future of an illusion. *Standard Edition*, 21:5–56. London: Hogarth Press, 1961.

———— Jung, C.G. (1974). *The Freud Jung Letters*, ed. W. McGuire. Cambridge: Harvard University Press, pp. 230–231.

Friedman, L. (1978). Trends in the psychoanalytic theory of treatment. *Psychoanal. Q.*, 47:524–567.

Gill, M.M. (1994). Conflict and deficit: Book review essay on Conflict and Compromise: Therapeutic Implications. *Psychoanal. Q.*, 63:756–780.

———— Hoffman, I.Z. (1982). A method for studying the analysis of aspects of the patient's experience of the relationship in psychoanalysis and psychotherapy. *J. Amer. Psychoanal. Assn.*, 30:137–168.

Gitelson, M. (1952). Emotional position of the analyst in the psychoanalytic situation. *Int. J. Psycho-Anal.*, 33:1–10.

Gray, P. (1973). Psychoanalytic technique: Ego capacity to view intrapsychic activity. *J. Amer. Psychoanal. Assn.*, 21:474–494.

———— (1994). *The Ego and Analysis of Defense*. Northvale, NJ: Jason Aronson.

Greenberg, J. (1995). Psychoanalytic technique and the interactive matrix. *Psychoanal. Q.*, 64:1–22.

Grubrich-Simitis, I. (1986). Six letters of Sigmund Freud and Sandor Ferenczi on the interrelationship of psychoanalytic theory and technique. *Int. Rev. Psycho-Anal.*, 13:259–278.

Grunberger, B. (1980). From the "active technique" to the "confusion of tongues." In: *Psychoanalysis in France*, ed. S. Lebovici & D. Widlöcher. New York: International Universities Press, pp. 127–152.

Hartmann, H. (1939). *Ego Psychology and the Problem of Adaptation*. New York: International Universities Press.

———— (1960). *Psychoanalysis and Moral Values*. New York: International Universities Press.

Heidegger, M. (1962). *Being and Time*, tr. J. Macquarrie & E.S. Robinson. New York: Harper and Row.

Heimann, P. (1950). On counter-transference. *Int. J. Psycho-Anal.*, 31:81–84.

Hoffer, A. (1991). The Freud-Ferenczi controversy—A living legacy. *Int. Rev. Psycho-Anal.*, 18:465–472.

Hoffman, I.Z. (1983). The patient as interpreter of the analyst's experience. *Contemp. Psychoanal.*, 19:389–422.

——— (1991a). Reply to Benjamin. *Psychoanal. Dial.*, 1:535–544.

——— (1991b). Discussion: Toward a social–constructivist view of the psychoanalytic situation. *Psychoanal. Dial.*, 1:74–105.

——— (1992a). Some practical implications of a social-constructivist view of the psychoanalytic situation. *Psychoanal. Dial.*, 2:287–304.

——— (1992b). Reply to Orange. *Psychoanal. Dial.*, 2:567–570.

——— (1994). Dialectical thinking and therapeutic action in the psychoanalytic process. *Psychoanal. Q.*, 63:187–218.

——— (1995). Review essay: Oedipus and Beyond by Jay Greenberg. *Psychoanal. Dial.*, 5:93–112.

——— (1996a). Merton M. Gill: A study in theory development in psychoanalysis. *Psychoanal. Dial.*, 6:5–54.

——— (1996b). The intimate and ironic authority of the psychoanalyst's presence. *Psychoanal. Q.*, 65:102–136.

Jacobs, T.J. (1986). On countertransference enactments. *J. Amer. Psychoanal. Assn.*, 34:289–308.

——— (1991). *The Uses of the Self*. Madison, CT: International Universities Press.

Kirshner, L.A. (1993). Concepts of reality and psychic reality in psychoanalysis as illustrated by the disagreement between Freud and Ferenczi, *Int. J. Psycho-Anal.*, 74:219–230.

Kohut, H. (1979). The two analyses of Mr. Z. *Int. J. Psycho-Anal.*, 60:3–28.

Kris, A.O. (1990a). Helping patients by analyzing self-criticism. *J. Amer. Psychoanal. Assn.*, 38:605–636.

——— (1990b). The analyst's stance and the method of free association. *Psychoanal. St. Child*, 45:25–42. New Haven, CT: Yale University Press.

——— (1992). Interpretation and the method of free association. *Psychoanal. Inq.*, 12:208–224.

——— (1994). Freud's treatment of a narcissistic patient. *Int. J. Psycho-Anal.*, 75:649–664.

Kris, E. (1951). Ego psychology and interpretation in psychoanalytic therapy. *Psychoanal. Q.*, 20:15–30.

——— (1952). Aesthetic ambiguity. In: *Psychoanalytic Explorations in Art*. New York: International Universities Press, pp. 243–264.

Laplanche, J. (1976). *Life and Death in Psychoanalysis*. Baltimore, MD: John Hopkins University Press.

Lear, J. (1990). *Love and Its Place in Nature: A Philosophical Interpretation of Freudian Psychoanalysis*. New York: Farrar, Straus & Giroux.

Levenson, E. (1988). Show and tell: The recursive order of transference. In: *How Does Treatment Help?*, ed. A. Rothstein. Madison, CT: International Universities Press, pp. 135–144.

Levine, H.B. (1994). The analyst's participation in the analytic process. *Int. J. Psycho-Anal.*, 75:665–676.

Lewin, B. (1946). Countertransference in the technique of medical practice. In: *Selected Writings of Bertram Lewin*, ed. J. A. Arlow. New York: The Psychoanalytic Quarterly, 1973, pp. 449–458.

Lilla, M. (1995). *New French Thought in Political Philosophy.* Princeton, NJ: Princeton University Press.

Lipton, S.D. (1977). The advantages of Freud's technique as shown in his analysis of the Rat Man. *Int. J. Psycho-Anal.*, 58:255–274.

Loewald, H. (1960). On the therapeutic action of psychoanalysis. *Int. J. Psycho-Anal.*, 41:16–33.

Lum, W.B. (1988a). Sandor Ferenczi (1873–1933)—The father of the empathic-interpersonal approach: Part one, Introduction and early analytic years, *J. Am. Acad. Psychoanal. Dyn. Psychiatr.*, 16:131–154.

———— (1988b). Sandor Ferenczi (1873–1933)—The father of the empathic-interpersonal approach: Part two, Evolving technique, final contributions and legacy. *J. Am. Acad. Psychoanal. Dyn. Psychiatr.*, 16:317–348.

Manent, P. (1995). *An Intellectual History of Liberalism.* Princeton, NJ: Princeton University Press.

McLaughlin, J.T. (1981). Transference, psychic reality, and countertransference. *Psychoanal. Q.*, 50:639–664.

———— (1987). The play of transference: Some reflections on enactment in the psychoanalytic situation. *J. Amer. Psychoanal. Assn.*, 35:557–582.

———— (1988). The analyst's insights. *Psychoanal. Q.*, 57:370–389.

———— (1991). Clinical and theoretical aspects of enactment. *J. Amer. Psychoanal. Assn.*, 39:595–614.

Mitchell, S.A. (1993). Aggression and the endangered self. *Psychoanal. Q.*, 62:351–382.

———— (1995). Discussion of Brenner: Knowledge and authority in analytic practice. Scientific meeting, New York Psychoanalytic Institute, October 10.

Natterson, J. (1991). *Beyond Countertransference: The Therapist's Subjectivity in the Therapeutic Process*. Northvale, NJ: Jason Aronson.

Nunberg, H. (1951). Transference and reality. *Int. J. Psycho-Anal.*, 32:1–9.

Orange, D.M. (1992). Perspectival realism and social constructivism: Commentary on Irwin Hoffman's "Discussion, Toward a social-constructivist view of the psychoanalytic situation." *Psychoanal. Dial.*, 2:561–565.

Orgel, S. (1995). A classic revisited: K.R. Eissler's "The effect of the structure of the ego on psychoanalytic technique." *Psychoanal. Q.*, 64:551–570.

Panel (1994). The Development of Psychoanalysis by Sandor Ferenczi and Otto Rank (1924). Reporter: A. Hoffer. *J. Amer. Psychoanal. Assn.*, 42:851–862.

Putnam, H. (1981). *Reason, Truth and History*. Cambridge: Cambridge University Press.

Renik, O. (1993a). Technique in light of the analyst's irreducible subjectivity. *Psychoanal. Q.*, 62:553–571.

———— (1993b). Countertransference enactment and the psychoanalytic process. In: *Psychic Structure and Psychic Change: Essays in Honor of Robert S. Wallerstein*, ed. M. Horowitz, O. Kernberg, & E. Weinshel. Madison, CT: International Universities Press, pp. 135–158.

———— (1994a). Commentary on Martin Stephen Frommer's "Homosexuality and psychoanalysis," *Psychoanal. Dial.*, 4:235–240.

———— (1994b). Publication of clinical facts. *Int. J. Psycho-Anal.*, 75:1245–1250.

———— (1995a). The role of an analyst's expectations in clinical technique: Reflections on the concept of resistance. *J. Amer. Psychoanal. Assn.*, 43:83–94.

———— (1995b). The ideal of the anonymous analyst and the problem of self-disclosure. *Psychoanal. Q.*, 64:466–495.

Sandler, J. (1976). Countertransference and role-responsiveness. *Int. Rev. Psycho-Anal.*, 3:43–48.

Schwaber, E. (1983). Psychoanalytic listening and psychic reality. *Int. Rev. Psycho-Anal.*, 10:379–392.

Stein, M.H. (1981). The unobjectionable part of the transference. *J. Amer. Psychoanal. Assn.*, 29:869–892.

Strachey, J. (1934). The nature of therapeutic action of psychoanalysis. *Int. J. Psycho-Anal.*, 15:127–159.

Tarachow, S. (1962). Interpretation and reality in psychotherapy. *Int. J. Psycho-Anal.*, 43:377–387.

Thompson, C. (1943). The therapeutic technique of Sandor Ferenczi: A comment. *Int. J. Psycho-Anal.*, 24:64–66.

Wallerstein, R.S. (1990). The corrective emotional experience: Is reconsideration due? *Psychoanal. Inq.*, 10:288–324.

CHAPTER 3

Psychoanalytic Dialogue: Kleinian Theory Today

(1977). *Journal of the American Psychoanalytic Association* 25:371–385

The caption "Kleinian Theory Today" implies the possibility that Kleinian thought has evolved, that is, that the theory of today differs from the theory of the past. I gather that there is a first and second phase of Melanie Klein's work, the first having to do with particular vicissitudes of the destructive drive and with sadistic fantasies very early in life; the second, with the coordination of the psychic state of the infant with that of psychosis. A knowledge of the history of ideas enriches our understanding of them and will enlighten us in regard to the development of Melanie Klein's views.

The clearest succinct statement of Mrs. Klein's basic theoretical position I found in a panel discussion on the Mutual Influences in the Development of the Ego and the Id (Klein, 1952): "I have for many years held the view... that the ego functions from the beginning and that among its first activities are the defense against anxiety and the use of processes of introjection and projection... I have also repeatedly expressed the view that the ego establishes object relations from the first contacts with the external world... fantasies operate from the outset... and are the mental expression of the activity of both the life and death instincts" (pp. 51–52). With reference to this last, she says,

"I differ from Freud in that I put forward the hypothesis that the primary cause of anxiety is the fear of annihilation, of death arising from the working of the death instinct within" (p. 51).

In the Kleinian schema, it seems to me, all development in infancy is motivated by anxiety and perhaps only by anxiety. Investment of objects occurs because the death instinct must be externalized. Libidinal investment is thought of almost solely as a defense against aggression. Subsequently, alternating processes of projection and introjection occur, which result in a "world of good and bad objects, both built up within the self or ego and in the external world." These first objects are called part objects because they are derived from the mother's breast. The first consolidated psychological state, which she calls the paranoid-schizoid position, is associated with persecutory anxiety. This situation is advisedly called a "position," as Dr. Segal pointed out, because it is not meant to be a stage in development, but "a specific configuration of object relations, anxieties, and defenses which persist throughout life." This holds for all the Kleinian positions. The fundamental characteristic of this first position is that bad persecuting objects predominate. There is already at this period of infancy an attempt at defense by idealization and splitting, which means not only keeping the good and bad images separated, but splitting the images into bits. A further complication arises because the idealized object is envied and thus attracts to itself an increase of destructive drive. After the fourth month of life, if this "position" is more or less overcome, a good total-mother internal object is established. But this, too, is endangered by the destructive impulses, and the result is the onset of depressive anxiety and guilt, the fear of the loss of the whole good object—what Klein calls the "depressive position." Various manic and reparation mechanisms deal with this position defensively.

44

In instinctual terms, these processes are thought of as oral incorporation and anal expulsion, concepts derived from Abraham (1924). However, partly because of the idea of inherited primal fantasies, as well as what Edward Bibring, in his critique (1947), called an idea of the spread of instinctual tension, genital sensations and oedipal fantasies are also involved from the beginning. In addition, the early introjects, both persecuting and comforting, form the core of the superego.

In thinking of the theory as a whole, what we seem to have is an interesting developmental theory of the recovery in severe child psychosis. I borrowed from that theory in 1964 in my attempts at such explanation in a four-year-old psychotic boy, particularly the representation of a fused self-object image of a body content, the feces. There are, nevertheless, some glaring differences, inasmuch as I put my emphasis upon an undifferentiated phase, or a symbiotic form of preobject relation, which has a background in normal development in a form not included in Klein's ideas. I was also impressed by the fact that oedipal conflicts were not present early in those children.

Edith Jacobson (1971) gave specific credit to Mrs. Klein for her description of the end-products of structural regression and disorganization, as well as for the emphasis on the aggressive drives in psychotic conditions. The problem is one I believe Dr. Segal has addressed herself to in her book, namely, to tease apart normal from pathological development, the difficulty of which has led to the charge that Mrs. Klein has postulated that every infant is psychotic, or functions, in fantasy at least, in a psychotic fashion. The answer given by Mrs. Klein (1930) does not seem adequate: "In my opinion, fully developed schizophrenia is more common and especially the occurrence of schizophrenic traits is a far more general phenomenon in childhood than is usually supposed. One of the chief tasks of the childrens' analyst is to discover and to cure psychosis in children" (p. 248). One must similarly ask for an explanation of Dr. Segal's statement, "Infantile neurosis is a *defense* against underlying paranoid and depressive anxieties" (1964, p. xiii).

To return to the issue of development itself: maturation and development in the ordinary sense of the movement from a less to a more complex organization, from a less to a more differentiated functioning seems to be largely absent from Klein's delineation of the psyche in infancy and childhood. Maturational processes as ordinarily understood in psychoanalysis, either in psychosexual development or in the ego and its apparatus, seem to find very little place in her theory. One wonders, for example, about turning passivity into activity, about taming anxiety from a traumatic state to a signal of danger, the place given to the development of language, or the differences between experience in the preverbal and verbal periods. Mrs. Klein has talked about the difficulty of putting primitive experience into words. The language of internal objects may have been her attempt to do just that. Dr. Segal achieved this beautifully in her 1949 paper on "Some Aspects of the Analysis of a Schizophrenic." If we compare this work with Nunberg's papers (1920), (1921) "On the Catatonic Attack" and "The Course of the Libidinal Conflict in a Case of Schizophrenia," substituting for his central thesis of the loss of the object world and its restitution, the effort to regain the good object and make the vicissitudes of aggression more explicit, the clinical theory in both would be very similar. I must add at this point a question regarding the place of the concept of regression in Kleinian ideas: Is what she sees clinically a reflection of a fixation in infancy or an arrest in development, modeled upon but not the same as, normal early infantile states?

To return for comparative purposes to the theory of the development of object relations: In the Kleinian conception, the motive for seeking an object in the external world is the necessity to externalize the dangerous death instinct; anxiety impels the infant to project—to invest—its aggression in the mother. In contrast, I believe that most Freudian analysts think that the infant's anaclitic needs, upon which the libidinal investment leans, because they are gratified from the outside, result in diminution of need tension and the perception and differentiation of, and response to, the mother as an actual object, so that gradually a separate object image is established. The infant thus acquires a more adaptive capacity to deal with anxiety: an external object complements the infant's biological helplessness.

One is again led to an important difference in emphasis concerning the actual mother—that is, of the real environment in infant development. The Kleinian emphasis is on the modifying role the real object has upon the primarily important internal fantasy life, particularly upon the destructive cathexis and distorting effects of these fantasies. Most other theoreticians in this area—Spitz, Mahler, Benedek, for instance—emphasize the fundamental role of the real mother as the external ego or beacon of orientation and buffer, the other half of the symbiotic unit in the building-up of object relations, ending in Benedek's (1938) "confident expectation." The circular interaction of maturation and nurturing brings about the earliest developmental differentiating steps, such as the formation of the body ego.

The outcome in this area of object relations, according to Klein, is the establishment within of a good maternal image, constantly threatened by the destructive drive. Other investigators have grappled with the same problem. Hartmann (1952) and Anna Freud (1952) conceive of a stage of a need-satisfying object, which gradually gives way to a phase of object constancy, a development that requires neutralization of the drives, especially of the aggression toward the first love object, the mother. Melanie Klein conceives of a similar process with a beginning relationship to part objects, confusion between self and object, which goes on to the establishment of a whole object that can be ambivalently cathected, that is not split, and eventually becomes, as I noted, a predominantly good image. The fundamental difference arising from the hypothesis of a pervasive destructive drive and a differentiated ego at birth, defending itself against what Klein calls psychotic anxieties, cannot be set aside. Also, as Zetzel (1956) pointed out, it is difficult to conceive of the Kleinian mechanisms of introjection and projection unless this differentiation of self from object and of inside from outside already exists.

This brings up another question, namely, is any distinction made between the formation of self- and object representations and the mechanisms of introjection and projection with their accompanying primitive anxieties. Dr. Segal does write about introjective identifications that result in what she says are the objects' becoming assimilated into the ego or the self, whereas other hypothesized internalized fantasies remain as separate internal objects, these latter entering into the complex relationships to each other which make up much of Kleinian psychology. I think we can agree about primitive ego-ideal formation and forerunners of the superego. But the conceptualization of independent structures in the manner Klein describes, unless considered gravely pathological, leads us again to serious differences of opinion about normal development. The original conceptualization seems to have been Ferenczi's (1912). He gave it the name identification and defined it as the urge to discover objects in the external world that correspond to one's own body, to begin with, primarily for the purpose of libidinal pleasure. Alice Balint (1943) demonstrated that this discovery of the external world via the similarity to one's own body was, in addition, motivated by an attempt to master the world outside of the self. These images are the forerunners of symbol formation. However, according to Mrs. Klein, what sets this mechanism going, in addition to the above, is the anxiety coming from the urge to destroy the bodily organs and objects and the symbols that stand for them, requiring further displacement and the addition of new symbols. This use of the term identification is very different from the mechanism conceived of, for example, by Jacobson (1964), which makes comparing ideas very difficult. It is helpful to keep Dr. Klein's usage in mind for it is a consistent idea in her work. In any case, has Mrs. Klein, by scrupulously adding the contribution of the aggressive drive, enlarged our understanding? Can this contribution be integrated with Freudian metapsychology, as Brierley predicted?

It should be clear by now that I think Mrs. Klein's major contribution is precisely this search for the vicissitudes of the aggressive drive in normal development and in clinical work. The instances most likely to lead to fruitful areas of investigation are in the psychoses, particularly when we choose to view them, as Bak (1954) did, as diseases of aggression.

There are other areas where, at first sight and taken strictly as written, there can only be complete disagreement with Mrs. Klein—for example, the inherited primal fantasies, or the dating of complex mental processes and developmental stages such as the Oedipus complex to the first year of life—"under oral primacy," as Mrs. Klein states. Here again, however, if we turn to the area of severe neuroses and psychoses—and I am among those who do look for correlation between severest disruption of psychic structure and its earliest maturation and development—we find an interesting overlapping of themes. Greenacre (see especially, 1950), (1958), (1967) found that in infants subjected to massive trauma, particularly overstimulation,

49

there occurs premature activation of the genital organs, defective ego functioning, particularly in the form of the tendency to primary identification and to severe anxiety, all of which lead to peculiar malformations and intensification of the Oedipus complex, endowing it with the burden of the pregenital patterns. In overstimulated females, the long preoedipal attachment to the mother that Freud found to be incompatible with Klein's reconstructions can be distorted by premature genital cathexis.

I have a whole series of other questions that come from a close reading of Dr. Segal's book. I'll ask three here. First, whether, in some clinical instances, the most primitive defenses, such as splitting in the sense of good or bad object or self-images, the material could not be just as well and perhaps sometimes better explained by what one might call higher-level defenses that develop later, such as isolation. Second, I'd like to ask for further clarification of the Kleinian explanation of envy, to me a very complex affect, particularly from the direction of the issue of regression and progression. Bibring (1947) called Mrs. Klein's placing of the vicissitudes of this affect so early in life "retrojection." Certainly, the oral aggression and the effects of oral deprivation influence the envy of the newborn sibling and, later, penis envy. But is this present in the same form in the nursing infant or is it a retrospective fantasy? An alternative explanation is the one used by Freud (1918) in connection with the Wolf Man—the deferred action of a trauma—and I can imagine this explanation for weaning trauma. Third, the other familiar category of problems resides in the use of terms—for instance, projection. Does finding objects in the external world that can be identified with parts of the body require projecting parts of the self into the object, and is this the same as the mechanism of projection of warded-off drive as a defense?

Let me now turn to three related questions. First, with regard to the theory of anxiety: As I understand it, in Freud's change from the first or toxicological theory of anxiety, in which repressed libido is transformed into anxiety, to the second theory of anxiety as a signal of danger, an important alteration was that the core concept of anxiety was not to be related to the instinct itself, but rather to the rising need-tension which could lead to a traumatic state. The hierarchy of danger situations: automatic anxiety (that is, the traumatic state itself), loss of the object, loss of love, castration anxiety, and guilt, has made a vast contribution to contemporary psychoanalysis. In Klein's theory, there seems to be a return to the first theory of anxiety in which the damned-up instinct, in this case, the destructive or death instinct, is the source of anxiety. Again, the place of aggression was not integrated in 1925, e.g., regarding object loss and guilt. In any case, in what way can Klein's theory of anxiety be related to Freud's second theory?

The next question has to do with the anaclitic theory of object relations I have already described. In contrast, we have Klein's theory of the turning to objects because of the destructive drive, which otherwise would destroy the organism itself. What role does seeking an object out of need and for gratification play in the development of object relations?

The final question has to do with a clinical vignette, presented here in order to inquire of Dr. Segal how she would understand a regressive process that I consider the refusion of self and object, partially defensive, partially a longing for reunion with the mother in a severely disturbed patient. Briefly: an intermittently psychotic young woman, while talking about her erotic interest in the analyst, found her eye caught by a cutglass door knob on the door to the exit of the office. She began to feel anxious, the cutglass seemed to her to become part of the walls of the room, the walls seemed to close in

51

upon her, and she suddenly bolted from the room. Other related pieces of behavior were her urges to eat the entire amount of whatever was in front of her, such as the contents of the refrigerator; when she had consumed all, she not only felt terribly disgusted but, in fact, became stuporous. After the stuporous fits, she had to perform certain exercises that would produce pain in her limbs. I am interested in whether Dr. Segal sees any role, as I did, for the concept of the loss of boundaries of the self, and the effort to regain them.

Finally, I would like to quote from Freud (1915) a passage I think is relevant to Klein's ideas, but not usually discussed in connection with them, namely, his concept of the purified pleasure ego:

Thus the original 'reality-ego,' which distinguished in-internal and external by means of a sound objective criterion, changes into a purified 'pleasure ego,' which places the characteristic of pleasure above all others. For the pleasure-ego the external world is divided into a part that is pleasurable, which it has incorporated into itself, and a remainder that is extraneous to it. It has separated off a part of its own self, which it projects into the external world and feels as hostile... At the very beginning, it seems, the external world, objects, and what is hated are identical. If later on an object turns out to be a source of pleasure, it is loved, but it is also incorporated into the ego; so that for the purified pleasure-ego once again objects coincide with what is extraneous and hated... this hate can afterwards be intensified to the point of an aggressive inclination against the object—and intention to destroy it [pp. 136–137].

This primitive reaction has seemed to me a better way to help explain certain extreme regressive states than the externalization and/ or projection of a death instinct. This phase passes, of course, into a second reality ego which distinguishes inside from outside.

It is clear that, although I find some of the Kleinian ideas valuable, others are very puzzling and of questionable validity.

DR. SEGAL COMMENTS:

I shall take up only three of Dr. Furer's points.

1. That Melanie Klein sees developments as due to anxiety and anxiety only and that she sees bad objects as predominant in the paranoid/schizoid position.

    I do not think that this is correct. She certainly sees anxiety as a spur to development, but certainly not the only one. She certainly does not see bad objects as predominating in the first phase. This would be more Fairbairn's view and even Freud's, as in the passage quoted by Dr. Furer. On the contrary, Melanie Klein emphasizes the importance of the libidinal drive and the ideal object for healthy development.

2. I cannot agree that we neglect "autonomous ego functions like speech." What I said about my work on symbolism and Bion's thinking should indicate how much attention we pay to those processes. The point is that we do not see them as *autonomous* ego functions, but as functions developed in close connection to object relationships. Speech in particular cannot be seen out of context of object relations.

3. Can you attribute to the infant a concept as complex as envy? To my mind, primitive envy is not at all a complex affect. Far less complex, for instance, than jealousy, which necessitates a complex triangular whole-object relationship. One could see envy as the other side of what Freud views as primitive narcissism— the hatred for the source of life when it is recognized not to be

one's self. Narcissistic rage and envious rage may be the same phenomenon.

DR. FURER COMMENTS:

The crucial concept of projective identification has to be included, and, in this instance, I would like to say something about the much-discussed matter of terminological confusion. Putting these two words together brings to mind a familiar concept which Freud described in superego formation: the projection of the child's aggression onto the prohibiting object and the internalizations of the prohibitions, as, for example, the prohibitions of the father altered by the projected aggression. This, of course, is not at all what was meant by Mrs. Klein, who derived the term from instinctual modes emphasized by Abraham and Ferenczi, but to which she has given her own cast. During the oral phase, psychic contents or introjects, libidinally or aggressively invested, although particularly the latter, which are considered dangerous, are expelled from the self and into the mother. The origins of the destructive fantasy may be oral, but also anal in the sense of excrement as potentially destructive, and even envy as derived from the Oedipus complex. The process is meant, according to its instinctual mode, to injure, but is not clearly differentiated from its defensive purpose of controlling and taking possession of the object. With the hatred of the self-directed toward the mother, the danger is now controlled except for the persecutory fear; and, here again, the identification is, on the model of Ferenczi and Balint, neither a partial nor total identification as an ego mechanism in development of defense but, as I understand it, rather the selection of an external equivalent to its bad self. So a Kleinian aggressive object relation, or, as I would call it, preobject relation of a primitive sort comes into being. I must conclude that concretized language is being used in the sense that the bad parts of the self enter the mother. This fits, to my mind, the psychic activity in psychoses that to some extent is regressive and concretized, has a prototype in early development, but is not the same as in infantile functioning.

The other concept to be explicated is that of splitting, and Dr. Segal seems to be attempting to find a normal and a pathological form of splitting. I agree with her, as do others, that the ego emerges out of chaos, as Freud (1915) described in his passage on the purified pleasure ego, or as Glover (1956), Mahler and Gosliner (1955), and Jacobson (1964) have described the maturation of self- and object representations as cohesive images which later can be split defensively in severe regression. Again, was the defensive character present in infancy? A further extension of the splitting idea that I have wondered about is its presumed basis for repression, that is, as a prototype. Incidentally, Freud and others consider repression a later defense by the ego. In any case, I wonder whether denial, the ostrich that Freud (1900) described in Chapter Seven, comes closer to a psychology that is based in intrapsychic conflict, than the Kleinian description which sometimes sounds more like an interpersonal psychology even though it is expressed in terms of internal objects.

Another cross-over of themes is in the area of envy and gratitude in relation to preoedipal aggression. The cross-over I think is with Jacobson's idea of the preoedipal value of power in regard to the parents that, as I understand it, results in a particular kind of aggression in the child, a devaluation of the object that leads to ego-ideal formation in idealization that preserves narcissism. However, it is again the underpinnings and the timing, the advanced ego state, and the continual operation of a primitive destructive drive, the wish to spoil the breast because it is envied as an infantile fantasy, which create a problem of disbelief.

Dr. Segal's attempts to deal with some of the criticism appears in Chapter 4 of her book (1964), where she states: "In psychological illness regression occurs not to a phase in development that was in itself normal but to one where psychological disturbances were present." However, she must then add, "From the observations of infants from birth we are now increasingly able to diagnose schizoid features in early infancy and foresee future difficulties." One must ask, Is this the case? And what is the evidence? As I understand it, the pathological form of the paranoid-schizoid position goes beyond the splitting of good and bad which presumably can then become integrated, but extends to fragmentation and "no tidy split." The additional idea suggested by Bion (quoted by Segal) of the disruption of links between any function or organ is difficult to understand, although one is reminded of the severe disorganization in autistic children.

I question the idea of symbol formation introduced by Dr. Segal as the outcome of object loss—"creative work," as she says, the setting up of substitutes called symbols, in order to spare the object. Rather, I think, following Ferenczi and Jones, of this process as a combination of maturation and conflict between id and ego. A similar issue arises in the idea that renunciation of an instinctual aim can only come about as the result of mourning, that is, as the result of giving up the love object, not in terms of an aim-inhibited drive or alteration in the drive-defense conflict.

There is a consistent new theme in Dr. Segal's chapter on Reparation: steps in maturation and development are included in her thinking. She writes of accepting the idea of separateness of psychic reality, of renunciation of omnipotence and magic, lessening of splitting, withdrawal of projective identifications, and allowing one's objects to be free.

56

But these can only occur if the particular primitive defenses do not have predominance and if affective states are no longer in an unmitigated form. Reparation, like gratitude, is a very complex affective response, with early prototypes, perhaps, but it is not an affect in early infancy. The vicissitudes of affects later in life are not only developmental, but come out of intrapsychic conflict and defense.

References

Abraham, K. (1924). A short study of the development of the libido viewed in the light of mental disorders In: *Selected Papers*. New York: Basic Books, 1953 pp. 18–501.

Bak, R. (1954). The schizophrenic defense against aggression. *Int. J. Psychoanal.* 35:129–134.

Balint, A. (1943). Identification In: *The Early Years of Life*. New York: Basic Books, 1954 pp. 92–127.

Benedek, T. (1938). Adaptation to reality in early infancy. *Psychoanal. Q.* 7:200–216.

Bibring, E. (1947). The so-called English school of psychoanalysis. *Psychoanal. Q.* 16:69–93.

Bion, W. R. (1957). Differentiation of the psychotic from the non-psychotic personalities. In: *Second Thoughts*. New York: Basic Books, 1968 pp. 43–64.

Bion, W. R. (1962). *Learning from Experience*. New York: Basic Books.

Ferenczi, S. (1912). Symbolism In: *Contributions to Psychoanalysis*. New York: Basic Books, 1950 pp. 253–282.

Freud, A. (1952). Mutual influences in the development of the ego and the id, Introduction. In: *The Writings of Anna Freud* 4:230–244 New York: International Universities Press.

Freud, S. (1900). The interpretation of dreams. *Standard Edition 5*. London: Hogarth Press, 1953.

———— (1915). Instincts and their vicissitudes. *Standard Edition* 14:111–140. London: Hogarth Press, 1957.

———— (1918). From the history of an infantile neurosis. *Standard Edition* 17:3–122 London: Hogarth Press, 1955.

Furer, M. (1964). The development of a preschool symbiotic psychotic boy. *The Psychoanal. Study Child* 19:448–469 New York: International Universities Press.

Glover, E. (1956). *On the Early Development of Mind*. New York: International Universities Press.

Greenacre, P. (1953). Special problems of an early female sexual development. In: *Trauma, Growth and Personality*. London: Routledge.

New York: International Universities Press, 1952. pp. 237–259.

———— (1958). Early psychical determinants in the development of the sense of identity. In: *Emotional Growth*. New York: International Universities Press, 1971 pp. 113–128.

———— (1967). The influence of infantile trauma on genetic patterns. In: *Emotional Growth*. New York: International Universities Press, 1971 pp. 260–300.

Hartmann, H. (1952). The mutual influences of the development of the ego and the id. In: *Essays on Ego Psychology*. New York: International Universities Press, 1964 pp. 155–181.

Isaacs, S. (1948). The nature and function of phantasy In: *Developments in Psycho-Analysis*. ed. J. Riviere. London: Hogarth Press, 1952 pp. 67–121.

Jacobson, E. (1964). *The Self and the Object World*. New York: International Universities Press.

———— (1971). *Depression*. New York: International Universities Press.

Jones, E. (1916). The theory of symbolism. In: *Papers on Psychoanalysis.* Boston: Beacon Press, 1961 pp. 87–144.

Klein, M. (1921–1945). *Love, Guilt and Reparation and Other Works.* New York: Delacorte, 1975.

———— (1946–1963). Envy and Gratitude and Other Works. New York: Delacorte, 1975.

Mahler, M. & Gosliner, B.J. 1955 On symbiotic child psychosis. The *Psychoanal. Study Child* 10:195–212 New York: International Universities Press.

———— Pine, F. & Bergmann, A. (1975). *The Psychological Birth of the Human.* Infant New York: Basic Books.

Nunberg, H. (1920). On the catatonic attack. In: *Practice and Theory of Psychoanalysis.* New York: International Universities Press, 1948 pp. 3–23.

———— (1921). The course of a libidinal conflict in a case of schizophrenia. In: *Practice and Theory of Psychoanalysis.* New York: International Universities Press, 1948 pp. 2459.

Rosenfeld, H. (1965). *Psychotic States.* New York: International Universities Press.

Segal, H. (1949). Some aspects of the analysis of a schizophrenic. *Int. J. Psychoanal.* 31:268–278.

———— (1957). Notes on symbol formation. *Int. J. Psychoanal.* 38:391–397.

———— (1964). Introduction to the Work of Melanie Klein New York: Basic Books.

Spitz, R. A.(1959). *A Genetic Theory of Ego Formation.* New York: International Universities Press.

Strachey, J. (1957). Editor's note to "Instincts and their Vicissitudes." *Standard Edition* 14:111–116 London: Hogarth Press.

Zetzel, R. (1956). Concept and contents in psychoanalytic theory In: *The Capacity for Emotional Growth*. New York: International Universities Press, 1970 pp. 115–138.

CHAPTER 4

Enactment Panel Discussion

(1999). *Journal of Clinical Psychoanalysis 8:62–70*

There is an aspect of the history of thinking, which is obvious from reading the contemporary literature, of which this panel is a part, that should now be made explicit: The era of the domination of American ego psychology, which found its culmination in the ideas of Heinz Hartmann, is over. In fact, for many analysts Hartmann's ego psychology, far from dominating, need no longer even be included in contemporary discourse. It may be true that the basic precept of Freudian theory, intrapsychic conflict, lives on in modern conflict theory, as defined by Charles Brenner. And, even though modern conflict theory is now understood not to exclude but to include object relations—a long-standing misunderstanding which has now been resolved—the focus of analytic discourse these days has shifted to the role of the object in the psychoanalytic situation.

The cutting edge of psychoanalytic interest as illustrated by this panel concentrates its attention on a particular aspect of the psychoanalytic situation: the analyst-patient relationship. The larger interest now is in the psychology of the analyst, the new clinical subject—or, as others would have it, the dual object, the analytic third, or the coconstructed object. This trend has gone so far that: Dr. Chused repeatedly had to remind the panelists that the ultimate goal of psychoanalysis is to understand how the mind of the patient works. What is clearly now a new paradigm in analytic technique is the mutual influence of patient and analyst, which, it is claimed, is an uncharted region requiring expeditions of students for its exploration. Moreover, there is now a new goal of analysis: the importance of the patient's life via the analyst's influence; not as the ultimate end of the treatment, but moment to moment in the sessions.

As I have discussed elsewhere (1998), there is an early precedent in analytic history for both this interest and approach. Sandor Ferenczi became a participant analyst—the first interrelationist, as it were. He began with what he called "active therapy," forbidding the patient his libidinal outlets, so as to concentrate libido in the analytic situation (1930). Most important, however, in the development of his technique was his determination to cure his patients and to make their lives better. He emphasized the analyst's influence in curing patients. He ultimately extended the curative goal to include himself, with the result that at the end of his life, he called his treatment "mutual analysis." As he put it, the Freudian method, the analysis of resistance, intrapsychic conflict, and unconscious fantasy, was only the beginning; the true curative work came after that. His specific contribution was that the pathogenic trauma of childhood, after its repetition in the analytic situation, would then be removed by the analyst who would provide a corrective emotional experience because he would not be like the hypocritical parents who denied their sexual interests in the child.

There is another area of psychoanalysis that seems to me to have been relegated to the background, as if never known; namely, that the analyst is qualified to analyze the patient not only because he is a figure of authority, but also because he is someone who has been analyzed and therefore knows his own heart and mind. For example, the impact of the training analysis after termination was studied over a period of fifteen years by a COPE committee of the American Psychoanalytic Association consisting of Drs. Brian Bird, Victor Calef, Francis McLaughlin, Martin Stein, and myself (Furer, 1985). There were two outstanding findings of that study that seem to me to be relevant to the topic of enactment: In the approximately five years following the termination of the training analysis, almost all of our thirty-two subjects, because of troubling emotional reactions to their patients, and because of emotional obstructions to their work, carried out fairly intensive self-analyses. In most instances, as one might expect, the subjects reported that there remained aspects of the relationship, or transference, to their analyst that had to be further understood and corrected. In 1985 I said that these nagging remainders, whether cherished memories or experiences of betrayal, were both unanalyzed and powerful because they were "real events" in the analyses. Now I would call them enactments and not be as struck that the post-termination analytic work included efforts to understand the analyst as well as the self. The term *enactment* adds clarification to a known phenomenon.

The other important finding was that transference experience was not simply remembered but, as reported by Dr. Arnold Pfeffer (1961), was readily aroused. This was so even in our format, a group discussion of two investigators and eight analysts talking about the effect of the training analysis on their analytic work. In the light of the new paradigm, transference (interminable) not only sensitizes the analyst to the patient's transference but shifts attention to the ever present countertransference enactments by the analyst as a necessary component of the work (Bird, 1972).

It is incumbent upon me as a witness to the training at the New York Psychoanalytic Institute in the 1950s to comment on the observations about this period made by Drs. Chused and Ellman.

Dr. Chused remarks that her childhood memory "tells it all": "If you were analyzed it was expected that you would be as close to psychic perfection as possible."

Yes, there was perfectionism and hero worship at the time. Even now psychoanalysis seems to have its heroes. But in the 1950s this was in fact recognized by many of the individuals in question, particularly by Dr. Phyllis Greenacre in her well-known paper, "Problems of Overidealization of the Analyst and Analysis" (1966).

A related memory of Dr. Chused is that there was "desperate longing for a saviour" to arise out of psychoanalysis. There is no doubt that the second generation of analysts who were my teachers felt analysis to be a revolutionary and powerful tool, as did the Prague circle of Fenichel and others. They were idealists who believed in the transformation of man and society through psychoanalysis (truth) and socialism (social justice). However, in my experience, many of the Europeans, for example, Dr. Jacobson, who had been imprisoned, and others who had lost family members, held a tragic view of life.

The perfectibility of man, as one commented to me, was a strange American notion.

Dr. Chused also talks about "set techniques," and that the words of teachers and training analysts were followed religiously. This was not so in my experience. I had six supervisors who had very different personalities and certainly very different ways of analyzing, despite their more or less agreement about theoretical positions as articulated by Hartmann, Kris, and Loewenstein. In my discussions with a colleague who shared four of these supervisors, the differences among them as people and the differences of their impact on their patients was very clear to us. But it was part of our private educational experiences. In my recollection, it was not formally discussed.

A final correction has to do with Dr. Edith Jacobson, who is referred to by Dr. Ellman as an "outsider" at the New York Psychoanalytic Institute. On the contrary, Dr. Jacobson was a respected "insider" who taught at the Institute from the earliest time I can remember until her illness forced her to retire. Her book, *The Self and the Object World* (1964), was considered by us to be a definitive text and a continuation of the concept of mind that originated with the structural hypothesis as elaborated by Heinz Hartmann. Moreover, it is my belief that Dr. Jacobson's writings on what Dr. Ellman considers to be the equivalent of enactment, had to do with her ideas about psychotic conflict; that is, the patient's requirement of interaction with the world around him, including the analyst, to preserve stability. This point of view is presented in her Freud Anniversary Lecture at the New York Psychoanalytic Institute (1967). In that lecture she dissociated herself from Searles who felt that one had to regress with one's patient to a mutually symbiotic dependency. She stated, "Searles expresses his opinion that I am afraid of symbiotic situations. I admit that I prefer oceanic gratification of a different nature to such experiences with patients" (p. 62).

A telling example of the difference in thinking between today and the 1950s is a clinical vignette by Ernst Kris (1951) in which he changed his wording of an interpretation to a patient from "your demand for love" to "your need for love," having in mind the patient's greed. Kris decided that it was his preconscious that made this correction, which was, in fact, a slip. He had not noticed the change, until the patient reacted with intense emotion and informed Kris of it. Today one would think of this as an enactment, and in this case, although I believe not in all cases, only recognized after the enactment-slip had taken place. Today we would assume that this had something to do with the analyst's feelings about the patient which changed his ideas. I believe that we go too far in concluding that this is the sum and substance of the analytic relationship and that it is the effective vehicle of cure, although it was a poignant experience and probably a corrective one for both.

In regard to the panelists, I find my position most closely articulated by Dr. Chused, probably because of similar experience in our development as analysts. I too was a child analyst for many years. In addition I undertook and supervised the treatment of very disturbed preschool age young children (Furer, 1967). Their communication was of course nonverbal, which required a sensitivity to its various manifestations; the use of body, sounds, facial expressions and so on, present in all human interaction, but clearly more so in children. The influence of the therapist on these mute young children, and on the mother-child pair, was enormous, as it was from supervisor to therapist to mother-child unit, and of course in the reverse direction as well.

I agree with Dr. Ellman's speculation about idealization leading to disillusionment and abandonment. In our analyst-subjects, there was much criticism about what was felt to be an enforced idealization of analysis, particularly of training analysis and the training analyst, which they called "elitism," or the imposition of an ego ideal that created strong negative feelings. The latter in most instances was not adequately analyzed.

I take exception to the position taken by Dr. Renik, that enactments are only known after they occur and in addition that analysts cannot evaluate the intensity or impact of enactment upon patient or analyst. I believe that one can anticipate certain kinds of enactments given what seems to me each person's specific limited templates. I continue to hold to the ego's role in consciousness, in both altering and modifying our participation. For Dr. Renik, self-disclosure is a logical extension of his assumptions. I believe that self-disclosure may be an added tool to help the patient understand the transference when it cannot be done in any other way. Disclosure may be required for a particular patient to be aware of the analyst's involvement in order for that patient to acknowledge his own; for example, when the narcissistic injury of one-sidedness is beyond the patient's capacity to bear. It is impressive to me, in agreement with Dr. Hoffman, that self-disclosure which goes against the cultural norm of psychoanalysis often results in a moving emotional experience as in many of Dr. Renik's examples and in Ernst Kris' slip. Renik's goal, to negotiate a corrective emotional experience which would benefit the patient's life, is at the far end of the therapeutic spectrum, a relational and experiential effect in contrast to the effect of insight. Dr. Renik buttressed this point by noting that experiences that happen spontaneously and without awareness are often the most effective. This emphasis in technique is expressed in his definition of analytic expertise: Analysts are now experts in collaborating with their patients, rather than experts in knowing their patients' minds. This omits altogether the analyst as expert in knowledge of his own mind and heart.

I think that it is fair to say that Chused and Ellman, and even Rothstein, adhere to what Hoffman has called "the conservative critique of the blank screen concept," which holds that the analyst can "dichotomize interpersonal experience in general, and the experience in the analytic situation in particular, into veridical and distorted," and in addition which "accepts the possibility of transference that is not linked to countertransference" (Hoffman, 1996). But Renik I believe adheres to the radical belief that the transference, and in fact all the data emerging from the psychoanalytic situation, is coconstructed, created by interacting contributions of both patient and analyst.

All communication contains an attempt to influence. That attempt is more obvious and more compelling in children, in children's intimate relations, and clearly in children's transference. This is a developmental point of view which is insufficiently represented in the panel. However, in both creative work and analytic work there is a two-step process. The rendering of emotion and desire in words involves reason and insight and adds to ego mastery. It is the relativity of the weights of these various elements at different moments that I find in Dr. Chused's thinking and not in Dr. Renik's.

The older theory has been turned on its head, as it were. The analyst's neutrality and abstinence were supposed to facilitate transference. Originally the frustration of drive discharge resulted in its flowing back to the original objects and original templates. Now the participation of the analyst is what enhances and intensifies the patient's experience, and it is inevitable. Most important to me is Dr. Chused's point that even in a two-person event, the unconsciously motivated interaction by either party can well have a different meaning for each participant. This is in direct disagreement with the idea that the experience is coconstructed or results in the creation of an "analytic third" (Ogden, 1985). I would consequently agree with Dr. Chused's narrow definition of enactment as those instances in which the patient's attempt to actualize the transference stimulates a repressed conflict in the analyst which leads him to respond inadvertently in a manner that supports the patient's perception. This would only *appear* to be an interpersonal event.

An analyst can certainly deceive himself, and at times self-awareness may be helped by the patient's accurate perceptions of the analyst. But to turn around Dr. Dale Boesky's provocative phrase, I would say that if the analyst and eventually the patient and the analyst together do not ultimately become aware of the large fraction of what is determined by the unconscious in their relationship, then the analysis has a long way to go (Boesky, 1990).

The emphasis on enactment should give greater weight to the transference, both of the patient and the analyst. But it seems to me that in this new paradigm there is a down-grading of the power of the transference, of its repetitive nature and its limited organization. For example, the emphasis by Renik is on the importance of the analyst's conscience, and Chused also talks about a standard of analytic behavior, rather than what is of importance to me, the recognition of the analyst's preferred transference potentials which by now should be well known to him. Analysis makes for greater tolerance, not for better character (Hartmann, 1960). The example given by Dr. Chused, in which she feels she violated that standard by pushing an idea on the patient, I think neglects the transference power within the patient. As Kris (1951) pointed out long ago, one cannot expect the patient to respond to the analyst's conscious intent in an interpretation, but the patient will associate to a transference potential that the analyst had not recognized.

Finally, a comment on common ground and differences among analysts. It is now clear that we are witnessing a convergence of ideas from various modifications or corrections of classical thinking. But when the suggestion is made that the convergence should progress to the point where distinctions in theory between various schools should be altogether dropped, this seems to me to be inimical to intellectual discourse. A similar point is made by Dr. Chused when she inveighs against the tendency to homogenize analysts from different disciplines whatever their prejudices as influenced by their subcultures. She notes that this would deprive us of their uniqueness and of their potential contributions. The differences among us sharpen our views, open our minds, and lead us to test ideas in our own experience. Common ground, it seems to me, leads to eclecticism in its pejorative sense, a situation where ultimately one's theory is chosen to fit the patient's material at any given time, and then, in a circular fashion, the material is taken as evidence for the theory.

References

Bird, B. (1972). Notes on transference: Universal phenomenon and hardest part of analysis. *J. Amer. Psychoanal. Assn.*, 20:267–301.

Boesky, D. (1990). The psychoanalytic process and its components. *Psychoanal. Q.*, 59:550–584.

Ferenczi, S. (1930). The principle of relaxation and neocatharsis. *Int. J. Psycho-Anal.*, 11:428–443.

Furer, M. (1967). Personality organization during the recovery of a severely disturbed young child. In: *Borderline Personality Disorders: The Concept, the Syndrome, the Patient*. New York: International Universities Press, 1977.

———— (1985). Transference terminable and interminable: 37th Brill Memorial Lecture. New York Psychoanalytic Society, November 26.

———— (1998). Changes in psychoanalytic technique: Progressive or regressive. *Journal of Clinical Psychoanalysis*, 7:209–235.

Glover, E. (1955). *The Technique of Psychoanalysis*. New York: International Universities Press.

Greenacre, P. (1966). Problems of overidealization of the analyst and analysis. In: *Emotional Growth*, Vol. 2. New York :International Universities Press, pp. 743–761.

Hartmann, H. (1960). Psychoanalysis and Moral Value. Freud Anniversary Lecture Series of the New York Psychoanalytic Institute. New York: International Universities Press.

Hoffman, I. Z. (1996). The intimate and ironic authority of the psychoanalyst's presence. *Psychoanal. Q.*, *65:102–136.*

Jacobson, E. (1964). *The Self and the Object World.* New York: International Universities Press.

———— (1967). Psychotic Conflict and Reality. *Freud Anniversary Lecture Series of the New York Psychoanalytic Institute.* New York: International Universities Press.

Kris, E. (1951). Ego psychology and interpretation in psychoanalytic therapy. *Psychoanal. Q.*, *20:15–30.*

Ogden, T.H. (1985). Analyzing forms of aliveness and deadness of the transference-countertransference. *Int. J. Psycho-Anal.*, *76:695–710.*

Pfeffer, A. (1961). Follow-up studies of the satisfactory analysis. *J. Amer. Psychoanal. Assn.*, *9:698–718.*

CHAPTER 5

The Analyst's Subjectivity and the Analyst's Objectivity: A Discussion of Current Issues in Psychoanalytic Technique

(1998). *Journal of Clinical Psychoanalysis* 7(2):237–252
(with Owen Renik, M.D.)

Ed. Note: The following discussion has been excerpted and edited from the minutes provided by the Secretary, Dr. Steven Wein, for whose assistance we are indebted. The statements have been further screened and approved by the various participants.

Precirculated Papers

Ed. Note: Dr. Renik graciously provided to the Institute copies of two of his most recent papers entitled (1) "A Note on the Analyst's Subjectivity and Objectivity" (in press,) and (2) "Getting Real in Analysis" (1996). These had been copied and circulated privately to the Faculty prior to the meeting. In both papers Dr. Renik gave detailed clinical vignettes illustrating his current technical innovations, including considerable interaction with and self disclosure to the patients.

Present at the Faculty Meeting were Edward Nersessian, M.D., Chairman; Steven Wein, M.D., Secretary; Drs. Sander Abend, Henry

Bachrach, Leon Balter, Francis Baudry, Antonio Beltramini, Charles Brenner, John Crow, Jerome Ennis, Aaron Esman, Manuel Furer, Karen Gilmore, Daniel Goldberg, Marianne Goldberger, Lisa Goldsmith, Richard Gottlieb, Robert Grayson, George Gross, William Grossman, Theodore Jacobs, Robert Lupi, John McDevitt, David Milrod, Wendy Olesker, Arnold Rothstein, Eslee Samberg, Albert Sax, Lester Schwartz, Theodore Shapiro, Ronda Shaw, Richard Weiss, Martin Willick, and Herbert Wyman.

In the first paper, the prominent vignette involved a male patient who perceived from the couch that Dr. Renik's voice had suddenly become more distant, as if he had turned his head in another direction. Dr. Renik realized he in fact had done this and so informed the patient (Renik, in press). The discussion below makes the context clear.

As to the second paper, for reasons of confidentiality Dr. Renik is unable to provide the full text. We are able to supply only the following detail: The controversial vignette involved Dr. Renik's direct advice to a patient to disregard a minor illness in favor of attending an important family function. Among the patient's reactions to this intervention was her feeling that Dr. Renik as a person might be as aggressively domineering and bossy as her father had been. Dr. Renik suggested that she monitor his behavior for signs of this attitude. For the rest, the ensuing discussion will make the context clear.

Introduction

Owen Renik

We are all inevitably parochial, because we are educated and work in particular analytic subcultures. It is important that we talk to people with whom we disagree. I am not advocating an atheoretical "anything goes" approach to psychoanalytic technique. I am proposing a change in theory. I think we have evidence that current techniques do not work well enough. Therefore, traditional conceptions of technique need to be reviewed and revised. It is in this spirit that I offered the precirculated material for discussion here.

Formal Discussion

Manuel Furer

First, let me express my appreciation to Dr. Renik and others who are working in the same vein, for an indirect influence of my teaching of psychoanalytic technique. They have brought about an alteration of the psychoanalytic atmosphere that has made it easier for candidates to include, even in a group setting such as a class, the expression and discussion of what Dr. Renik has called absolute intersubjectivity, or the subjectivity of the analyst—what I think of as countertransference analysis.

I do not see this evening as a debate, but rather as an opportunity for us to learn more about Dr. Renik's positions, and consequently these few words are by way of opening remarks. Dr. Renik proposes and argues for a different set of procedures in analysis—a new paradigm in technique that meets his goal of improving the patient's life more efficiently and effectively than is the case using what we consider standard procedure. I want to say at the outset that I have no disagreement with Dr. Renik's observation of intersubjectivity as I understand it; an ongoing continuous communication and a potentially helpful emotional relationship between analyst and patient, whether positive or negative, as was described by Ferenczi in the 1920s (1919, 1920, 1928, 1930) and by Bird in the 1970s (1972).

Dr. Phyllis Greenacre (1954) once said that if you put two people in a room and enjoin them not to communicate, a social relationship will develop (p. 671). If we compare that hypothetical situation to that of psychoanalysis, where on the part of both patient and analyst there is an enormous effort both to communicate and to restrain communication, the inevitable social relationship must become even more complex and certainly more intense. This experience may not be unique, as Drs. Brenner and Renik point out, except that Brenner emphasizes that it is different because the transference is analyzed and not responded to; perhaps already a point of difference (Brenner, 1976, 1987).

My point is that it is the contending forces in the psyche (i.e., intrapsychic conflict, one of Freud's earliest and most lasting discoveries) that is the major factor in this experience. With the result that as Freud (1914) put it in the technical papers, in a manner still conceptually valid, the transference replaces the neurosis, so that the analysis of the transference is indispensable for the analysis of the neurosis and of conflicts that produced the neurosis. This is perhaps another difference, because Dr. Renik, it seems to me, emphasizes maladaptive past relationships and not intrapsychic conflict as the major factor.

Of course, these conflicting sexual and aggressive forces have been directed toward the primary objects. The outcome of conflict has become embedded in the psyche, and the repetition of past experience is consequently filtered through that particular psyche. In Dr. Renik's work, it seems to me, the reappearance in the present of a disordered, unhappy, or unattended to experience in the past is purposefully accentuated by the analyst's participation with the patient, not only to bring it into sharper focus, but via corrective emotional experience in the broad sense as one of the vehicles of cure. This emphasis—I agree here with Lawrence Friedman (Panel, 1995a, b)—will at the very least lessen the importance of the investigation of what is unconscious.

In regard to technique, Dr. Renik has come to the conclusion that since he cannot know about the impact of his subjectivity on the patient until after it has happened, it is imperative for reasons of equality, honesty, and effectiveness, to introduce that subjectivity, particularly via self-disclosure, as part and parcel of psychoanalytic treatment, as well as in response to emergency reactions as described by Gitelson (1952). At this point Dale Boesky's reminder of the limitations of self-knowledge comes to mind: "The recent trends toward revelations of counter-transference, of the analyst's feelings about the patient, or behavior with the patient, as understood by the patient particularly, are deceptively honest" (1990, p. 569). My position is that even though our passions are involved, countertransference enactment is not operational at all times in an analysis. Its significance or effect in the sense of determining the productions of the patient or the analyst at his work is not inevitable, but variable. It is a potential, not necessarily activated in the analyst or acted on or known to the patient.

My view is that the outcome of our intrapsychic conflicts over drive derivatives can usefully be thought of as relatively autonomous. For example, I agree with Brenner (1985) that, in the analyst at work, sadism and voyeurism and their accompanying defenses, such as reaction formations, are likely to be prominent and most of the time in balance—sometimes not. The breakthrough of Dr. Renik's urge to be domineering illustrates this point. How to deal with this in one's self is obvious; in regard to the patient it is a thorny issue. Dr. Renik's patient helped by supplying an understanding of him, superficial or limited though it may have been. Dr. Renik's invitation of her continuous monitoring of his behavior is consistent with his procedures. But I ask Dr. Renik to elaborate on the purpose of this procedure as it relates to a theory of psychic change.

I will state in an oversimplified fashion the differences in our thinking. My procedures and the goal and objective of my technique is based upon the theory of the working of the mind and of pathogenesis that I find most convincing, shared by most of you and known to Dr. Renik. It seems to me that Dr. Renik either feels no need for theory, or is caught in a dilemma between his agreement with our ideas and his wish to change them—or he is not yet ready to change our theory in accordance with what he sees as the effectiveness of his current procedures.

If I understand Dr. Renik correctly, he finds that interaction, the influence of the analyst, and corrective emotional experience in the broadest sense, all of which require knowing the analyst as a "real" person, are not only effective, but constitute the most important active ingredients of cure. This implies a different theory of pathogenesis as constituting something closer to a continuation of past maladaptive influences into the present—without, however, any explanation of why this is the case. My theory on the other hand would not allow for the minimizing, but would require the analysis of resistance, the elaboration of fantasies, and the construction of the content of the contending forces in the unconscious.

In regard to the clinical material, it is always difficult to question an analyst's understanding of his patient. That understanding is not an intellectual task; one does not know the context of the past experience in the analysis, and only to a limited degree the immediate experience. I will try to focus on how Dr. Renik's thinking informs his procedures. To take one example: In the paper "Getting Real in Analysis" (1996), Dr. Renik tells us that his thinking began with his belief that the patient was using poor judgment, to her disadvantage, in not calling her friend about her decision not to attend Thanksgiving because she would harm the children. He already knew about her self–abnegation derived from her experience with her mother. As I understand Dr. Renik's procedure, the better way to psychoanalyze the patient, is to think of improving her life, and also "to get real"—to make evident the true interaction— an analyst helping a patient. He presents what he considers reality testing—he tells the patient how he handles having a cold and going to work. In addition he makes the interpretation of her wish to be close to her mother, but via a maladaptive method. She is moved and reveals what to me is a consciously withheld transference fantasy—that Dr. Renik will also get tired of her. It seems to me that this transference fantasy quite consistently is corrected later on when he asks her to monitor his potentially domineering behavior. My question is why not let her go on and elaborate her fantasy to understand its conflictual nature and its unconscious content?

This sequence seems to me to pervade the material. After a moving interchange with the analyst, a consciously withheld fantasy is revealed. Consistently, Dr. Renik also requests the conscious perceptions of his patient, "What do you really think of me?" recalling Merton Gill's recommendation in his last writings (1994). In essence this takes the place of the analysis of the patient's resistances, her mechanisms of defense that might well reveal why she is withholding, and further details of both her conscious and unconscious conflicts; for example, other reasons than the mother's perceived behavior for her projection of aggression onto the mother and the analyst. I assume that Dr. Renik believes that the material moved quickly into crucial areas, that is, the repetition of the distorted relationships with primary objects as a consequence of being real, and perhaps close. Her gratitude is reasonable, but her appreciation of the fact that he did not insist upon her adopting his point of view, seems to me to be precisely an idealization of the analyst that he wishes to avoid. This complex emotional experience, truly cocreated, is consequently more difficult to analyze, in my opinion.

How she gets to the next associations regarding her sadomasochistic fantasies in regard to her father is not clear, but the subsequent enactment of their disagreement about the meaning of girls in her high school teasing her seems to me to follow. My point is that reality testing is not the issue but rather an affective interchange that eventually leads the analyst to enlist the patient in a corrective emotional experience. Although a single incident it seems to me paradigmatic of Dr. Renik's technique. It is reminiscent of Ferenczi's goal of reconciliation in the present to replace alienation in the past (Ferenczi, 1931, p. 137).

To pose one more question about procedure: Does what Dr. Renik calls reality testing have to be introduced because of the extent of the analyst's participation—though I should remind you of Dr. Renik's argument that his participation follows from his conclusion that one only knows one's subjectivity after it happens. Dr. Renik will remember Dr. Lawrence Friedman's question "How do you know when to restrain yourself and what to restrain?" (Panel, 1995a, b, p. 519). My theory would require me to focus on the more–or–less conviction of the patient's belief in regard to transference ideas and what function the move–or–less conviction serves in dealing with the anxiety derived from conflict. I believe this is Dr. Stein's precept: That these latter issues would be interfered with if the analyst confirmed or denied what was realistic in the patient's thoughts (Stein, 1966, p. 882)—not to mention the value of the patient's untrammeled elaborations of conscious fantasy or what I would call daydreaming.

Dr. Renik's approach is indicated by his statement that, "Only when a patient is able to expose his or her sincerest convictions about who the analyst really is can the patient consider how his or her experience of the analyst may have been effected by the past" (1996). As I pointed out, this seems in Dr. Renik's argument to be a step beyond the overcoming of resistance, to the curative effects of what others have called authentic interaction. The emphasis is upon changing the effects of the past rather than reconstructing a childhood neurosis and unconscious fantasies for their explanatory value, as Kris put it (1956). Dr. Renik's method seems to me to be offering a royal road to the past via the present, as in, "it was when she examined, very carefully, what she really thought about my character that she became aware of her conflicted sexual interest in her father" (Renik, 1997). This is in keeping with his idea that the patient's avoidance of judgment about the reality of her ideas is a procrastination that impedes the analysis.

At one point, Dr. Renik asks questions to which only theory can provide an answer. He asks, "How does the patient both repeat the maladaptive patterns in the analysis and forge new adaptive ones? How does the patient experience the analyst as an old transference object and a new mutative object offering new interactions?" (1997).

The symptomatic adaptation, the symptoms themselves, as I've said, become the transference. The relationship to so–called new objects that to others are mutative in the sense of fostering developments, to me means without the intrusion of symptoms, so that the way is open for Freud's "common unhappiness" rather than "hysterical misery" (Breuer and Freud, 1893–1895, p. 305). The patient's insight has made the analysand more independent of unconscious influences. The alternative is for the analyst to offer new and better ways to live, either by identification or "real experience" with the analyst. Does Dr. Renik believe that he is offering us only better procedures, or also better theory or a different emphasis in theory? Is this illustrated by the first patient, Ethan, when he says, "I wish I had had this with my Dad" (Renik, 1997), although he adds, "I wonder how much of the problems between us was with him and his need to be a big shot, and how much was me and my guilt about playing up to my Mom?" (Renik, 1997). It seems to me Dr. Renik requires the first to get to the second, the patient's reflecting on his own psychology. But is the emotional response not also considered part of what is curative—a new experience with the analyst? Finally, Dr. Renik asks, what is the ultimate objective of clinical analytic work, and we all agree, it is to cure the patient. However, Dr. Renik says, "longstanding controversies within our field remain active and unresolved because the various partisans prioritize their objectives differently and therefore pursue with objectivity different enterprises under the name of psychoanalysis" (Renik, in press).

To me this is precisely the issue. What are our convictions up to this point about the evolution of the workings of the mind that helps us understand how it produces maladaptive or pathological outcomes? Consequently, our objective ultimately is for the patient as a vehicle of cure to understand his own psyche. Dr. Renik's ultimate objective seems to me to be of a different order that: "Two imperfect people who care about each other can manage to sustain their relationship in the face of mutual disappointment" (1993, p. 151).

I prefer Ferenczi's conclusion earlier in his work as to the preferred outcome of analysis.

A special form of this work of revision appears to occur, however, in every case I mean the revision of the emotional experience which happened in the course of the analysis. The analysis itself gradually becomes a piece of the patient's life history, which he passes in review before bidding us farewell.

In the course of this revision it is from a certain distance and with much greater objectivity that he looks at the experiences which he went through at the beginning of his acquaintanceship with us [Ferenczi, 1928, p. 97].

General Discussion

Owen Renik

Dr. Furer has indeed touched on the major points of controversy. I want to emphasize that in my opinion many parts of psychoanalytic theory are not in need of revision. For example, I am not proposing changes in the theory of pathogenesis. Compromise formation remains, for me, a useful way to describe motivation. I would, however, like to reconsider the nature of the clinical analytic and therapeutic processes and the analyst's tasks.

An analyst is irreducibly subjective. The influence of the analyst's subjectivity may be variable, but the analyst cannot know at any given moment how much his or her idiosyncrasies are influencing the clinical process. Therefore, the patient needs to be invited to monitor the analyst—not as a matter of political or moral principle, but because it is effective. An analyst cannot hope to know what his or her blind spots are; and authorizing the patient as a consultant is an attempt to be methodologically sound, not an attempt to be democratic. Important data will not be brought to the analyst's attention unless the patient is encouraged to comment on the analyst's actual person, and traditional conceptions of technique inadvertently discourage this. Investigation of the "real analyst" is not a substitute for investigation of "transference," but is a way of facilitating investigation, as I think my clinical examples illustrate.

The question is how best to make the analyst's subjectivity a legitimate topic for discussion in the clinical setting, in order to correct for limitations imposed by the analyst's subjectivity. This kind of interaction does not impede analysis; it helps the patient to consider what is going on within his or her mind.

Robert Grayson

Dr. Renik to me is unclear in his definition of terms. What is the definition of subjectivity?

Owen Renik

The analyst's subjectivity refers to all of the personal psychological factors that may affect his observations and actions, i.e., his values, interests, wishes, anxieties, etc. Taking it into account means doing what Einstein suggested in physics about studying the inextricability of the observer from the data observed.

Sander Abend

I would like to respond to Dr. Renik's statement that our central goal is to invite the patient to be as candid as possible about his reactions to the analyst, and that standard technique does not encourage this. It is not clear to me that the conscious invitation will be experienced by the patient at face value, nor responded to only at that level. What is critical is not what the patient says, but the analyst's clinical assessment of the patient's responses. To analyze the patient's reluctance to express himself in a candid way is our central task.

Owen Renik

I think that the ground rules we establish facilitate or inhibit the patient's self–expression. Of course it is a matter of judgment for the analyst what to reveal or not to reveal, and this judgment on the analyst's part, too, has to be subject to discussion between the patient and the analyst. A lot of this is creeping into practice, but we need a theory that systematically describes it. We have not been taught that a good technique for one patient is not necessarily good for another.

Theodore Shapiro

I would like to ask why Dr. Renik does not cite Harry Stack Sullivan as a significant precursor to his position, as Dr. Furer cites Ferenczi. Another point, I'm not sure that Dr. Renik's use of the case vignette supports his arguments. Case vignettes only show our clinical virtuosity but offer no firm proof of our theoretical positions because they are used as exemplars and not as empirical demonstrations. As to psychoanalytic education, we all need quite a few years of practice to learn how to be an analyst. Candidates in particular must be taught first how to listen. They need a lot of time doing that before they can interject their own reactions without causing significant confusion.

Owen Renik

I agree that Sullivan was a great contributor, ahead of his era in many ways, but by the time I had discovered him, our theory had already gone beyond him! I would disagree with Dr. Shapiro's approach to candidates. We should not hesitate to teach them from the beginning how best we think we work. Of course, in our vignettes, we do not offer evidence for our views, only illustrations of our views.

Theodore Shapiro

And therefore it is not sufficient just to present a case without demonstrating what the indications are to intervene in a particular way in a particular case.

Theodore Jacobs

If we focus only on intrapsychic conflict we may miss the scanning that the patients do of the analyst and the analyst's communications. This gets entangled in the transference, but is not the same thing as the transference. Dr. Renik is trying to pay attention to this. Our technique calls for restraint, neutrality, abstinence. But with some patients this leads to resistance. In such instances we may need a different approach to engage these patients. Some patients need more of us, and Dr. Renik is on the "more" side. An important question, however, is whether this engagement becomes part of the analytic work or remains a powerful therapeutic force in itself.

Edward Nersessian

Isn't it possible that we could end up with the same material even without any of these techniques of self–disclosure?

Owen Renik

The question is what is the best means to the end that we all share. We should take a more experimental attitude to technique. We know a lot less than we think we know about how to get where we want to go.

William Grossman

I would caution against any assumption that we all end up in the same place regardless of the technique used. Every seemingly rational statement has an unconscious meaning. As Congreve said: "No mask like open truth to cover lies/To go naked is the best disguise" (1694; cited in Rosenberg [1974]). The consequences of any technique are many. The outcome reported is only one moment of outcome. The crucial question is how it would be different if the patient came to it in a different way. Fenichel said in 1941 that we should be real, but people mean different things by that. I do not understand why certain of Dr. Renik's interventions were necessary. What are the consequences of Dr. Renik's having intervened? Making one thing explicit also makes it less clear what else is also implicit. I would agree of course that the same could be said of an intervention within the classical approach. And certainly that different analysts will use the same theory in different ways. Not all ego psychologists behave the same way. The question is not did you do the wrong thing. The question is how do we know the consequences of following a particular technique.

Owen Renik

What is crucial is how we feel about the relationship between thought and action, about the difference between discovering unconscious truth versus creating new truth in the therapeutic situation.

Charles Brenner

There is a difference between a relatively superficial understanding of a patient's transference and a more profound understanding of transference wishes, fears, and conflicts.

The latter on a profound level is less likely to be reached spontaneously by the patient. They must be interpreted, i.e., brought to the patient's attention by the analyst. The question is what interpretation is most likely to accomplish the desired result. Dr. Renik realized from his patient's associations that it was Dr. Renik's having turned his head to one side that reminded the patient of what his father did when bored. Dr. Renik therefore told the patient (in effect), "Yes, my attention was distracted briefly and I turned my head to one side. When I did so you thought I was bored, like your father." Another appropriate intervention would have been, "You heard my voice coming from somewhere else and you thought I was bored like your father." I would ask Dr. Renik why he preferred the intervention he had made, which included a degree of self–disclosure, to an intervention such as the above alternative, which says nothing about Dr. Renik's having been distracted briefly. Why does Dr. Renik think that his having told his patient that his attention had been distracted was more likely to help the patient achieve a more profound understanding of the nature and origins of transference wishes, fears, and conflicts than was likely to be achieved by an intervention that did not include such self–disclosure? Doesn't the suggested alternative intervention, for example, leave open more possibilities?

Owen Renik

Not in my opinion. One does not necessarily leave open possibilities by being minimalist with one's own input. Often, more opportunities are opened up when the patient knows where the analyst is coming from.

Charles Brenner

You introduced to the patient a new idea, an idea that thus far had not come from him: "I'm not like your father." What advantage was there in your doing so?

Owen Renik

I would rather describe the sequence of ideas not as having been introduced by me to the patient, but as generated by an interaction between myself and the patient, as follows: Renik: "I'm not like your father." The patient: "Even though you think you're not like my father, I'm telling you that you are more like him than you realize, and that as a result I'm so uncomfortable in this room with you that I'm picking a fight with you."

Manuel Furer

Why was the patient unaware of all of this before this "interaction"?

Owen Renik

Who knows? The question is whether it is more useful to try to let a process "unfold by itself," or to accept that interaction can facilitate increased self–awareness for the patient.

References

Bird, B. (1972). Notes on transference: Universal phenomenon and hardest part of analysis, *J. Amer. Psychoanal. Assn.*, 20:267–301.

Boesky, D. (1990). The psychoanalytic process and its components. *Psychoanal. Q.*, 59:550–584.

Brenner, C. (1976). Transference. In: *Psychoanalytic Technique and Psychic Conflict*. New York: International Universities Press, pp. 108–133.

——— (1985). Countertransference as compromise formation. *Psychoanal. Q.*, 54:155–163.

——— (1987). Working through: 1914–1984. *Psychoanal. Q.*, 56:88–108.

Breuer, J., & Freud, S. (1893–1895). Studies on Hysteria. *Standard Edition, 2*. London: Hogarth Press, 1955.

Congreve, W. (1694). The double dealer. In: *Congreve's Comedies*, ed. E. Rump. New York: Penguin, 1985.

Fenichel, O. (1941). *Problems of Psychoanalytic Technique,* tr. D. Brunswick. New York: Psychoanalytic Quarterly.

Ferenczi, S. (1919). On the technique of psycho–analysis. In: *Further Contributions to the Theory and Technique of Psychoanalysis,* ed. M. Balint. New York: Basic Books, 1960.

———— (1920). The further development of active therapy in psycho-analysis. In: *Further Contributions to the Theory and Technique of Psychoanalysis,* ed. M. Balint. New York: Basic Books, 1960.

———— (1928). The elasticity of psycho–analytic technique. In: *Final Contributions to the Problems and Methods of Psycho-Analysis,* ed. M. Balint. New York: Basic Books, 1955.

———— (1930). The principles of relaxation and neocatharsis. In: *Final Contributions to the Problems and Methods of Psycho–Analysis,* ed. M. Balint. New York: Basic Books, 1955.

———— (1931). Child–analysis in the analysis of adults. In: *Final Contributions to the Problems and Methods of Psycho–Analysis,* ed. M. Balint. New York: Basic Books, 1955.

Freud, S. (1914). Remembering, repeating and working through. *Standard Edition,* 12:145–156. London: Hogarth Press, 1958.

Gill, M. M. (1994). Conflict and deficit: Book review essay on Conflict and Compromise: Therapeutic Implications. *Psychoanal. Quart,* 63:756–780.

Gitelson, M. (1952). The emotional position of the analyst in the analytic situation. *Int. J. Psycho–Anal.,* 33:1–10.

Greenacre, P. (1954). The role of transference: Practical considerations in relation to psychoanalytic therapy. *J. Amer. Psychoanal. Assn.,* 2:671–684.

Kris, E. (1956). The recovery of childhood memories in psychoanalysis. *Psychoanal. St. Child,* 11:54–88. New York: International Universities Press.

Panel (1995a). Towards a definition of the term and concept of interaction. Reporter: D. M. Hurst. *J. Amer. Psychoanal. Assn.,* 43:521–537.

Panel (1995b). Interpretive perspectives on interaction. Reporter: S. D. Purcell. *J. Amer. Psychoanal. Assn.,* 43:539–551.

Renik, O. (1993). Countertransference enactment and the psychoanalytic process. In: *Psychic Structure and Psychic Change: Essays in Honor of Robert S. Wallerstein,* ed. M. Horowitz, O. Kernberg, & E. Weinshel. Madison, CT: International Universities Press, pp. 135–158.

———— (1996). Getting Real in Analysis. (Typescript).

———— (1997). Getting Real in Analysis. Paper presented to the Faculty, New York Psychoanalytic Institute March 10.

———— (1998). The analyst's subjectivity and the analyst's objectivity. *Int. J. Psycho–Anal.* 79:487–497.

Rosenberg, S. (1974). *Naked Is the Best Disguise: The Death and Resurrection of Sherlock Holmes.* Indianapolis: Bobbs-Merrill.

Stein, M. (1966). Self observation, reality, and the superego. In: *Psychoanalysis—A General Psychology: Essays in Honor of Heinz Hartmann,* ed. R. M. Loewenstein, L. M. Newman, M. Schur, & A. J. Solnit. New York: International Universities Press, pp. 275–298.

———— (1981). The unobjectionable part of the transference. *J. Amer. Psychoanal. Assn.,* 29(4):869–892.

CHAPTER 6

The Furer Symposium: Editors' Introduction

Herbert Wyman MD and Stephen Rittenberg MD
(2000). *Journal of Clinical Psychoanalysis* 9 (4):407–408

We are glad to publish an issue of the Journal devoted entirely to the presentation and discussion of clinical psychoanalytic case studies. This is in keeping with our stated goal of meeting a universally felt need for greater access to clinical data.

We have another goal, not explicitly stated, but equally important: to provide students of psychoanalysis, present and future, with vivid samples of psychoanalytic technique as it is taught and practiced by the foremost clinicians of our time. All too often in the past, because of the difficulties inherent in the publication of clinical data, the clinical work of our leading analysts has been hidden from us, leading to a lopsided picture of their contributions to analysis. A prime example of this is Heinz Hartmann, who many remember only as a complex theoretician of ego psychology, but who in his time was also known to his colleagues as a superb clinician. Because of his clinical skills, Hartmann was chosen as the first Director of the Treatment Center at the New York Psychoanalytic Institute. Similarly, Otto Isakower's exceptional clinical acumen is preserved not in the literature but in the memory of his colleagues and students.

The clinical excellence of Dr. Manuel Furer is known far and wide by his students and colleagues, but has also been underrepresented in the literature. We are pleased to remedy this situation, at least in part, by offering in this issue a fine sample of Dr. Furer at work. We are doubly pleased because Dr. Furer's contributions occurred at a Symposium organized for the very purpose of honoring his work in psychoanalytic technique.

The first section of this issue is devoted to the Furer Symposium, which is made up of two case presentations and their discussions by Dr. Furer and a distinguished panel that includes Drs. Judith Chused, Jay Greenberg, Helen Myers, and Shelley Orgel. Also included is a transcript of the open floor discussions that followed the formal presentations. In the second part, readers will find a demonstration of excellent clinical work in the form of a case presentation by Dr. Naemi Stilman, with accompanying discussions by Drs. Herbert Wyman and Kerry Sulkowicz.

CHAPTER 7

Introduction to the Symposium

Albert Sax MD

(2000). Journal of Clinical Psychoanalysis (9)(4):411–413

The format of this discussion will be case presentations. The moderator will be Dr. Carl Kleban, a faculty member of the New York Psychoanalytic Institute and Clinical Professor of Psychiatry at the New York University Medical School. Dr. Kleban organized this Symposium as Chairman of our Extension Division.

The first case will be presented by Dr. Susan Epstein, the second by Dr. Peter Dunn. The panelists are Dr. Judith Chused, Dr. Jay Greenberg, Dr. Helen Myers, and Dr. Shelley Orgel.

I should like first to discuss Manny Furer's theoretical and clinical contributions, and what he has meant to the New York Psychoanalytic Institute. Manny's interest in child development led him first to work with the legendary child psychiatrist Loretta Bender at Bellevue Hospital, New York City, then, importantly, with Dr. Margaret Mahler. Manny Furer was a significant participant in and contributor to Mahler's studies of early childhood. His early papers were on childhood psychosis, superego development, and the separation-individuation phase. It may not be generally known, but it was Manny Furer who coined the phrase "emotional refueling" to describe the toddler's behavior in returning to the mother for the renewed strength that fosters further development. So, too, Manny in his innovations and contributions has always returned to the fundamental principles of classical psychoanalytic theory, whence comes the rigor and strength of his thinking.

It may also not be generally realized, but Manny was a candidate at the New York Psychoanalytic Institute while already contributing to Mahler's work. He graduated from the Adult Program in four years, and from the Child Program a couple of years later. Shortly thereafter he was appointed Training and Supervising Analyst—probably the youngest in our history. He has been honored with both Brill and Freud Lectureships. His 1985 Brill Lecture, entitled "Transference: Terminable and Interminable" demonstrated the persistence of the analytic transference in all aspects of our work. His 1995 Freud Lecture, entitled "Changes in Psychoanalytic Technique" (1998), is a historical survey of Ferenczi's influence on psychoanalysis, particularly with reference to current alternative theories and technical modifications. It is this interest that has led to the present Symposium.

Dr. Furer has himself participated in many studies and symposia—notably a fifteen-year study of the training analysis. During a recent panel on Enactment he made a comment that may be fairly taken to sum up his psychological and intellectual philosophy: "It is now clear that we are witnessing a convergence of ideas from various modifications or corrections of classical thinking. But when the suggestion is made that the convergence should progress to the point where distinctions in theory between various schools should be altogether dropped, this seems to me to be inimical to intellectual discourse" (1999, pp. 68–69).

Manny Furer's leadership has been highly significant to the New York Psychoanalytic Institute, and has been responsible for the enormous changes that have taken place here. He has served two six-year terms as Chairman of the Educational Committee (in itself an unusual accomplishment). Between these terms he was Chairman of the Faculty for two years. During these fourteen years he has guided and encouraged the following developments: the method of choosing training analysts was changed from a closed process of committee selection to an open process of clinical evaluation, which can be self-initiated; the curriculum was thoroughly revised; a psychotherapy training program was instituted; an externship for graduate students in psychology was created; a neuroscience program was inaugurated; and a new Psychoanalytic Foundation was instituted. Furthermore, Manny has continually encouraged younger people to assume more control of the Institute and Society.

For all this we thank you, Manny. I can't think of a better way to honor you than a symposium where you can engage in the intellectual discourse you love.

References

Furer, M. (1985). Transference: Terminable and interminable. AA Brill Lecture, New York Psychoanalytic Society.

—— (1998). Changes in psychoanalytic technique: Progressive or retrogressive. *Journal of Clinical Psychoanalysis*, 7(2):209–234.

—— (1999). Comments on the Enactment panel. *Journal of Clinical Psychoanalysis*, 8(1):62–70.

CHAPTER 8

Furer Symposium Opening Remarks

(2000). *Journal of Clinical Psychoanalysis* 9(4):414–419

The meeting today approaches perspectives on contemporary variations in technique, practice, and theory, through consideration of two analytic cases; one is presented by Dr. Epstein and the other by Dr. Dunn. I expect the discussion will explore a continuum of positions and proclivities in theory and technique and that we shall all leave better informed.

I will focus on one of the current controversies, the issue of the participation of the analyst in the analytic process. In the forty years that I have been in practice, there have been many changes in psychoanalytic technique. Two recent experiences were, to me, telling illustrations of one of these developments. A patient who was analyzed by me years ago, and had recently returned for additional analysis, said to me one day, "Analysis seems to be friendlier than it was twenty-five years ago"—a correct perception. Note, at that point he said analysis, not yet the analyst. He had also changed compared to the stoic he had been. He could now express affection and the wish for affection more easily to me.

The second experience was a presentation made to our faculty by Dr. Michael Singer, the Chairman of the Certification Committee of the American Psychoanalytic Association. Dr. Singer, in arguing for a terminated case as a requirement for certification, said that the

Committee wanted to know how the analyst experienced mourning for the loss of his patient, how he handled not only the patient but himself.

The inclusion of the analyst's participation was also evident in a class on advanced technique, which I taught over many years. Expression of reactions to the patient by candidates, whether straightforward countertransference from particular people in their past, or more complicated responses to the patient's behavior, which included the analyst's conflicts as well as his current life realities, all were much more openly expressed than during previous years.

I want to state in summary form certain positions in regard to this change so that my convictions are made clear. (A fuller exposition of these ideas may be found: in my paper, "Changes in Psychoanalytic Technique: Progressive or Retrogressive" (1998); in a discussion with Owen Renik published in the same issue; in a discussion of the Panel on Enactment in this Journal; and finally in an essay on Glenn Gabbard's book, *Love and Hate in the Analytic Setting*, entitled "Passion's Risk" (2000).

As was pointed out by Brian Bird in 1972, transference as an aspect of mental functioning is a powerful motivating force in life as well as in psychoanalysis. Transference is the repetition of the neurosis, including the repetition of early object relations distorted both by intrapsychic conflict and resistance to the recovery of the memory of childhood conflicts. These convictions derive from Freud's 1914 paper: "The patient does not remember anything of what he has forgotten but acts it out. He produces it not as a memory but as an action. He repeats it without of course knowing he is repeating. We must treat his illness as a present day force" (p. 150).

Freud added in 1925 that transference is "A universal phenomenon of the human mind, and in fact dominates the whole of each person's relations to his human environment" (p. 42).

100

In my 1984 Brill lecture at the New York Psychoanalytic Institute, entitled "Transference: Terminable and Interminable," I referred to the conclusion of a study of completed training analyses to the effect that the transference that develops during analysis does not disappear. It can be reactivated under certain conditions, whereupon as often as not it is relatively quickly recognized and understood. It was clear that a crucial aspect of transference was that the patient wished the analyst to play a role, to interact either in fulfillment of the patient's wishes or as portions of the patient's psyche. In the past, the wish for the analyst as a transference object to respond to the patient was assumed; now, with the focus on the analyst's participation, new weight has been given to the analyst's responses.

Our psychoanalyst-subjects in subsequent self-analyses undertaken in the course of problematic work with their patients, found it necessary to try to understand their former analysts' reactions as well as their own prior transferences. The analyst cannot be thought of as a fully objective observer. He is an informed participant observer, a fact that was not given its full weight in certain periods of analytic history, despite its prior historical recognition. To this point I quote Ferenczi (1919), "The doctor is always a human being and as such liable to moods, sympathies, and antipathies, as well as impulses. Without such susceptibilities, he would, of course, have no understanding of the patient's psychic conflict" (p. 186).

Bird (1972), refers to the reciprocal transference in the analyst as essential to the analytic process. He adds, "Each analyst's concept of transference derives variably but significantly from his own inner experience and so transference probably means many different things to many analysts" (p. 271). Ideological differences, Bird states, may well arise out of what was "actually said and done in response to transference reactions," how transference was handled both from the patient and in the analyst.

Ferenczi, in response to Freud's statement that he could not treat certain immoral people, said that such patients could easily, as we would express it today, actualize the response of the analyst in order to be sent away.

Self-awareness and self-analysis in regard to the analyst's activity or in response to the patient, whether empathic or transferential, can lead to further understanding of the patient as well as to an understanding of one's self. This was originally proposed by Paula Heiman in 1950, and is particularly emphasized and conceptualized in their own way by contemporary Kleinians with the term *projective identification.* The patient puts his feelings into the analyst who thereby experiences them as his own, but the feelings in reality come only from the patient.

There is inevitably a corrective emotional experience built into analysis by the basic circumstance that the patient is not reacted to as in his prior life, but is simply analyzed. There are other universal aspects of the analytic experience, such as the narcissistic gratification inherent in the unique concentration on the patient by the analyst. This was thought to be an unanalyzable aspect by Dr. Annie Reich (1951).

In my opinion, such participations are not central to the work nor to the therapeutic effect. The efforts by the analyst to build a technique upon participatory elements in order to make it more effective, both downgrades the analytic importance of transference and makes the analysis of transference more problematic (for another version, see Friedman [2000]).

In regard to the analyst-patient interaction, I place myself among those analysts described by Irwin Hoffman (1983) who maintain the "conservative critique of the blank screen concept," whereby the analyst can "dichotomize interpersonal experience in general, and experience in the analytical situation in particular, into veridical and distorted portions" (p. 393).

I also accept the possibility of transference that is not linked to countertransference. But I cannot agree with the more radical current belief that all of the data of the analytic situation, including the transference in particular, are co-constructed by the interacting contributions of patient and analyst, which is how I understand inter-subjectivity.

There are times, of course, when the transference and counter-transference can be said to collude, which may give the appearance of an interpersonal event, but I would agree with Dr. Chused's point of view that this interaction can well have a different meaning for each individual (1992). However, it remains more important to me, as stated by Ferenczi, that

> [E]very patient without exception notices the smallest
> peculiarities of the analyst's behavior, external appearance
> or way of speaking, but without prior encouragement, not
> one of them will tell him about them, though failure to do so
> constitutes a crude infringement of the primary rule of analysis
> [p. 3].

More recently, Merton Gill (1994) emphasized the patient's accurate perceptions of the analyst and also the importance of focusing upon these perceptions. To me, this admonition, like Ferenczi's comment, is a useful reminder, but one must keep in mind that transference repetition and distortion are primary.

There are a number of recent ways of thinking about technique that I seriously question: first, that enactments cannot be known until after they occur, and that they are not only inevitable, but important elements in cure, as stated by Boesky and Renik (1993); no doubt such experiences are often emotional and dramatic and can be useful to the work. For me, potential enactments can be anticipated, especially if they are habitual and not emergency reactions (Gitelson, 1952).

Second, although emotional experiences are necessary elements in insight, without an outcome that includes, as Kris (1956) put it, a fuller understanding of the patient's mind and past, we will not achieve the therapeutic effect for which we strive.

In regard to the latter, I will conclude with another quote from Ferenczi (1928):

A special form of this work of revision appears to occur, however, in every case; I mean the revision of the emotional experience which happened in the course of the analysis. The analysis itself gradually becomes a piece of the patient's life history which he passes in review before bidding us farewell. In the course of this revision it is from a certain distance and with much greater objectivity that he looks at the experiences through which he went at the beginning of his acquaintanceship with us [p. 97].

References

Bird, B. (1972). Notes on transference: Universal phenomenon and hardest part of analysis. *J. Amer. Psychoanal. Assn.*, 20:267–301.

Chused, J. (1992). The patient's perception of the analyst: The hidden transference. *Psychoanal. Q.*, 61:161–184.

Ferenczi, S. (1919). On the technique of psychoanalysis. In: *Further Contributions to the Theory and Technique of Psychoanalysis*, ed. M. Balint. New York: Basic Books, pp. 177–188.

——— (1928). The elasticity of psychoanalytic technique. In: *Final Contributions to The Problems and Methods of Psychoanalysis*, ed. M. Balint. New York: Basic Books, pp. 87–101.

Friedman, L. (1978). Trends in the psychoanalytic theory of treatment. *Psychoanal. Q.*, 47:524–567.

——— (2000). Modern hermeneutics and psychoanalysis. *Psychoanal. Q.*, 69:225–265.

Freud, S. (1914). Remembering, repeating, and working through. *Standard Edition*, 12:145–156. London: Hogarth Press.

——— (1925). An autobiographical study. *Standard Edition*, 20:3–7. London: Hogarth Press.

Furer, M. (1984). Transference: Terminable and Interminable: A Fifteen Year Study of the Training Analysis and Its Impact on Future Analytic Work. *AA Brill Memorial Lecture of the New York Psychoanalytic Society* (Unpublished).

——— (1998). Changes in psychoanalytic technique, progressive or retrogressive. *Journal of Clinical Psychoanalysis*, 7:209–252.

———. (2000). Passion's risk. A review of Love and Hate in the Analytic Setting by Glenn Gabbard. *J. Contemp. Psychoanal.*, 36:148–155.

Gill, M. (1994). *Psychoanalysis in Transition: A Personal View*. Hillsdale, NJ: Analytic Press.

Gitelson, M. (1952). The emotional position of the analyst in the psychoanalytic situation. *Int. J. Psycho-Anal.*, 83:1–10.

Greenacre, P. (1960). Regression and fixation: Considerations concerning the development of the ego. In: *Emotional Growth*, Vol. 2. New York: International Universities Press, pp. 162–182.

Heimann, P. (1950). On countertransference. *Int. J. Psycho-Anal.*, 31:81–84.

Hoffman, I. (1983). The patient as interpreter of the analyst's experience. *Contemp. Psychoanal.*, 19:389–422.

Kris, E. (1956). On some vicissitudes of insight in psychoanalysis. *Int. J. Psycho-Anal.*, 37:444–455.

Ogden, T. (1994). The analytic third: Working with intersubjective clinical facts. *Int. J. Psycho-Anal.*, 75:3–18.

Reich, A. (1951). On countertransference. *Int. J. Psycho-Anal.*, 32:25–31.

Renik, O. (1993). Technique in the light of the analyst's irreducible subjectivity. *Psychoanal. Q.*, 65:553–571.

Strachey, J. (1934). The nature of the therapeutic action of psychoanalysis. *Int. J. Psycho-Anal.*, 15:127–159.

Sterba, R. (1934). The fate of the ego in analytic therapy. *Int. J. Psycho-Anal.*, 15:117–126.

CHAPTER 9

Case Presentation: The Case of Ms. X

by Peter Dunn MD

(2000). *Journal of Clinical Psychoanalysis* 9(4):482-490

Ms. X, a 30-year-old actress and acting teacher, was referred to me for analysis because of stage fright. Ms. X enjoyed a promising career through her twenties, but for the four months before she sought treatment she was unable to perform because of fear of forgetting her lines. Her analysis lasted for six years and terminated when she married and moved to another city. I will present a summary of the history she gave me in the first month of weekly face-to-face consultations and then two detailed vignettes from the analysis that followed. The first vignette describes a complex transference-countertransference enactment revolving around the patient's anxiety about first using the couch. The second vignette, from the third year of the treatment, clarifies some of the genetic roots of the earlier enactment.

Ms. X was an attractive young woman with the engaging, trained speaking voice of an actor. She was not histrionic in her dress or manner. Rather, she appeared serious and disciplined. She approached the prospect of beginning the analysis with the kind of rigor with which she told me that she approached her work in her master classes. She began by stressing that her career was her main concern. She was a graduate of a famous acting conservatory and had worked in regional theater since completing her schoolwork. She was regarded as having considerable promise and attracted the interest of Y, a well-known theater director. She was accepted as a member of his repertory company and received a favorable review in a prominent publication. Such a review typically gave a head start to an acting career. She had "buzz." She and Y became romantically involved and she moved into his apartment. They began to talk about getting married. "Just when things were going great," she started to forget her lines during rehearsal. She became "glassy" while she was on stage and her mind would "lose focus." Y was, by and large, unsympathetic to her emotional distress. It was clear to me, though Miss X did not say so, that she thought that she was about to lose both her acting career and the relationship with Y if she did not get over her anxiety symptoms. She worried that she was going to end up an "old maid teacher," which for her was a fate "worse than death."

When I asked about her previous history of treatment, Ms. X told me that she was "new to therapy," but had recently seen an array of doctors. She started with her family doctor who prescribed a beta blocker medication for performance anxiety. When this did not help, she asked the advice of the high school guidance counselor who referred her to a psychopharmacologist who suggested that she see a psychoanalyst. The psychoanalyst in the town where she attended acting school referred Ms. X to me with the recommendation that she be analyzed.

When I asked about her early life, the gist of the history she gave me was that she was the youngest of three children, and the only girl, from a Midwestern farm family. She had two brothers who were four and ten years older than the patient. The parents' marriage was troubled when the patient was growing up. Mother was angry and dramatic. Father was distant and unmoved by the mother's hysterics. The father marched to his own beat, spending much of his free time on

108

his hobbies (e.g., tinkering in his woodworking shop, growing roses). At this stage, Ms. X always smiled when she spoke of her father. She compared him to Jimmy Stuart: tall, handsome, straightforward, and only talking when he had something significant to say. When she spoke of her mother, Ms. X's voice betrayed fear and contempt. Mother was all talk, attention seeking, and manipulation. Mother threatened suicide many times when she did not get her way. If this did not work, she would take to bed with migraines. Ms. X had many memories of feeling obliged to comfort mother after the marital fights.

From an early age, Ms. X was considered the "good child" in contrast to her middle brother who had temper tantrums and did poorly in school, and to her oldest brother who was chronically truant. The family lived on a farm removed from the local town and her brothers and their friends were her main playmates when she was not at school. She resented it when she was left out of their play. When I asked her about early symptoms she mentioned only periods of feeling "gray." I had the impression that she was often alone on the farm when the brothers were with their friends, her father was at work, and her mother was depressed or ill. It was during these times, starting in early grade school, that Ms. X began to develop an interest in the theater. She put on imaginary plays with herself as the star.

Ms. X's mother had wanted to be a violinist as a young woman but she had never developed her talent; instead she was a housewife. Disappointed in her own ambitions, mother was very supportive of the patient's nascent acting abilities. Throughout Ms. X's childhood, mother took her for acting lessons and prepared her for auditions and performances. Ms. X felt she was "Mom's prize cow." Except for the school plays, Ms. X had only a limited social life through high school. Most of her time was spent on the farm keeping her mother company and playing with the brothers when they were free. Theater work was her salvation. The other children in the plays were her schoolfriends and she inevitably developed a crush on whichever male teacher directed the production or coached her in acting.

When Ms. X was 14 her mother was diagnosed with a malignant melanoma and had a wide excision that proved curative. Ms. X remembers being shocked that, "My hypochondriac mother actually got something so serious." Though the mother never had a recurrence, the patient went through adolescence convinced mother was going to die prematurely, and this increased the mother's influence over her, making it harder for her to have a full adolescent rebellion.

The patient left her hometown to attend an acting school, at age 18. The parents separated soon after. The father soon married a woman twenty years his junior and the mother was briefly hospitalized for depression. Ms. X was entirely sympathetic about the father's decision to leave the marriage but she was afraid to visit the father.

She feared that mother would make a suicide attempt if Ms. X (or her brothers) saw her father and his new wife.

Vignette 1

In the fifth consultation session I told Ms. X the reasons why I agreed with the referring doctor that analysis was the treatment of choice for her. She responded as if I had thrown a drowning woman a life preserver. She readily agreed to a four-day-a-week schedule at a fee of $10 a session.

When I told Ms. X she could begin the analysis on the couch the next session, her affect changed as on a dime. No more the pleasant, somewhat naïve, cooperative Midwestern young woman, she became combative and sarcastic. "Couch!" she said with genuine surprise

110

and distress. "I didn't know I had to lie on a couch in analysis." She reminded me that she came from a small and unsophisticated town where they think that, "People who go to analysis and lie on couches are crazy." She was "suspicious of the procedure" and was only trying it because she was desperate about her career. She went on to say accusingly that she had not been properly informed by the referring doctor or me that she had to lie on a couch. She would never have agreed to analysis if she had been properly informed. Taken aback I asked her if she had seen the couch in the office of the referring analyst. She said she had, and added that she had been staring at my couch for the past five meetings. She also said that she had long talks with her boyfriend about his analysis and knew he used a couch. Still she had reached her own conclusion, which was that lying on the couch was optional.

I asked her what distressed her about the couch and she said it reminded her of Woody Allen movies where neurotics talk interminably about their problems while looking ridiculous. She was "results oriented" and not a "navel contemplator." Also, the couch seemed "theatrical" like something you would see in a Broadway play. I asked her if the alarm she felt about using the couch was similar to the alarm she felt about going on stage in the theater. She agreed that there were similarities. She said that the idea of lying down on the couch "plain scares me." She asked me to make a suggestion as to how she should proceed. I said, "You can begin the analysis now and see if we can get to the bottom of understanding the fears or you can sit up and we can talk about it more."

The next session Ms. X came in and marched to the couch like a condemned prisoner going to the gallows. She looked at the couch and lay down. For most of the first four months, the patient lay flat as a board and was hardly able to talk. When she did speak she stuck to the description of her stage fright, which she repeated without much modification and without adding anything new. The sessions often degenerated into her cataloging her symptoms: her dread before saying her lines, her attempt to start memorizing scenes, her mind becoming hazy, her thoughts blocking, her body feeling mechanical and out of her control, her wish to flee. The only intervention that appeared helpful during this period was to point out the similarity between her fears in the analysis and her fears on the stage. When she seemed serious about stopping the treatment she responded to my suggestion that perhaps if we could understand why she was so frightened on the couch she would also know more about her fears on the stage so she could overcome them. However, her primary sense was that she was being forced to stay on the couch by me. When she asked if she could sit up I had to point out that she had the feeling that she was not free to get up even if she wanted to.

As her anxiety continued relatively unabated, I told her my impression about its cause. I reminded her that in the last of the face-to-face consultations, I had told her that the way to overcome her fears was to begin the analysis. I said that I thought that this must have made her feel that if she did not lie down I would think she was afraid. She interrupted me here to say, "A chicken. I thought you would think I was a chicken." I went on to say that she must have felt forced to lie down because she didn't want me to think of her as a "chicken." So she's caught between lying down and feeling scared and sitting up and feeling ashamed and defeated. So she ends up feeling trapped. Ms. X responded that this reminded her of an incident from high school in which she was hesitant to go out on stage to do an improvisation. When her mother saw that she was going to give up her turn the mother embarrassed her by telling her that if she were too nervous she should give up performing altogether. She went on stage but resented her mother thereafter. I told her that I thought she was reacting to me the same way.

The following session Ms. X announced that she was beginning to feel that it was more her choice whether she would proceed with the analysis on the couch or not. She was struck by the strong memory of her mother "forcing" her on stage. She reported a dream of the previous night.

She was moving to a new apartment. Maybe it was her boyfriend's apartment. Her mother and father came in all upset and nervous and they were worried that she had made a hasty decision about moving to this apartment. Then her mother and the family doctor sat down next to her on the bed. The doctor was writing notes on a music pad. Then her mother started to undress her and she tried to resist but Mom and the doctor forced her down on the bed and she couldn't get up. Then the doctor started to make a pass at her and she was frightened. She tried to push him away.

After recounting the dream Ms. X said that she wanted to sit up and asked if it was okay. I said that she must feel that I am like her mother and the doctor in the dream forcing her to lie down even though she is feeling she doesn't want to. She lay back down and said the part where her mother took off her clothes reminded her of an episode from age 2. The family was at a professional photographer's studio. Everyone was dressed in fancy clothes but her mom wanted her to show off her pretty petticoat. She was very embarrassed. She paused and said she lost her train of thought. I said that I thought her losing her train of thought—forgetting what was on her mind—was the only way she could think of right now to keep her privacy and avoid having to expose her thoughts and feelings to me before she wanted to. She was especially concerned that she would be put in an undignified position like she was as a child in the photo studio. Ms. X responded that the dream was clearly about the analysis but the doctor reminded her of a doctor she had when she was a little girl. She had remembered that the doctor in the dream was a pediatrician who left town when she was about 5. There were rumors that he molested children. She had read yesterday morning about a dentist who put children to sleep and then molested them.

As Ms. X began to explore her associations to the dreams her anxiety and elective mutism abated. She related complicated feelings of resentment about being made to perform on stage and in the analysis. She focused intently on the mother who exposed her to situations which had intensified her exhibitionist conflicts. The mother encouraged her to join with mother's dreams of living the life of a performer but the mother herself was highly conflicted about the patient's success. At this early point in the analysis it was clear that lying on the couch at my request had been the "day residue" for a fantasy of being forced by her mother to expose herself to a forbidden object who is variously pictured in the dream and the associations as the analyst, the patient's pediatrician, the photographer, the dentist, and her boyfriend Y.

Vignette 2

Throughout the second year of the analysis the patient was convinced that I opposed both her wish to become a lead actress and her wish to marry a famous director such as Y. She was convinced that I wanted her to have only a teaching career and date men her own age. What

114

she thought she heard me say—no matter what I did say—was "How dare you want these things when you are nothing special."

The need to see me as similar to her mother was interpreted in a number of different ways over the first three years. In ascribing her mother's views to me she was finding a way to continue her ambivalent closeness to the mother and to assuage her guilt about abandoning the mother to pursue a career. The compulsive need to see me as the mother also allowed her to keep her mother in the analytic room so that she did not have to feel that she was alone with a man. This need to see others like the mother was not solely a transference phenomenon. In Ms. X's everyday life she found so many other people to be "just like Mom," that it occurred to me that she was trying to make the mother appear as a more ordinary or typical person than the mother in fact was. I found it helpful to interpret to the patient that in being so certain that I (and so many other people) was just like the mother, she was normalizing the mother. She started discussing awareness that her mother's virulent opposition to her career and relationship were "unusual" and that her family was "different." She began to face the degree of the psychopathology in her family. It emerged that the middle brother could not sleep through the night. The older brother could not hold a job. Only the father initially escaped this revisionist history.

By the third year, the relationship with Y had ended and she began dating a younger man, R. She also began taking acting lessons with a well-known teacher named Duncan who had a reputation as a flirt. During one of the lessons Ms. X discovered that Duncan's wife was observing the lesson through an open side door. This was the day residue for a dream in which Ms. X's landlady breaks through the double doors to her apartment and accuses her of being a whore. Several months before the patient had this dream, I had moved my office to a new set up where the office was a studio apartment connected by double doors to my family home. I related the double doors in the dream to the double doors that connected my home apartment to my office. I related the landlady to my wife. She acknowledged she was worried that my wife resented low-fee patients. She said she was afraid she was going to run into my wife and see the resentment that she imagined was there. She feared that my wife would think that she was coming to analysis to flirt and not to get better.

The following session the patient announced that she had decided she would not tell me anything further about her feelings toward me. When I asked her how she had reached this decision, she answered, "You'll make a pass at me." I was struck by the surety in which she said this. She did not say that "You might make a pass at me." But that "You will make a pass at me." I pointed out to her and asked what she made of the certainty. She replied, "Why the hell should I trust you? My own father was off the wall." She had always presented her father as a paragon and I asked her how he was crazy. "He was off the wall, crazy. You once said that my sexual fears had come from early childhood. It wasn't like that at all." Ms. X then recounted a series of events from the period that mother was hospitalized for melanoma surgery and father was caring for her. Father drank heavily. He would hide in her closet so that he could observe her getting dressed. "Can you imagine peeping on your own daughter?" She paused and said, "So why the hell should I feel so comfortable with you for god's sake?"

In the following sessions her mood was subdued. She was astonished that this dissociated memory returned with such force. The patient began to talk about other experiences with the father that appeared "odd" to her in retrospect. For example on a recent camping trip her father had said to her, "Don't worry, I won't make a pass at you." In a phone conversation he had said, "Why don't we get married if things don't work out with my wife." As the idealized view of the father began to crumble Ms. X began to understand more about mother's perpetual concern that she not be too close to father.

The patient recalled a summer when she was 7 years old and alone with father while mother was in the hospital for minor surgery. The father had insisted that she sleep on the porch in the hammock. She remembered awakening in the middle of the night with the feeling that "There is a hole in the hammock and someone is sticking their hand through." Her associations turned to the beginning of the analysis and her fear when I told her that she should use the couch.

CHAPTER 10

Discussion of Dr. Dunn's Case

(2000). *Journal of Clinical Psychoanalysis* 9(4):491-494

Once again I will address myself to the technical issues, particularly the analyst's response to the patient, and only cursorily to the data of the case relevant to this issue.

Dr. Dunn's example of the first enactment in this analysis, telling the patient that she could begin on the couch, joins the issue very clearly. One might say following Boesky and Renik that Dr. Dunn could not know the meaning of his action, its meaning to the patient, and its impact until after it had happened. The second point that may be made is that their emotional involvement, the meaning of which neither party is aware, is an important carrier of the therapeutic effect. As Boesky put it, without such unintended interactions the analysis will not proceed to a successful conclusion. According to Renik, the distinction between analyst and patient cannot be made on the basis of either party's actual involvement, that is, the extent to which either one expresses or experiences emotional responses.

My counterargument is that human interaction and emotional involvement are givens if not warded off by the analyst. What is more important is that all such interaction, including communications, have unconscious purposes and meanings; second, that there is a difference, a distinction between analyst and patient not only by the reality of one seeking help from the other, but also crucial to me, the nature of their

119

transference, presumably at the very least better known by the analyst and likely to be more intense in the patient. The latter, I believe, is what the material demonstrated, a preformed transference that immediately became evident. This, of course, can be made dramatic involuntarily by the analyst motivated to varying degrees by countertransference. When such interaction is valorized, it is my belief that what informs our technique, the transference as repetition of childhood conflicts, is potentially devalued. In addition, the overvaluation of what I will call mutual enactment will more likely result in denial of aspects of the transference and consequent sequestering of cherished memories about interaction with the analyst. We found such an outcome in many of the subjects of a study of training analyses. These sequestered, cherished memories that arose out of unanalyzed enactments had to be dealt with by our analyst subjects when they were activated later as countertransference reactions.

My point about the power of transference is illustrated by Dr. Dunn's attempt to reassure and diminish the patient's reaction by asking her whether she didn't know that analysis included the couch. She responds that she had been *staring* at the analyst's couch for the past five meetings. She had also been discussing this issue with her boyfriend, a displacement from the performed transference as well as a continuation of it in life.

Dr. Dunn returned to the coercive stance in the instance when he asked does she wish to begin the analysis and to understand the problem that is crucial in her life, or does she wish to sit up and talk about the couch. The subtext being to do nothing or not much. This apparently egalitarian approach or the reducing of the gradient between analyst and patient or the removal of the analyst's authority, to my mind is as stated, determined by personal factors; that is, Dr. Dunn's need for a patient and his response to the patient's reaction

120

to him. The recommendation for an egalitarian mindset and behavior is both futile and potentially obfuscating to both patient and analyst. The "tilted relationship" (Greenacre, p. 630) because of the reality of the situation and of transference, is nicely demonstrated in this case despite the analyst's evident involvement.

There is an interesting clinical fact that is sometimes forgotten, that the patient on the couch will reproduce the symptoms of the neurosis. If this is thought of only in terms of an enactment, important data of intrapsychic conflict will be lost. The analyst is the audience for her performance on one level and the voyeur in transference on a deeper level, which activates her symptoms in the analysis. As reported and important to note, the form of her resistances is of equal importance in understanding her psyche; that is, both portions of the intrapsychic conflict.

Consistent with our approach at this Institute, the analyst interprets her resistance and the defensive portion of the symptom of memory gaps to ward off anxiety in her dream of being held down and undressed.

This transference fantasy of the analyst as voyeur and lover was brought to her attention by the patient's friend. Here the contemporary focus on enactment may have clarified his understanding of the patient. Old fashioned as some may think, exploring the surface via her associations about this reported conversation might have told Dr. Dunn more about her defenses; for example, as revealed later, turning to women to ward off men.

In the second vignette, what was most interesting to me was the analyst's intuitive sense that there was something going on other than the analysis of her superego. He approached the matter first by understanding that her generalizing her maternal transference was a defense by denial—"normalizing" the mother but not the father.

As described by Ferenczi and Kris this mixture of intuition, but also careful attention to associations and rational thought, is precisely the analyst's psyche at work. We see the same functioning by the analyst when he notices that the patient states that she is certain he will make a pass at her rather than questioning that as a possibility.

The superego with its meaning as connection to the mother, as well as representing the mother's condemnation of her, are both resistances that return with full force; when analyzed, each repeat results in further release of repressed erotic feeling.

Covering all bases, one might say the analyst's initial questioning of her certainty may also have served as a suggestion that there was something unsaid that she was certain about, namely, the father's hiding and observing her as she undressed at night. Her response to this material was to ask her mother about her father once she was able to express her own concerns about him in the analysis. In the past, one would have understood this as the same defense to include the mother and consequently an acting out in life. We can now consider a mutual enactment, not to my mind something I would call reconstructed, of the patient's and the analyst's wish to know or even the more sexualized version of their curiosity and voyeurism. The added complexity and burden for the analyst is to include his self analysis, though this is often done preconsciously. The ultimate outcome that I look for is the further understanding of the patient's psyche that includes anticipating future enactments (for an opposite point of view see Renik).

The important point to me is that analysis fosters an observing ego via identification as originally described by Sterba. The patient identifies with the analyst as part of the analytic relationship. Today, we emphasize that this is a portion of a more complex interaction that inevitably includes shared instinctual impulses and susceptibilities as stated by Ferenczi; to Sterba's experiencing ego of the patient we must now add the experiencing ego of the analyst which does not vitiate Sterba's contribution.

Such interactions, although inevitable and meaningful, do not, as thought in the past, necessarily create greater resistance nor as some hold at present, does it foster the progress of the analysis despite the claim that interaction provides information that cannot otherwise be obtained, since I am doubtful about this claim.

I return to my conviction that to help the patient understand his psyche and to relieve his symptoms, it is best to rely upon the analysis of the resistances plus the one small step, as Freud recommended, in pointing to the repressed or dissociated memories and instinctual impulses. The most convincing arena for the analysis of the neurosis and of intrapsychic conflicts is the transference, representing the reliving of the past in the present, as Dr. Dunn has demonstrated.

References

Greenacre, P. (1974). The role of transference: Practical considerations in relation to psychoanalytic therapy. In: *Emotional Growth*, Vol. 2. New York: International Universities Press, pp. 627–640.

Part Two: Psychoanalytic Training and Education

CHAPTER 11

Editor's Note

"Transference: Terminable and Interminable" was publicly presented by Dr. Furer to the New York Psychoanalytic Society as the A.A. Brill Honorary Lecture for 1985.

Dr Furer listed the paper as "unpublished" in the bibliography he prepared for the *Journal of Clinical Psychoanalysis* Vol 9, No 4, 2000. It remained unpublished thereafter. However, the paper remains important, since in it Dr. Furer reports his experience as a member of the Study Group on Training Analysis, and also expresses his own views on the impact of the Training Analysis. For Dr. Furer, the personal analysis is the core of psychoanalytic training, and the transference is the core of the personal analysis. This "interminable transference"—particularly in its negative aspects—has a lasting impact both on the individual analyst and his/her theoretical orientations and professional organizations.

Dr Furer's views on these perennially controversial topics were well known locally within NYPSI and so may well be shared with the broader psychoanalytic community.

CHAPTER 12

Brill Lecture by Manuel Furer
Transference: Terminable and Interminable

November 26, 1985

This lecture will be on the one hand, a report of a study into the current status of the training analysis and on the other, my ideas about the durability of the transference from the point of view of psychoanalytic technique.

In the course of the lecture, I will go back and forth between the two subjects, using the data. of the study to illustrate and support my hypotheses. Transference as it develops in the analysis is durable and continuous in the psychic organization of' the former patient.

Transference is active and to some degree conscious in the former analysand of a training analysis, as evidenced in me material of the study to be presented tonight.

I shall focus on the durability of the transference from the point of view of psychoanalytic technique rather than as a consequence of biological factors which Freud emphasized, and which he felt made analysis interminable, except as a practical matter. In my opinion, it is the transference as organized in the analysis which previous follow-up studies, and the one I shall describe, demonstrate to be a continuously active mental structure subject to various vicissitudes after the analysis. To define transference, I quote from the postscript to the Dora case:

129

the productive powers of the neurosis are by no means extinguished (by analysis). They are occupied in the creation of a special class of mental structures, for the most part, unconscious, to which the name transference may be given. What are transferences? They are new editions or facsimiles of the impulses and fantasies which are aroused and made conscious during the course of the analysis, but they have this peculiarity that they replace some earlier person by the "person of the physician."

There are three other points about transference in Freud's thinking that are relevant to this:

1. The patient's neurosis is created in a new form in the analytic situation which Freud called the transference neurosis.
2. The thoughts and feelings may well have been experienced in consciousness for the *first time*, in the analysis, and
3. From Freud's paper "Dynamics of Transference":

> The longer an analytic treatment lasts, and the more clearly the patient realizes that distortions of the pathogenic material cannot by themselves offer any protection against its being uncovered, the more consistently does he make use of one sort of distortion which obviously affords him the greatest advantages. Circumstances tend towards a situation in which finally, *every conflict has to be fought out in the sphere of transference.*

The data which stimulated these reflections and indeed the impetus to take on this lecture derives from my participation in an investigation into the current status of the training analysis lasting some ten years. This study was undertaken by the Study Group on Training Analysis—a subcommittee of the Committee on Psychoanalytic Education of the American Psychoanalytic Association.

The procedure we elected was that of a series of weekend-long seminars consisting of two Study Group members and eight recent graduate analysts, two from each of four Institutes.

We began with a discussion of standard practices in the various institutes such as fees, reporting/non-reporting, assignment or personal choice of analyst, etc., and then invited the participants to talk about their training analyses, and how these analyses affected their psychoanalytic work.

This was only one portion of the work of the Study Group, and only one source of data, but it was the most enlightening for the subject of this lecture.

There were, in addition, discussions by the Study Group investigators, Drs. Brian Bird, Victor Calef, Francis McLaughlin, Martin Stein, and myself, which, over the years, informed my thinking on transference, on psychoanalytic education and on the problems of evaluation and research in these areas. Dr. Calef died some two years ago. He was a man with a lively and imaginative intelligence, and also with a strong sense of his professional responsibilities.

He felt it was the obligation of each one of us to use the data in some way that would not only contribute to our individual development as analysts, but also be communicated to the psychoanalytic community how Dr. Calef fulfilled his obligation in a number of published papers, Dr. Stein communicated some of his responses in a lecture in this hall, Brian Bird and Francis McLaughlin in various papers and discussions, and tonight submit this lecture as partial fulfillment of my own obligation.

The second source of ideas is my experience as an analyst, the third, the Introductory Course on Technique at the New York Institute that I have been teaching for the past several years, including the contributions from students in that seminar. From the literature I cite particularly Freud's *Papers on Technique:* the paper "Analysis Terminable and Interminable," Brian Bird's review of Freud's contributions, and his own Ideas in "Notes on Transference, Universal Phenomenon and Hardest part of Analysis" (1974), and more recently, John Kaluber's paper, "The Role of Illusion in Psychoanalytic Cure," delivered in 1981.

Freud once believed that analysis of intrapsychic conflict could inoculate the patient against all future pathological outcomes of what Brenner has called psychic compromises.

In the paper "Analysis Terminable and Interminable" (1937), Freud revised this optimistic assertion, and stated that biological forces, particularly the quantitative strength of instinct, the predisposition to conflict inherent in the aggressive drive or death instinct, and the distortions of the ego in the defensive struggle, made such inoculation impossible. Ferenczi, in 1922, believed to the contrary, that the training analysis, in contrast to other analysis, if it were complete enough, would be able to accomplish this immunization and, in addition, would produce a consensus about correct psychoanalytic technique.

Ernst Kris seemed to believe that if memory of the training analysis could be retained, that is, knowledge of the structure of the neurosis and of the reconstruction of memories of the past, that such memories would replace the transference, and something like an inoculation would be operative.

He was writing not only about pathological outcomes in regard to symptoms, but in regard to the analyst's personality engaged in psychoanalytic work. Today, many analysts conceptualize a model of the mind in which all compromise formations in the psyche remain, although altered by analysis in regard to the balance of forces.

Consequently, we consider the outcome of intrapsychic conflict in particular contexts at a particular time and under particular circumstances. I am not attempting tonight to add to the discussion of the theory of transference, except to restate my opinion that in addition to its source in the repetition of the past, it becomes a new organization in the psyche as a result of the analysis. The complex set of compromise formations that make up transference present distinctive problems in the training analysis and results in both adaptive and maladaptive functioning in the future analyst. An example of adaptive functioning of this organization is the availability and the readiness for transference in the analyst at work as emphasized by Bird.

Before going on to the findings of this study, I want to make a few remarks about changes in emphases or priorities in psychoanalytic technique in the history of our discipline. It may be artificial, and in a sense illogical to separate intellect, understanding, and explanation—the explanatory arts as Freud called them—from emotion and experience which came to mean experiencing in repetition in the analysis, that is, in transference as well as in memory. However, it seems to me that in the history of psychoanalytic technique, the predominance of one or the other—explanation or experience—is evident. In the early years of clinical theory, there was chimney-sweeping or abreaction of affect; subsequently, there were periods of didactic instruction of the patient and, in that sense, the analyst serving as a model. There was then a very sharp reaction towards the preeminence of emotional experience in the analysis in the book *The Development of Psychoanalysis* by Ferenczi and Rank, 1922:

By analyzing in the transference these as it were abortive wishes which continue to struggle for fulfillment. In the unconscious, but which the ego has long since discarded will give the patient an opportunity to experience these wishes intensely for the first time, in order, with the help of the conviction which he thus acquires, and avoiding the formation of pathological reactions, to place him in the position of obtaining an adjustment in reality.

They meant that the emotions experienced were the subject of primal repression, that they had never reached consciousness and that the special features of the transference enable these emotions to reach consciousness for the first time, to be abreacted, as well as explained. This emphasis continued, I believe into the thirties, with Strachey's conviction that only transference interpretations were effective. History after that is more mixed, but it seems to me that during the heyday of ego psychology in the forties, fifties, and early sixties, the effectiveness of explanation, understanding, and reconstruction came back into prominence. There was also considerable interest in basic human development that many analysts believed influence the analysis but existed outside of transference—the so-called therapeutic alliance. The current preoccupation with transference is another swing of the pendulum towards experience and emotion. Changes in emphasis reflect emerging psychoanalytic theory, for example, in the recent past, ego psychology and psychic development, and, of course, also reflect larger social and cultural changes, and are also a matter of new generations of analysts.

To turn to the findings of the study of training analysis, there were some outstanding impressions: First, the training analyses discussed with the Study Group had been very significant experiences in the lives of our graduate participants; second, transferences were still active in more or less conscious form. This was expressed three to five years after termination of analysis at the time of the first set of seminars. In a second set of weekend seminars with the same individuals, held some three years later—that is six to eight years after termination— transference emotions, although altered in many of the participants, continued to be expressed. And can say anecdotally, a very recent attempt to present some of this material in a seminar setting, brought forth memories of transference by a number of analysts thirty- plus years after the termination of the analysis, that is transference interminable.

There are some special features of the individuals that made up our groups that should be noted. We had asked each institute to recommend six representative recent graduates from which we would select two. At the time of our first meetings, it became obvious that the individuals selected were already very successful professionals and highly regarded colleagues. Second, the members of the seminars are advisedly called participants, because in the discussions they served both as subjects of the investigation, and at the same time as participants in the study— that is, in addition to their memories of the training analyses, and of their Influence on their current work, they participated in evaluating the material presented and in giving opinions concerning the role of the training analysis in psychoanalytic education. There was also a great deal of criticism, not only of the training analysis, but of the Study Group and how it went about its investigation.

This seminar format, it should be noted, was such that whatever came to mind in regard to the training analysis either became the subject of great interest (and I should say of candid reflection and candid spontaneous expression) taking up most of the time, and consequently producing most of the data, or, if a matter of less

interest was introduced, the subject rapidly faded from the discuss
ion.

As expected from previous follow-up studies of former patients, such as those done by Arnold Pfeffer, activation of the *content* of the training analysis, and of transference to the members of the Study Group, or to the Study Group as a whole did occur, *but* to a very limited degree. For example, there were some dreams reported by the participants, both before and after the seminar meetings, and various parapraxes; for example, slips in action that represented the wish to continue the weekend longer than time permitted, and a mistake in regard to a purported break in confidentiality. In fact, the type of memory presented, the relative lack of genetic and dynamic formulations or descriptions of change over time, except in a most general way, led Calef to conclude, "The personal psychoanalytic experience does not permit an adequate recognition and recollection of its content or its process." Strikingly, the memories which appeared to carry the most feeling were those interpersonal interactions between the graduate participants and their analysts that seemed to have occurred either outside the analytic situation, or if within the analytic situation, not to have been a subject of the analysis. At first these memories were considered to be aspects of outside reality between analysand and analyst, in contrast to transference, an aspect of psychic reality. The responses of participants to these memories, to quote Calef, were "Enthusiasm, criticisms, skepticism, fault-finding, forgiveness, idealization." I should note in passing that we also received many long letters in response to our invitation to communicate post-conference thoughts that repeated these memories and opinions.

Briefly, two. aspects of these memories are predominant in our data: (1) the relatively severe criticism of errors in technique and empathy, and (2) the nearly ubiquitous complaint of what they called the "imposition of ego ideals" by the analyst including variously, specific values, general expectable values such as truth, honesty, ultimately psychoanalysis itself, and the particular value of the elitism inherent in the analyst's position as an analyst of candidates.

To consider first, technical errors and failures in empathy: specific examples cannot be adequately disguised and thus must be generalized or taken from other contexts. The range of criticism was wide and included both complaints about lapses in the analytic attitude and exaggerations of the analytic attitude. In regard to the latter, most of the participants asserted at one time or another, in the course of our meetings, that the analyst should have been more humane, more caring, more open and honest in acknowledgement of the patient-physician relationship. Examples of errors in technique, on the one hand inadvertent, and on the other an acknowledged technique in a training analysis, include expressions perceived as compliments, an explanation of the analyst's way of working, a new friendliness of manner and/or a new instructional tone in the analysis of termination, an occasional opinion on a professional topic, an offer to lend a decorative object the analysand had admired, a comment about the analysand's patient in response to the analysand's associations, received as supervisory advice rather than the required analytic communication, and material to be used in a publication mentioned in passing. The issue, however, is not simple. In some instances, a similar interpersonal interaction of a seemingly positive nature, a compliment, for example, was accepted at face value by some of our graduate participants and seemed to be sustaining, and by others was experienced as a cover-up of a kind of negative counter reaction: "I am saying this or doing this so you will not be angry when you leave."

As has been noted throughout the literature whenever training analysis is under discussion, the termination phase of this analysis is considered to be technically difficult. To raise again, or in some instances, to raise for the first time, painful affects at the point of termination of analysis *and* at the point of entry into a community shared by analyst and patient, seems to offer too many opportunities for dilution, evasion, and avoidance.

The result was a phenomenon that occurred in many graduate participants between the first and second series of seminars, something that I will call the self-analysis of termination. It should be made plain that these self-analyses were not carried out voluntarily but were in fact forced upon the individual, particularly upon the practicing analyst, because of uncomfortable emotional reactions, dreams, intrusive thoughts, difficulties in reaction to one's patients, and so on, directing the person to memories of his analysis.

In the main, the graduate participants came to a conclusion that Ferenczi had come to long ago, that it was the negative transference, the experience of hatred that at least so far as their memories went, which was left to the self-analytic capacity of the individual. For example, a candidate overcomes a work inhibition by imitating his analyst. He uses this imitation in class, in supervision, and in the analytic situation. This imitation is noticed by fellow students but is not remarked upon by the analyst. The candidate feels he has been spared professional humiliation by virtue of this imitation, and is grateful. The gratitude does not become a subject of the analysis. In later self-analysis of termination, he first understands the countertransference of his analyst, and exact as this understanding may be, only later understands this memory as a screen for his negative transference.

In another example, an analysand abandoned a habitual leisure activity during his analysis, and at the same time began to use figures of speech from that activity in his associations. Only after the analysis did the candidate experience the disappointment and anger that the analyst had never realized that this language referred to the cherished hobby. After this piece of self-analytic work had been accomplished, that is, the analysis of the transference as well as the recapture of the memory of the original teacher, did he again take up this activity.

At this point, I want to say that the almost unanimous opinion of our graduate participants was that the training analysis, if it is to be a true analysis, is an entirely therapeutic analysis which has to be judged by the single criterion of therapeutic change. Given this point of view, all the issues which concerned prior generations reporting or nonreporting, evaluation, assessment for progression, extra-analytic contacts, the candidate as captive patient, lower fees, and so on were considered not important, and, in fact, not relevant to the analysis. Most participants, in fact, accepted the educational practices and academic requirements of their respective institutes as standard, and at first were surprised and mildly disapproving to learn of variations from institute to institute. For example, assignment of personal choice in training analyst.

In almost every case, the training analysis was considered to have succeeded in the goals in regard to symptom or character that the graduate participants had had in mind when they began analysis.

To quote Dr. Calef again, "Most, in gratitude, having been benefited, stimulated, and interested by the experience, regardless of skepticism and criticisms, were able to use their personal analytic experience for what they wanted it for."

Dr. Calef, from his special viewpoint, concluded that very good therapeutic results did not necessarily signify that good analysis had been done, and added, perhaps analogously, that some of the consequences (the directions the seminars followed, and the material produced) seem to be the product of the readiness for transference and identification, and so a therapeutic result of the analysis, rather than an entirely satisfactory analytic one. However, there was evidence that the psychoanalytic experience freed the restrictions that had initially prevented the fulfillment of ambitions and goals.

and although

...the training analysis does not seem to have been designed at present to teach what analysis is or how It is to be conducted, it may be peculiarly designed to free those functions from the inhibitions that prevent learning what psychoanalysis is and how to conduct it.

At the time of the second set of seminars, it seemed that in many instances, self-analytic work or introspection had led to a mellowing of the responses to memories of the analysis and of the analyst. There were new traces of tolerance in the discussions, but at the same time, evaluation of the errors as such remained unaltered, the same criticisms were expressed and reaffirmed, as it were. Once again, and with equal conviction and confidence, the graduate participants voiced the determination not to allow the same kinds of errors to occur in their own work, and in general to do better than their analysts. In fact, many of the participants as recently appointed training analysts were preparing to do just that. Moreover, in this second set of seminars, the participants made apparent, despite the repeated criticism of their training analyses, that in the course of these analyses most had learned, however indirectly or as a byproduct, or as a natural consequence of good analytic work, a great deal about their own functioning with their patients. Also evident at the second set of seminars were distortions of the memories of the first seminars. The data demonstrated not just the way in which memory works, whether about the childhood past or the recent past of the transference, but also recapitulations of aspects of individual transferences.

My own scrutiny of this second set of seminars brought me to a disagreement with Calef's implication about the possible or even likely psychotherapeutic nature of these training analyses. The self-analytic work, the appearance in consciousness of certain transference reactions, particularly negative transference emotions, I concluded, must have had its basis upon significant analytic work during the analysis. Another note, important for what one might call psychoanalytic social history: our graduate participants, in the main, disagreed with the opinion Miss Anna Freud had given to the International Training Commission. In 1938, and confirmed again in 1983, that the training analysis was a hazardous undertaking because of the shared endeavor, the diminished anonymity of the analyst, and what has been called the syncretic function, that is the participation by the Training Analyst to *any* degree in the educational life of the student analysand. At the time of our studies, many of our participants who were on their way to leadership positions in psychoanalysis considered these very hazards as probable facilitators of the training analysis; for example, they felt that the likelihood of shared goals and Interests as aspects of identification made analysis of this issue more convincing.

To turn to the other major memory and criticism: the imposition of an ego ideal: elitism, as it inheres in the concept of training analysis as more complete or as in any way different from other analyses, and elitism in the training analyst as a special position. The combination of guilt, fear, envy, and so on, and the defenses to deal with their emotions were, of course, highly individual. In this connection, some members of the Study Group noted that moral issues as such did not seem to be of great interest to our group. Dr. Calef believed that every lifting of repression produced some sense of dishonesty. It seemed to me that the relatively intense feeling about the imposition of values represented just this superego or moral conflict. It may, in fact, have been exacerbated by the request by us to remember—perhaps felt as a command to remember. Consequences of the superego conflict were present, I felt, in the self-imposed demand to do better than their analysts, and in the denigrations of idealizations of their training analysts after the analysis. It also appeared to me that in addition to individual conflicts, a particular common experience was involved in the complaint of the imposition of ego ideals as well as in the complaint of elitism; namely that during the analysis, identification with the idealized analyst had brought the illusory anticipation of "power, glory, and love." After the analysis, with inevitable disappointments, the feeling was that the value of psychoanalysis had been imposed, and there was resistance to the hard work of introspection and self-analysis.

Throughout, some graduate participants would just as well have discarded the "elitism" of psychoanalytic work itself, and particularly the elitism of psychoanalytic work with candidates that is the training analysis Itself.

I now bring your attention to certain statements in the psycho-analytic literature that bear upon the issue of transference and its durability, from the point of view of psychoanalytic technique.

The first is Freud's statement in 1937 that only an unfriendly act on his part would have brought Ferenczi's negative transference into the analytic work. Ferenczi, who could well have been one of our typical graduate participants, stated: "The analyst ought to have known and to have taken into account the fact that a transference relation can never be purely positive. He should have given his attention to the possibilities of the negative transference."

Freud wrote, you will recall, that at the time of the analysis, the negative transference was not currently active in his patient and therefore was unavailable.

The second example is a paraphrase of remarks about training analysis by Anna Freud in 1983—*But what is wrong with the analysand being inspired by the training analyst to a love of the truth or to a conviction about psychoanalysis? Is that not one of the ways in which learning takes place, what happens, in fact, between good student and good teacher?*—This statement implies a seemingly benign value but, revived in memory, would well have been pointed to as an imposition of an ego ideal by our graduate participants.

The third example is the statement by Annie Reich that there is no way to analyze the narcissistic gratification that the patient obtains from the fact that his analyst listens to him conscientiously throughout his analysis. Again, some of our graduate participants would have accepted this and continued it into their own work without question, while others would have found a denial of the awareness of possible negative transference that became a shared sanctuary of analyst and analysand. For example, from our seminar: Was my analyst asleep? Only the opinion of another analysand, after the former's termination, could confirm his observation.

The fourth and final example is a quotation from Klauber's paper on the role of illusion in psychoanalytic cure: I will quote what a woman in her thirties, speaking of a quite new phase of tenderness between herself and her lover of many years' standing, said to me, as I noted it down immediately after the session:

"I don't know whether I love him more because I love you. I don't know whether I substitute him for you. I think that because I trust you, I can love him. Love comes from getting to know one's self, and it may refer to God, or to another person, but it is true."

Klauber considers whether she was expressing transference love, that is displaced from early childhood, as memory projected onto him, or did she love him, and concluded that the patient now believed that "Men with certain characteristics can after all be trusted." One of many possibilities I can imagine our graduate participants expressing might be, "That is all the love that he, the analyst, has given, and all that he will accept from her—an illusion." As Ferenczi would have said, he should have given his attention to the possibility of a negative transference. Not, of course, that Klauber might not have done so at some other stage of the analysis in some other. There is a great appeal to the psychoanalyst to explain the findings of the Study Group by specific transference-countertransference interaction, the shared sanctuaries of wish and defense. The clearest examples of the mixture of particular collusions of analysand and analyst occurred in the many avoidances, as I have mentioned, in the period of termination. During the analyses there were other examples of particular mutual transference expressions; for example, protections expected from the analyst in relation to the institute, some of which, in fact had been accommodated and others symbolic.

To look for more general explanations resulted in the following speculations: The first had to do with the emphasis given by the graduate participants to what they called real events and real interactions, which, as I noted, later became the subject of self-analysis. Let me call this an anchoring in reality that not only serves as screen memory for the organization of transference emotions, but reveals limitations to the resolution, certainly to the destruction of transference fantasies. Our usual explanation in operational terms is that the working through had not been completed. If completed, as Ferenczi hoped, this would result in resolution, destruction, and inoculation against pathological outcome in the future. Examples In the literature abound in regard to these realities, for instance, Freud's setting of a termination date for the Wolf Man, or contrariwise, instances where termination dates are altered for apparently good reasons. The complexity of transference-countertransference is always present but so is the inevitability of these reality-anchored experiences.

I will point to the current view that although analysis is carried out in a state of abstinence, that is, transference wishes are not fulfilled, anonymity, we have discovered, is not the same, and must be thought of in a much more relative sense. A more subtle influence on reality is contained in Bird's idea that a readiness to consider aspects of the transference in the patient, is dependent upon a readiness for such transference in the analyst.

In regard to Freud and Ferenczi, my own speculation goes perhaps a bit further than the personal affection that Freud obviously felt for Ferenczi and further than "the respect and admiration" of Ferenczi for Freud, that Freud perhaps had at the time a double view of his own work, one part of which I might even call an ego-ideal that was imposed: on the one hand, analyzing his patient, Ferenczi, on the other hand, his wish to have followers, and to found a psychoanalytic movement. Analysts, older and younger, in a way, have a dilemma with their own ego-ideal of analyzing, more pointedly of doing better than their own analysts, and yet analyzing the very expressions of that ego-ideal in identifications and in other expressions in the transference. The candidate, in fact, also has a dilemma: his therapeutic goal and endeavor, which must include autonomy, as well as the ego-ideal to become like the idealized analyst—all, I would agree with the graduate participants, make the analysis of the negative transference particularly difficult.

A second aspect of what I can only call human limitations refers to the intellectual side, one might say, the effects upon the analytic work of the limitations on any analyst's cognitive as well as emotional capacities. Explanatory arts, the structure of the neurosis, to my mind, pale in complexity to the repetition of the neurosis in the transference, a new psychic structure that is organized around, and includes, the person of the analyst. We conceptualize this, not only as facsimile of someone in the past, but as an ever-changing part of the neurosis that includes "all of his conflicts"; that is, aspects of intrapsychic conflict of all of the compromise formations of the patient's psyche now experienced in the psychoanalytic situation.

Subplots and subtexts within the transference expressions, and their varying intensities, the phenomena Freud considered current life within the analytic situation, are beyond cataloguing. Take, as an obvious instance, the matter of identification for which I used Miss Freud's statement in 1983, or the incorporation of the analyst into the superego that Strachey talked about, or the so-called new object in some current psychoanalytic thinking.

In regard to identification, outstanding in our data, was the relative lack of interest in the analysis of career choice among our graduate participants and, to our surprise, the evidence of shared career choice wishes—subspecializations, one might say, of analysand and training analyst that emerged only at the time of the seminars. We have also the matter of the so-called impossibility of analyzing adaptive ego-functions, particularly those in use by analyst and candidate in the valued career of understanding other human beings, or other so-called possible adaptive outcomes as in the example I gave from Klauber.

We need to be reminded repeatedly, as Martin Stein reminded us, that benign transference *is* transference. For example, the analyst encounters his analysand with his long-time girlfriend, who

146

is reintroduced as "wife." The analyst remarks by way of greeting or acknowledgement, "My, how you have changed,"—a witticism in regard to marriage. In the analysis this incident is duly noted: in the analysand's fantasy, "change" means that the wife is pregnant, and the analyst's remark is understood as approval of the patient's mother's pregnancy, whereas in the patient's childhood the mother's pregnancy was believed to have accelerated the course of an illness. No harm will come to this woman. Later, the memory or this piece of analytic work intruded into the work of the new analyst, and self-analysis revealed—in addition to an identification with the analyst's presumed defense against sadistic feelings—a piece of negative paternal transference, paternity the ultimate source of pregnancy, which had not been worked through in this context, and was anchored in reality until the self-analysis.

To summarize our findings: assuming that analysis takes place, and in the graduate participants who attended the seminars, we in the Study Group agreed that very good, very thorough, very intelligent analyses had taken place. In my opinion, as a consequence of these analyses, a complex structure was set up in the psyche of these analysands that had not been there before, although obviously the sources, the drive impetus and the defense resistance, alterations in the ego, and so on, were rooted in the childhood past. The analysis of this complex structure was therapeutically very useful to our participants and contributed a great deal to their understanding of themselves, of their neuroses, of their unconscious, and of other people, particularly their psychoanalytic patients. Depending on the framework from which it is viewed, desirable change took place, certainly from the point of view of these participants. The compromise formations in symptoms and behaviors, including this transference, was altered in large measure, adaptively as well. In many, a self-analysis of termination occurred,

147

and in others ongoing self-analysis occurred, the source for which was the memory of the transference during and after analysis.

Finally, to the conclusions that have come from the study of the data of our investigation into the current status of the training analysis, the discussions of the Study Group investigators, and my own thinking concerning mental functioning and transference, I will start with the beginning of the Study Group about fifteen years ago when we gave not only a sympathetic ear, but a tentative affirmation to the concerns and remediation offered by preceding generations of psychoanalytic educators.

You are aware, of course, that the training analysis as part of psychoanalytic education has been considered problematic and has been under periodic review about every five to ten years since the establishment of the International Training Commission in 1922. I begin with Anna Freud's description of the training analysis, written in 1938:

We do not hesitate to brand it as technically wrong if, for the purposes of therapy, an analyst selects his patients from his circle of acquaintances, if he shares his interests with them or discusses his opinions, either with them or in their presence, if he forgets himself far enough to judge their behaviour, to disclose his criticism to other people, and to permit it to effect decisions, if he actively manipulates the patient, offers himself to him as a pattern, and ends analysis by permitting the patient to identify with him personally and professionally. Nevertheless, we commit every single one of these deviations from classical technique when we analyze candidates. Further, we do not inquire frequently enough how far these deviations complicate the candidate's transference and obscure its interpretations.... We may thereby determine how far analytic success is diminished or endangered by these changes in the transference situation which seem to be imposed on the analytic setting under the conditions of training as they exist at present.

In response, I can say, first that these condltions of training as they exist at present, are considerably different from those described by Miss Freud. Of course, certain basic characteristics that make the training analysis different from other analyses, for example, sharing the same goals, the most important of which is competence in psychoanalytic work, will always be present. Furthermore, our data from the particular group of successful graduate participants indicates that successful analyses by any standards can be accomplished in the training setting.

The final conclusion that the Study Group came to was that the problem was not in the training setting that is, in the contaminations of the analysis, or in the so-called '"normality" of the candidates, the well defended character neurosis with adaptive outcome in life—the concerns of previous studies, but in the limitations of psychoanalysis itself. My reading of the data has led me to consider limitations to analysis in terms of the durability of the transference from the point of view of the psychoanalytic pair, and have emphasized that the core of the limiting process after the analysis, is the same as it was during the analysis, namely the analysis of the transference is a requirement which is forced upon psychoanalysts as an ego-ideal, and necessarily creates an ambivalent cathexis.

Thus, in the training analysis, we are not just after cure, the contemporary ideal, and not just after what Ferenczi required as the analysis of the most recondite areas of the patient's mind, but we are after this particular skill in introspection and self-analysis.

The limitations to this Ideal in our endeavors, we will, of course, try to overcome. And, in fact, our graduate participants, in their eagerness to talk about their training analysis and about the work on themselves they continued to do, were certainly trying to overcome the limitations to further insight. The seminar data, I might add, pointed to two major resistances: displacements of the transference from the training analyst to institutions and to other people and other experiences, and second, as I have emphasized all along, the issue that Ferenczi had to deal with, repeated by our graduate participants, the discomfort of hatred. As Bird wrote: "Hatred has always been one of the unsolved and perhaps insoluble problems of mankind causing troubles far beyond (but clearly also within) the field of psychoanalytic training."

In my opinion, the process of dealing with recurrent activations of transference, in practicing analysts, may be taking place most intensively in the first four or five years after termination. It is also probably facilitated by the many post-graduate study groups that have proliferated in recent years, even though, of course, the focus of these efforts is not self-analysis. Most of the graduate participants urged that our seminars be continued. We In the Study Group had undertaken a pilot project, intended to yield some recommendations about how to undertake such a study. It should be clear that our experiences were gratifying and useful both to the investigators ourselves, and to the co-investigators, the graduate participants. It seems to me that these groups can serve as a model for further work, perhaps as peer groups alone.

I will end with an opinion by Freud about analytic work and transference very early on in a letter to Fliess, Apr 16, 1900, five years before he wrote the postscript to the Dora case about transference:

E at last concluded his career as a patient by coming to supper in my house. His riddle is *almost* completely solved, he feels extremely well, and his nature is entirely changed: for the moment, a residue of symptoms remains. I am beginning to see that the apparent endlessness of the treatment is something of an inherent feature and is connected with the transference. I am hoping that this residue will not detract from the practical success. I could have continued the treatment if I had wanted to, but it dawned on me that such prolongation is a compromise between illness and health which patients themselves desire, and that the physician must therefore not lend himself to it. I am not in the least worried by the asymptotic conclusion of the treatment: it is more a disappointment to outsiders than anything else. In any case, shall keep my eye on the man.

Thank you.

CHAPTER 13

Interview with Susan Jaffe MD

Newsletter, New York Psychoanalytic Institute 2007

Ed Note: Dr Jaffe is a member of the Faculty of New York Psychoanalytic Institute

SJ: I'd like to hear your thoughts about psychoanalytic education,
specifically at our Institute.

Dr. F: I would put the analysis as the most important part. In the
1970s on a Cope Study Group. Eight institutes each sent two graduate
representatives. The question was: how did your analysis affect your
technique? It presupposed the idea that the most influential piece of
their education was the analysis. The graduates, after their analysis,
continued their self-analysis mostly in order to deal with the problems
that came up with their patients, at least that's what they told us, and
what we asked about. The outcome of a good training analysis is self-
analysis as stated by Ernst Kris.

The second piece of education is supervision. Transference is
a lifelong part of someone who has had a good analysis and your
transference to the supervisor is very important. Some supervisors
hit it off well with you and vice versa. For example, a classmate
and close friend and I had a supervisor who asked us to present

on alternate weeks. I felt the supervisor was more interested in my friend's way of working than mine. But another supervisor of mine was Berta Bornstein and that was a different learning experience. We had supervision on Saturday. It ran into lunch and so she invited my wife and two little girls over because it was also a social occasion. In all, I had six supervisors including Edith Jacobson. Another valuable piece of my education was discussing different styles of supervision with my classmates.

Curriculum is the third leg and is vital. At NYPI, we've kept up with the times. It's a pluralistic universe and the curriculum reflects that. My hunch is it's more interesting now than it was when I was a candidate. The teaching depends on the individual. When I was a candidate, the teachers were often Europeans and very formal and I think they made a greater impression than the teachers today. Everyone remembers Otto Isakower. He was a piercingly critical person. After class, I would drive Berta (Bornstein) and Isakower home and they would joke with each other in English and German, so he was very different outside of class. Dr. Leonard Straub, a classmate, was an incredible mimic and before the teachers arrived, for example, Ludwig Eidelberg, he would get up and imitate him. Aside from the obvious hostility, it made everyone in the class more comfortable. We had a somewhat different, interesting education in regard to the curriculum.

SJ: Did you primarily read Freud in class?

Dr. F: We had one class with Bert Lewin on Ferenczi and Abraham. That was the extent of our pluralism. We were taking in Freud's wisdom. If we spoke up it was mostly to have things explained. We rarely disagreed.

SJ: Tell me about your work with Mahler.

Dr. F: She was never a supervisor of mine so we didn't work together on an analytic case. We were co-investigators in a NIMH study of symbiotic psychosis in preschool age children, which would probably be called autism today. Margaret was a pioneer. People were reluctant to accept psychosis as a diagnosis in children. She was more than devoted to her ideas and work. She would say, I have no children. This is my baby. She was single minded. There was no obstacle she wouldn't knock over. I was invited to join her on the grant application while I was on the faculty at Einstein and Milt Rosenbaum, the Chair of Psychiatry at the time, said to her, now that you're doing this you have to give time to teach residents. She said, I came to do my research. Milt said, if you won't, you'll have to give the grant back. She turned to me and said, "Manny give the grant back", which is what we did. With her usual determination we got the grant reactivated and set up a clinic on Horatio Street.

She didn't rise in the hierarchy of our institute and took over a failing institute in Philadelphia that ultimately produced such well-known analysts as Cal Settlage, and Henri Parens. She invented piggyback supervision where a younger analyst sits in on her supervision and that of other older analysts in order for the observer to learn how to supervise. Margaret was always fastidious about contributions by others. She would always credit me with creating the term 'refueling'. She would correct people and tell them it wasn't her idea. It was mine.

SJ: How have you found teaching your course on 'Alternative Theories' to candidates?

Dr. F: I would like to push the course even further in regard to the individuality of the analyst. I will add the paper by Sandler where he writes about private and public theories. The candidates are encouraged to talk about their own countertransference responses as much as they are willing. We will continue to have the guests: Roy Schafer, Jay Greenberg, Marianne Goldberger and Paul Ornstein. in order to help the candidates develop their own form of being an analyst. Just as, for example, Roy Schafer is not an exponent of contemporary Kleinian theory, he decided that certain aspects of their ideas about technique could usefully be adapted to his work; so too, he and the others in discussing the candidates' cases present their individual variations of alternative theories of technique that influenced them.

The goal of the course is twofold: To understand something from the work of our guests and mine and Dr. Welner's that they can think about as modifications of their own analytic work and to realize that the participation of the analyst is inevitable and once recognized enlarges the understanding of the analyst, the patient, and the analytic process they are observing. I hope to end the course with a discussion with Dr. Larry Friedman about the epistemological basis of Freudian theory and practice.

CHAPTER 14

Editor's Introductory Note

Manuel Furer was known for his skill in mediating institutional conflicts, and for his rare ability to retain the confidence of opposing factions. The following memorandum gives evidence of these skills. The issue at hand was the method of election to the Educational Committee, which determined training policies at the New York Psychoanalytic Institute, in its role as the executive arm of the Faculty. Nominations for election to the EC at the time could only be made by the Faculty itself. This process, according to one faction among the Faculty, led to its exclusion. An amendment was proposed to allow nominations for EC election to be made not just by Faculty but by all NYPSI members from the floor. A supplementary amendment was made which while allowing nominations from the floor, would limit those nominated to be only members of the Faculty. There was considerable confusion whether the second amendment was properly proposed.

Memorandum to NYPSI Board of Trustees with editor's concluding note

Into this tense situation stepped Dr. Furer as Chairman of the EC.

MEMORANDUM FROM: Manuel Purer, M.D.

Since the Board meets on Wednesday evenings at the same time that the course I teach meets, I have prepared the following statement that I hope can be read if I cannot attend the meeting.

When Dr. Silberman brought the amendment which states that only faculty can be nominated and elected to the Educational Committee to the Board of Trustees for discussion, I felt that it would be bewildering to the membership if presented as it was proposed because no actual change would occur since anyone can see that only members of the faculty are nominated and elected, and the reason for this amendment would not be known to the membership.

After the amendment was presented to the membership by Dr. Silberman that is, read my contacts with the members indicated that the amendment was not only bewildering but misleading. Dr. Silberman had asked the Board to discuss the amendment with the view toward sponsoring it; we had neither the opportunity to discuss it and did not vote on whether to sponsor it. What happened was, however, that since the amendment was sponsored by Dr. Silberman himself as an individual, it was taken by some members as an official sponsorship since he is also the president of the Institute.

Before explaining what seems to me to be the issues involved, I would like to make a motion that a letter be sent to all the members stating the facts that is, that the memorandum was sponsored by Dr. Silberman as a member of the Society and not in his official capacity as president of the Institute. Therefore. he was not speaking for his committee, the Board of Trustees. I think it is unfortunate that whether our opinion would have been for or against, that once having been asked for that opinion we were not given the opportunity to discuss the matter and perhaps real a conclusion in a matter of this importance before it was presented to the membership.

To go directly to the heart of the matter, we all know this Amendment is presented only because it is linked to another amendment which does propose crucial change in actual procedure and is meant to deal with a real problem. I will present the facts as I see them. There are other members of the faculty present who may have another viewpoint. But what is important, I think, is that the Board and certainly the membership, which I think has been, again unfortunately, drawn into this without adequate information, are entitled to as comprehensive a presentation of the facts as is possible.

The facts and the problem as I see it as that there are factions on the faculty, and one of these factions feels that it is under-represented on the committees that make educational policy for the Institute. Although they are represented on some of the committees of the Educational Committee, they feel they are not sufficiently represented on the EC itself because they are not nominated to the EC. In fact, this is a faculty matter. Dr. Brenner I think properly brought the matter for discussion to the faculty. It was briefly discussed; as part of the discussion a few people suggested the amendment we are discussing now as an addition. However, as I remember it, there was not full discussion. I also do not remember a conclusive vote and more important, the faculty certainly did not reach the conclusion that they were unable to deal with this problem themselves. Herein lies my objection to the Board of Trustees sponsoring this amendment, although of course any such question of our sponsorship is too late since the amendment has been introduced. In any case, I think we have been, and now the membership is being asked to interfere and intrude in a faculty matter improperly. That is, the faculty has not, as far as I know, as a body or via representatives approached the Board or the president to say, "We have a problem. We are unable to resolve it by ourselves and we need your help. "

That is my first objection, second objection is more for the future, and for the record is what I had meant to say, but the fat is in the fire, Because I would hope that when and if the Board or anybody else may they would come up with a better proposed, which I believe, in the long run, contain serious hazards for the Institute. As I explained to a question from Dr. Earle at a previous meeting, it is not by chance that the by-laws read that any member may recommend a nominee to the Memorandum Nominating Committee for the Education Committee, but that this is not binding on that Committee, while quite the opposite obtains for the Board of Directors or the Board of Trustees, where any member may actually nominate by sending a name in writing or speaking up from the floor. This was not done haphazardly or because the framers of these by-laws did not have logical minds, but deliberately because of a principle, the principle being that the Education Committee is meant to be an executive committee of the faculty. That is, by giving the faculty, the majority of the faculty, the exclusive right to nominate, the potential members of the Education Committee are expected first to have the confidence of the faculty, and then, from among these the membership finally votes and chooses. The purpose as you can see is that there will be relatively small chance of conflict between the Educational Committee and the faculty. If this procedure is changed so that nominations come from the members, it need not necessarily follow but it may follow that people will be nominated and elected because of general popularity or some other issue not relevant to the faculty, either to become a small number, a large number, or perhaps a majority of the Educational Committee whose views on educational policy and perhaps other matters might well be at variance with or in conflict with the views of the majority of the faculty, the situation that I believe would be hazardous to the Institute.

This procedure—that is, the one that would follow the acceptance of these two amendments which cannot be separated—might solve in the short run the problem of under-representation of a faction of the faculty, but in the long run it seems to me that the cure is potentially much worse than the relatively minor disease.

Re: Memorandum to the Board of Trustees

Editor's concluding note:

Both amendments were subsequently defeated.

However, in subsequent years Dr. Furer, as head of the Educational Committee presided over several reforms and improvements, not only of such political frameworks, but also of the Training Analyst appointment process and the academic curriculum.

Part Three: Psychoanalysis and the Developing Child

CHAPTER 16

Psychic Development and the Prevention of Mental Illness

(1962). *Journal of the American Psychoanalytic Association* 10:606–616

Presented at the Fall Meeting of The American Psychoanalytic Association, New York, December, 1961. Chairman: Herbert F. Waldhorn, M.D.

Herbert Waldhorn pointed out that in the recent past psychoanalysis had mainly been concerned with the inevitability of neurotic conflict and the great complexity of overdetermination in mental functioning; consequently, the problem of the prevention of mental illness has seemed "awesomely unapproachable." However, with the recent advances in our knowledge of early psychic functioning deriving from both clinical psychoanalysis and psychoanalytic research in childhood, the time has come to attempt to rethink the problem.

To illustrate this change in point of view, he quoted Anna Freud from her Arden House talk in 1954, in which she stated that the emergence of neurotic conflicts had to be regarded as the price paid for the complexity of the human personality. In 1957, however, in her paper on "Child Observation and the Prediction of Development, " she paid tribute to the late Ernst Kris's ideas about prediction and the early spotting of danger, adding that prevention was feasible only if we could know the therapeutic steps which are appropriate to each age level and its disturbances, and to each special group of disorders. The new knowledge, which Kris had stressed and which now made such an approach to prevention possible, consists in the awareness of the mother's unique role in human life, the adaptive value of psychic conflict and function, the interaction of libidinal and aggressive drives, and the phase-specific and situation-specific mechanisms of defense.

In September, 1960, Anna Freud gave her revisions of her contributions to child analysis. She proposed a new method of diagnosis in childhood, which would be concerned with the assessment of lines of development, rather than with symptom formation, levels of achievement in the ego, or instinctual phase. She discussed the importance of progressive and regressive trends and again raised the possibility of developing specifically appropriate types of treatment and preventive intervention. It is time, Waldhorn stated, for the application of the now large amount of psychoanalytic knowledge concerned with early development and functioning.

In the first paper, "Problems and Opportunities in the Application of Psychoanalytic Knowledge of Normal Development, " Sibylle Escalona stated that the failure of past applications of psychoanalysis toward the prevention of neuroses was not only the result of the frequent misaplication of psychoanalytic knowledge but derived from the nature of psychoanalytic theory itself. In terms of prediction, psychoanalysis is not an inclusive theory of human behavior and has not concerned itself with the complex interactions between the social, physical, biological, experiential, and psychological factors that determine overt behavior. In fact, one of the most important contributions of psychoanalysis has been in an opposite direction—to the effect that there is no invariant causal link between specific traumatic events and specific predisposition to neurosis, that the same intrapsychic state of affairs may produce widely different observable manifestations, and that early psychopathology may lead to mental illness, but also to sublimation and enrichment of the ego.

Escalona concluded that we do not possess sufficient knowledge of the normal developmental processes definitively to identify the critical deviations which require preventive intervention. She then outlined a tentative tabulation of normal developmental acquisitions, normal defenses and coping patterns, phase-specific stress reactions, and phase-specific psychopathology, which could be used for this purpose. She presented the tables for the three earliest stages of development, which she called "preverbal, " "anal, " and "oedipal."

In summary, the preverbal stage is linked to the body, its separation from the outside, and the development of a selective strong tie to the mother. In this stage she listed such normal acquisitions as separation of the self from the outside, voluntary motor action, memory and anticipation, discrimination among reality objects, a selective strong tie to the mother, pleasure in exploratory sensorimotor play; normal coping patterns such as autism, self-stimulation, and stranger anxiety; stress reactions including disturbed body functioning, excessive withdrawal, self-stimulation and excessive stranger anxiety, and minimum pleasure in exploration. The phase-specific psychopathology included marasmus, physiological disorders, no strong tie to the mother, and minimum awareness of the body entity. The toddler anal stage included many more acquisitions such as mastery through movement, speech, voluntary choice, the awareness of affect, the awareness of dependence on the mother, and the transformation of passive into active on the action level. The phase-specific psychopathology of that stage includes hyper- and hypomotility, absence of pleasure in body movement, symbiotic clinging, and chronic play inhibition. Regressive psychopathology at the toddler stage includes withdrawal, excessive

169

autoerotic activity, and persistent stranger anxiety. In the early oedipal stage the important new acquisition is the capacity to turn passive into active on the ideational and not only on the action level, and the appropriate stress reactions are such ideational symptoms as phobias.

Escalona then illustrated the use of this type of developmental thinking on three levels of preventive action. First she considered the detection of developmental deviation, using the hypothetical case of a two-year-old whose movement is restricted. The repercussions of this type of hardship will be expected to have more profound effects in the toddler stage. Preventive action must be directed to providing opportunity for self-determined, unrestricted action in such areas as the use of the hand to express the acquisitions of that stage, e.g., choice and the normal battle with adults.

The second example had to do with the determination of appropriate preventive action in relation to unavoidable noxious experience. In the hypothetical case of hospitalization in a two-year-old, whose individuation has begun, we will expect depression and regression requiring the phase specific action of rebuilding his trust in the world via his own mother. On the other hand, the two-year-old who has not yet fully cathected his mother can be supplied with a substitute object. In contrast, the anxiety of the five-year-old in a similar situation will be focused on bodily injury, and he can achieve mastery through words and play. The third example dealt with developmental diagnosis or the preventive use of treatment. The five-year-old with a phobic symptom and without deformity of the ego can be expected to respond quickly to interpretation. The five-year-old who shows regressed ego functioning requires longer treatment to return him to phase-adequate growth potential.

Sally Provence presented a paper on "Observations from a Longitudinal Study, " conducted at the Yale Child Study Center. She reported two cases of disturbed mother-child interaction in the first year of life from the point of view of early recognition of psychological difficulties and attempts at early therapeutic intervention.

Both mothers had expressed the fear during pregnancy that they would give birth to a damaged child. Later data suggested that each mother viewed the girl baby she bore as the defective part of herself. In the first year of life, both infants showed some deviation in development, without evidence of disturbance of the inborn maturational apparatus. In the first case, the efforts of the staff to improve the mother-child relationship were effective; in the second case, they were not. The first mother, Mrs. C., in the fifth month of her pregnancy, was described as a pleasant, childlike young woman, eager to become a part of the study. Later it was learned that to her the study represented an attempt to get help with her feelings of deprivation and worthlessness, and the protection against gratifying prohibited erotic and aggressive impulses toward the child. She was hospitalized for severe nausea and vomiting during her second trimester and felt happy at being taken care of. She delivered at term, after a prolonged labor, and the 7 lbs. infant was in good condition at birth. Twelve hours after birth, the infant had a high-pitched cry, reacted minimally to stimulation, was somnolent, and had poor sucking and rooting responses. However, by six days of age, these disturbing signs had disappeared, and she was described as a vigorous and well-formed infant. However, she was easily startled and hypertonic, and it was felt at the time that she would be a difficult baby to live with, especially for an anxious and inept mother; and so it developed. The mother was totally unable to enjoy the child whose normalcy she doubted despite repeated reassurance to the contrary. She was unable to make decisions regarding the daily care of the child, required frequent contact with the pediatrician, and could implement instructions only of the most specific and direct nature.

A change occurred some days after a staff examination of the infant at five months of age, when the mother expressed her continuing concern about the child's normalcy, although the child had become more socially responsive, physically attractive, and, most strikingly, already displayed a discrimination of strangers, and a marked preference for the mother. Five days later, Mrs. C. called to express her newfound happiness with the child's progress, namely, the social responsiveness and the preference for the mother which had been pointed out to her at the testing time. It was concluded that the change in the mother's attitude had been brought about by the above-described developmental step, which the mother received, not as a demand upon her, but as flattering attention. During the next few months Mrs. C. showed a growing pleasure in her child, a disappearance of her fears of retardation, and an increasing capacity to make everyday decisions. It was concluded that this woman had been helped because she had been able to recognize and express her wishes for attention, care, and guidance. These had been supplied in ways that fitted to her personality—as specific concrete advice, repeatedly available.

In contrast, in the second family, Mrs. D. and her infant daughter, Ann, the recognition of the potential pathology came primarily from the observation of disturbed and delayed development in the infant at eight months of age, and only secondarily from the mother. Mrs. D. had combined a full-time career with her marriage, and this unplanned pregnancy had brought a radical change in her mode of living. She was delivered of a 5½ lbs. girl, a healthy, pretty, doll-like infant who easily attracted attention from the staff. She expressed a belief in strictness with rather than babying of children. The infant was easily comforted by holding, but after a few weeks the mother reported that

Ann preferred not to be held. The staff concluded that although the mother might manage efficiently, she would give little of herself to her infant. Development was normal and without incident until six months of age, when it was noted that Ann had poor control of her trunk and poor mastery of large body movements. By eight months of age, gross motor functions were significantly retarded; there was delayed language development and a less than normal interest in toys. More importantly, she reacted to her mother's approach with vigorous crying. Concerted efforts by the staff allowed the mother to express her feelings of depression and loneliness, but these were later denied. Psychotherapy was advised, but rejected. The pediatrician attempted to teach the mother to stimulate the infant in more favorable ways. From nine to thirteen months the infant improved, which the staff attributed primarily to a visit of Mrs. D.'s brother and to the fact that Mr. D. spent more time at home. The staff asked themselves why they did not earlier recognize the mother's detachment from the infant and her depression. They believed it was due to the fact that in the presence of adults the mother was able to mobilize herself and present a competent appearance. Advice offered to this mother seemed to have been taken as a confirmation that the observers were not interested in her, but only in her child.

In both cases the research and service staff were aware early in the study of potentialities for disturbances of maternal attitudes and functioning, and were thus forewarned. Mrs. C., the first mother, had a baby who was sensitive and hypertonic during the first three months, a source of great tribulation and no pleasure whatever to the mother; yet, by dint of openly expressing her needs, doubts, fears, and great wish for guidance, Mrs. C. was able to benefit from the interventions of the staff at that time; moreover, she could take pleasure in the child once it afforded her the gratification of exclusive social response. Mrs.

D., the second mother, expressed her theories of strict child rearing to the staff, but was wary and evasive in interviews; the existence of pathology was noticed only in a retardation of the infant's motor, adaptive, and social development in its eighth month of life. A closer look at the mother then revealed that she had concealed from the staff a considerable depression and detachment from the child. In this instance, staff interventions were unable to bring about an improvement in the mother-child interaction.

In her discussion, Provence raised the following questions: When is there sufficient evidence to diagnose disturbance in the mother-child interaction, and what type of intervention is correct? The conclusions from the longitudinal study were that although these disturbances might be predicted during the mother's pregnancy, one could make reliable diagnoses only when the mother could be observed with her infant, and the baby's developmental progress measured.

Provence pointed out that psychological problems in the mother differ in the extent to which they influence the infant. If this influence is an adverse one, there will be deviations in many areas in the infant's development because of the lack of differentiation in the infant's somatic and psychic apparatus. Specific disturbances in the mother, such as depression, may result in particular alterations in the mothering functioning, which in turn may produce specific syndromes in the infant, a relatively unknown area which is worthy of research.

In terms of preventive intervention, the author listed four possibilities: help through the professional people who provide infant care; direct therapy for the mother; the use of substitute mothers; and the enlistment of the baby's father. The first requires education of physicians, nurses, and social workers who deal with mothers and babies. In reference to direct therapy of the mother, we are reminded of Anna Freud's warning that the alleviation of a mother's withdrawal or depression by therapy may be too late to help her infant. The last two methods of a mother substitute and the assistance of the father, Provence believes, are thought of too infrequently and might have been the correct and only possible procedure in the second of the two families presented.

In the ensuing discussion Rudolf Ekstein and Theodore Lidz pointed out that Escalona and Provence were thinking of prevention as something instituted after deviation had occurred. They proposed that psychoanalytic theory could also be applied to the fostering of healthy development. Lidz said that guidance, if directed by our knowing the varieties of interaction between different types of mothers and different types of children, could be effective. He further stated that the entire family interaction, including the father, had to be considered; for example, in present-day isolated families, in order to give to her baby the mother must have the support of her husband. It was Escalona's view that considering the wide variety of cultural patterns, it was not up to us to decide upon the correct roles for parents. Margaret S. Mahler initiated a discussion of the role of pleasure in the development of autonomous functions in the study of normal development. Both Escalona and Lidz emphasized the survival value of this functional pleasure. Provence stressed the importance of the mother's response to these emerging functions and quoted Escalona to the effect that the mother's marvelously beneficial error transforms the "mama"-"dada" sounds into communicative speech.

Theodore Lidz, in his paper on "The Influence of the Family Environment on Psychic Development," pointed out the unique position of the family in human adaptation. Psychoanalytic theory, he felt, has not given due weight to the enculturating task of the family as an instrument in passing on such techniques as language, patterns of perception, and ways of interrelating developed by a particular culture to cope with its environment, and rewarded with survival of evolution. Psychoanalytic theories have tended to neglect the importance of who the parents are in actuality, of how they interrelate, and of the nature of the family they form in shaping the child's adaptive capacities and techniques. The harmonious functioning of the family has a central position in the organization of the evolving ego of the child. The family is not only the environmental setting in which the child develops, but it has the task of integrating the child's biological needs and innate patterns with social and cultural requirements.

Lidz considers the family to be a true small group with an organic unity, which can be understood only if one takes into account that the action of any member affects all the others. As a special small group, the family has certain characteristics. First, it is composed of two generations, each with different needs, tasks, and prerogatives. The parents who come from different families must merge themselves into a new unit. The children are dependent on the parents, form intense emotional bonds to them, introject their characteristics and yet must learn to live in such a way that they can emerge to start their own families. The parents as a coalition act as a guide for the children. Second, the family is composed of two sexes with different roles. The feminine role leads to emphasis on interpersonal relations and emotional harmony. The masculine role leads to emphasis on adaptive leadership and protection. Third, the bonds between the family members are held firm by erotic and affectional ties. Erotic gratification accompanies nurturant care of the children and must be progressively frustrated lest the bonds become too firm. Fourth, the family forms a shelter against the remainder of society and at the same time must transmit the ways of that society for the time when the children emerge from the family.

In order for the family to carry out its functions, the parents must be able to form a coalition, must maintain the separation of generations and of their sex-linked roles, and must be capable of transmitting specific methods of adaptation suited to their particular society. It is Lidz's thesis that one major reason for inadequate ego integration in the child arises because the parents' ways of interacting lead to faulty family organization.

The child requires two parents, one of the same sex for identification and one of the opposite sex as the primary love object. If they do not form a coalition, neither parent can properly carry out their individual functions. When the parents are chronically at odds the growing child may invest its energy into bridging the gap between them, or in trying to satisfy the discrepant needs of both. The result may be the incorporation of irreconcilable introjects and a split in ego and superego structures.

The division between the generations, with the older generation acting as the educators, works to safeguard against role conflict within the family. It was a regular finding in the families of disturbed patients that these boundaries between the generations were not maintained. In general, the child's phases of development such as the oedipus complex are seriously interfered with by the actual participation of the parents, for example, their own jealousy and incestuous wishes toward the child.

Inadequately defined sexual roles in the parents lead to confusion in sexual identity in the child, which is a factor in both neurosis and schizophrenia. The particular pattern of these relationships may make some families more difficult for the development of a boy, others for a girl. Lidz stated that in the contemporary family the sharing of role tasks has become more necessary and acceptable, but that there is still need for the parents to support each other in their primary gender roles. In conclusion, Lidz pointed out that in a time of great change in the family and society, it is important to consider what are the essentials of good family structure, for these need to be safeguarded in order to prevent mental illness.

The last paper was "Psychoanalysis and Education—Past and Future," by Rudolf Ekstein and Rocco L. Motto. Surveying the relationship of psychoanalysis to education from its beginning in the period during and after World War I through the present, the authors describe a first phase in Europe that lasted until the beginning of the Second World War, a second phase in America and England starting after the Second World War, and a third phase which they believe may be presently in the making.

The first reception of psychoanalysis in general was hostile, so that in the period prior to World War I there were few attempts to apply analysis to education. In the revolutionary period after the war there was a breakdown of old institutions and a questioning of old educational methods which offered psychoanalysis an opportunity to extend its contributions. A certain number of educational experiments, usually with war orphans, were originated by psychoanalysts, such as Bernfeld in Germany and Schmidt in Russia. The general spirit of liberation also led to the publication of many enthusiastic books and articles, such as *The Liberation of the Child*, written by Fritz Wittels in 1927, which were essentially protests against the suppression of instinct in the Victorian society. In this period there also developed a fear of traumatizing the child (for which psychoanalysis was more directly responsible), as exemplified by Bernfeld's definition of infancy as the phase of life which leads from the trauma of birth to the trauma of weaning. At the same time, in *Sisyphus: Or the Boundaries of Education* (1925), Bernfeld recognized the limits of education and the complexity of its task since it must take into account both the unconscious forces in the child as well as the reaction of society to these forces.

Within the psychoanalytic movement centers for training and thus of influence began to develop. The first organized expression of an effort to relate psychoanalysis to education was the founding of the *Zeitschift für psychoanalytische Pädagogik* which started in October 1926, and continued until the invasion of Austria in 1938. In the lead article of the first issue by Schneider, therapeutic psychoanalysis is presented as "posteducation" and psychoanalysis in general as a new means of education to be applied by teachers. Ekstein pointed out that this lack of differentiation between psychoanalysis and education has presented many theoretical and practical dilemmas from that time on.

In this first phase, the main source of interest in the application of psychoanalysis to the life of the child came from teachers who became the first child analysts. Anna Freud gave a series of lectures to teachers in 1931 in which she said that psychoanalysis did three things for pedagogues: it criticized the existing educational methods; it pointed to the importance of the relationship between the child and the educator; and it supplied educators with the knowledge of the use of analysis as a therapeutic method for those children who suffered injuries inflicted by the educational process. By the late 1930s, the psychoanalytically oriented educator, instead of stressing the liberation of instincts and a crusade against the faults of parents and educators, became concerned with creating an optimum situation which was to avoid pathological trauma as well as the extremes of indulgence or strictness. In 1936 special techniques deriving from psychoanalysis for educators were described by Editha Sterba, who recommended that teachers use interpretation to deal with situational crisis in order to help the child with a current educational task. Ekstein made the point that this approach focused on symptomatic disturbance rather than on the ordinary educational situation where the educator acts primarily as a teacher. On the other hand, in these years child analysts in Vienna began to experiment with the application of psychoanalytic understanding to the classroom situation.

However, starting in 1938 the European analytic organizations were being broken up and new ones had to be built in the United States and England. The political upheavals in Europe and the Second World War influenced psychoanalysts to consider the relationship of psychoanalysis to education in the light of the social system. Alice Balint, in her book *The Early Years of Life* (1931), had already pointed out that there are no absolutes in pedagogy or mental hygiene. The society, no matter what its nature, whether free or tyrannical, produces its underpinnings in educational measures. On the other hand, reforms in education necessarily bring about a change in civilization even when that was not necessarily the conscious intention, making of education a revolutionary science. It was Erikson, however, who with his book *Childhood and Society* (1950), has led the way in attempting to understand educational systems culturally as well as analytically.

At the end of the war the second phase of the relationship between psychoanalysis and education began. *The Psychoanalytic Study of the Child* was founded in America, the heir, it seems to the authors, to the *Journal of Psychoanalytic Education*, but now with a significant difference in stress more on study and research. The social scene for psychoanalysis in America and England was quite different from that in Central Europe. Instead of a complete focus in private practice, there was much more involvement with general psychiatry and the community through social agencies. As far as education is concerned, the authors quote Oberndorf who felt that the influence of John Dewey's theory of instrumentalism and learning through doing, which allowed for a maximum freedom of initiative rather than subordination to the teacher, paralleled the influence of Freud and prepared American education to accept psychoanalysis. The aid to teachers, however, came primarily in dealing with deviant children and educational problems. Ekstein pointed out that the first volume of *The Psychoanalytic Study of the Child* contained the subheading, "Problems of Education." In subsequent volumes the papers dealing with education refer rather to therapeutic nursery schools and analytically oriented education as therapeutic measures. This general tendency, as exemplified by Pearson in his volume on *Psychoanalysis in Education* (1954), was to lead teachers to analytic training after which they generally became therapists despite that author's hope that they would prefer to employ their knowledge in the field of education. Ekstein added that the psychoanalytic training of teachers, although it might tap the resources of people who were talented and gifted with children, would not approach the problem that he thinks is crucial— the strengthening of education as a positive and creative force.

The author then proposed a third phase in the relationship between psychoanalysis and education which would focus on the essential task of the school—learning; this would include, as Peller stated in 1956, the acquisition of knowledge and skill for growth and enrichment and for meeting the tasks of life. They hope this can be carried out in the spirit Kris wrote about in 1948, where there would be "a process of communication between experts trained in different skills in which cross-fertilization of approaches is likely to occur." In keeping with these ideas the authors, who are connected with the Reiss Davis Clinic in Los Angeles, have set up an institute for the collaboration of teachers and psychoanalysts. In the discussions and meetings of this institute, the analysts, rather than offering themselves as models for identification, are intended to become resource persons to work together with teachers in order to develop a better understanding of the teaching process so as to apply psychoanalytic concepts both to the teaching process and the acquisition of teaching skills. Specifically, they will consider teaching methods as they apply to different age groups as well as teaching difficulties and methods concerned with special subject matter. As their goal, the authors quote from Freud's discussion of the case of Little Hans, in which Freud proposes that education "aim instead [of suppressing the instincts] at making the individual capable of becoming a civilized and useful member of society with the least possible sacrifice of his own activity." Freud adds, however, "What practical conclusions may follow from this and how far experience may justify the application of those conclusions within our present social system are matters which I leave to the examination and decision of others.

"The authors conclude that educational techniques are more influenced by psychoanalytic considerations when the society lives in a period of peace without anxiety. The return of peace or the breakdown of social systems was in the past accompanied by social experimentation. However, in time of stress and "the ascendancy of fear" education of the individual is subordinated to certain social goals which may not be compatible with psychoanalytic influence. whether the effect of the social forces of the latter situation, which is our time, can be overcome by the work and inspiration of dedicated educators and psychoanalysts is for the future to determine.

In the discussion Provence reiterated that one has to consider the influence of a child's deviant equipment on the parents. Lidz cited a study by Goldfarb on families of psychotic children; Goldfarb found that the family interaction in the families where the child was brain-damaged was fairly good compared to the gross derangement in families where the child was not brain-damaged. Waldhorn questioned the concept of the internalization of family structure and pointed out that a skewed family setup does not necessarily result in neurosis.

Many discussants were interested in Ekstein's hoped-for third phase of a contribution of psychoanalysis to education. Escalona suggested that psychoanalysis might be able to investigate the underlying state of affairs in reference to educational techniques and come to a decision as to their usefulness, but she doubted that psychoanalysis could contribute in suggesting techniques. Manuel Furer also doubted whether psychoanalysis could be used directly as an aid in teaching subject matter, as, for example, attempts at present are being made to use the developmental psychology of Piaget; on the other hand, he wondered whether it could not contribute more in such ever-present but not always consciously apprehended areas as the transmission of values.

Edward Liss reminded us that psychoanalysis had made substantial contributions to progressive education. Hilde Bruch, investigating what a good teacher did do in the classroom, found that the teacher provided a continuity of warmth and an alertness to the level of functioning of each child with the capacity to communicate on that level. Stephen Fleck brought up the problem of the underachievers and the complex issue of the acquisition of pleasure in learning. Ekstein replied that for the moment the third stage was in its infancy; he is therefore satisfied with such tasks as emphasizing that a sustained relationship to a teacher is required for learning so that he can advise against a school changing teachers every six months.

CHAPTER 17

Some Developmental Aspects
of the Superego.

(1967). *International Journal of Psycho-Analysis* 48:277–280

Presented at the Annual Meeting of the American Psychoanalytic Association, Los Angeles, March 1964; a Panel on the Current Status of the Theory of the Superego.

The following observations of behaviour in childhood seem to throw some light upon the problem of the precursors of the superego and to reveal certain complex ego capacities that may be required for superego formation.

The particular ego capacity I would like to deal with at some length is that of empathy, which I would define in short as the capacity for making a partial identification with another person. In the instances under study here, this was seen as the capacity to experience the painful quality of an affect in the other person that may, in some instances, have been evoked in the observed person by an act of the observer. When a forerunner of the superego is involved, either the child ends up saying, "I am sorry," in actual words, or else this is to be understood from the nature of his consoling behaviour toward the object. Although one can also infer concern for the object—or, in Kleinian terms, the restitution of the destroyed object—from the child's behaviour earlier in life, the affective statement, "I am sorry," involves, I believe, a significant step forward in development. The child is conscious of the harm that he or someone else or something else has done to a person whom he loves; he is able to feel along with the person (empathize with the object), and then to express to the object his sympathy or concern. He is no longer simply overwhelmed by contagion, or merely shocked and blank in expression. He begins, on the contrary, with the expectation that, with his omnipotence, he can make it all better.

If one thinks for a moment in terms of the possible anxieties involved, one's thought is directed to the forerunners of the sadistic superego. In the "I am sorry," there is surely embedded the statement, "Don't be angry at me, even though I have hurt you."

To return to empathy in broad theoretical terms, in reference to ego development this capacity is based upon a very firmly established differentiation of self and object, side by side with a temporary merging, a form of regression. In this particular form—"I am sorry"— the experience can be likened, I think, to the affect of remorse, which arises from the positive libidinal aspect of ambivalence.

I regard this affective expression as a forerunner of the benign superego. I have observed its first appearance during the second year of life—that is, around 14 to 18 months. Interestingly, it is often taken up spontaneously by mothers in a kind of play that becomes established with their children. (During this same period, a toddler will injure another toddler, who will cry out in pain, without the least show of regret or remorse on the part of the attacker. Many toddlers will also attempt to hurt the mother when they have been themselves frustrated, yet will be very surprised if the mother registers a painful feeling. Sometimes, however, the toddler will look abashed and regretful.) The game that evolves often takes shape when the toddler forcefully refuses to do something the mother has requested. She then exaggeratedly imitates the child's own distress behaviour in a loud, crying-like tone. The usual response is for the toddler, who is at first shocked, to console his mother, often saying, "I'm sorry," and more often than not, also subsequently acceding to the mother's request. What is involved here is an obvious identification with the mother, not as the aggressor, but as the consoler; it is this identification I believe, that supplies one of the sources for the libidinal energies that are available to the later superego. Parenthetically, a half-year later such behaviour on the mother's part will not be such a surprise to the child; it rather becomes a kind of love-game, the important part being that the mother "caricatures" distress—pretends distress—which allows the child to go over and pat her with a broad smile, whereupon they embrace.

Another illustrative incident, having to do with a perhaps somewhat precocious 18-month old, occurred when the mother was staring out of the window, feeling extremely sad (not withdrawn) about the fact that her husband had left for the Army. Of course, there had been much talk about this, and the leave-taking itself may have been in the child's memory. In the midst of the silence, she went over to the mother and said, "I'm sorry," indicating that she knew the mother was sad, and making the same kind of stroking, consoling gestures to the mother that the mother had, at other times, made to her. It was particularly interesting that this should have happened at this time, because the earlier evidence of precocity had to do with this 1½-year-old girl's very acute response to having observed a boy's penis during the preceding month and her having expressed with acute distress the absence of one in herself; she had at that time received much consolation from the mother.

The following is an example of more complex ego-superego functioning in a somewhat older child, aged 5, who is very sensitive to the feelings of others. When he fights with his younger brother, he does not generally feel remorseful. On occasion, however, when his mother, because she thinks the younger brother has been the one at fault, scolds him, the older boy becomes very angry at her and very tender toward the younger brother, again with the statement, "I'm sorry." The reaction is, on the one hand, the result of his guilt feeling, and a displacement and acting-out of his wish to be consoled by the mother, which he re-enacts toward the younger brother. However, it also seems that it was through the intensification of his empathy—finding his own experience in that of the little brother—that his own guilt feelings were accentuated, which led to his acting-out of the wish for forgiveness.

This child's unusually sensitive empathic response has to be fended off for him to be able to express cruelty. There are common instances of the latter in analytic work—for example, a male patient who laid sieges of cutting criticism of his wife's posture. There were many reasons why he was not conscious of his cruelty; one of them was that to feel along with her, to be sympathetic, would have meant identifying with her castrated image. As he said, "But *she* really does have bad posture."

The final example comes from the case of a 4½-year-old psychotic boy. When he began treatment, about a year and a half before, he was almost completely withdrawn from human contact; he was often in a state of extreme distress, entirely inconsolable by any effort on the part of the mother. Without exception, adults had the curious experience of not being able to feel the quality of his forceful "affective" expression. During the following year, there were many developments that indicated an increasing awareness both of himself and of a separate and cherished object. His particular inanimate substitute for the maternal object was piles of things, such as piles of plastic numbers; the first obvious affect of sadness that we observed appeared when he was not able to find all his cherished numbers. The point of our ability to recognize his *sadness* was that, during this period, his affective expressions had changed, particularly in regard to the fact that they could now be empathized with by the adults; instead of their producing confusion and frustration in the mother, she was able to feel that he was pathetic and to offer consolation—which he at the same time was prepared to receive.

In this particular instance, the sadness at not finding the numbers built up into an angry rage, directed outwards at first toward some other types of number objects, which he started to destroy, and then suddenly at the therapist, whom he bit. She, caught unawares, drew back in fright. He turned away from her without any apparent affective expression, played in an isolated way with water for twenty minutes, and then, when he was soaked, was easily taken to the bathroom, which had previously been for him a place of great fear. When the therapist started to change his clothes, he suddenly looked at her quite sadly and said, "Sorry I," after which they played together; when the mother came in, he repeated, "Sorry I" to her.

A similar situation occurred sometime later, when the child was pushed somewhat beyond his capacity to communicate, that is, to show a separate functioning: when asked to make it clear, instead of disguising his newly acquired language, he again suddenly bit the therapist, who drew back in alarm and obvious pain. The boy looked like the young child in the game, very shocked; he suddenly stopped what he was doing, withdrew from the therapist, and played alone. He then soiled himself and was taken to the bathroom; and during the process of being changed he said, "Sorry I."

This expression heralded a change in the danger situation in this psychotic boy. The previous predominating fear of the loss of his body parts, reflecting his aggressive investment in the body image—a fear that he had been struggling with, in reference to toileting—had also been understood as having to do with fear of the loss of the object, not differentiated from his own body. Now there appeared manifestations of higher development: fear of the loss of the love of the object, that is, a conflict of ambivalence that produces remorse. I think that Klein may be correct in asserting that the earlier fear of the loss of the object may in fact produce attempts at restitution (especially in bodily symptoms, such as withholding faeces); but it is the ego's increasing capacity to sustain memory, to maintain the love of the object in the face of frustration, and to empathize, that results in the affects of remorse and later in guilt. The typical reaction to such an incident in an earlier phase of the treatment would have been a panic tantrum, involving an incredible amount of spasm of musculature, including the sphincters.

In reference to empathy itself—especially with regard to the child who noticed her mother's sadness at the window—I believe that what set off her response was the experience of separation from the mother because of the mother's interest elsewhere (the memory of her husband and her own feelings). The awareness of the anxiety of separation initiated a wish for incorporation, that is, of reunion with the loved object, which the child might have shown by many more primitive means, such as becoming sad herself, and no more. However, a change of function occurred, in that there was only a partial and temporary identification or partial refusion with the object, a sharing of the feeling; at the same time an appreciation of the object as a separate, feeling, being remained, which brought forth the child's attempt to console the mother—on the model, of course, of the mother's consolation of her. In terms of the drive economics concerned, every feeling of separation produces not only a longing for reunion, but an aggressive component; for the processes that are here described to take place, the capacity for a certain neutralization of this aggression, as well as a form of reaction formation, must have been established.

I think that this forerunner of the superego is better described as "identification with the comforter" (rather than with the mother as consoler, which may occur even earlier in life), because of the implication of the giving of strength. To console has rather the quality of simply feeling pain along with the sufferer, and thereby relieving it. The times in a child's life when this comforting portion of the mothering function is most poignantly experienced occur when the child is in severe pain or distress, often with an element of anxiety that he may be overcome. The mother, in empathizing with the child, that is, feeling the child's pain, is nevertheless not overcome by it, but rather able to comfort, to give strength to her child. She also consoles the child feeling along with him, and expresses her sympathy. I think that, in these instances, the child recognizes—not necessarily altogether consciously—not only the parent's comfort and consolation, but the sharing by the parent of the child's pain. Along with this goes an awareness of the parent's strength, as contrasted with his own, and the feeling that her strength can be imparted to him. This kind of experience is in contrast to the much more primitive form of affective communication that has been called "contagion," in which a strong affect in one individual simply stimulates the same affect in the other. In the experience just referred to, although the mother may be drawn into the child's experience, she shows her true concern for the child by offering comfort. As one"child put it, after a bout of severe pain, "Now I know you really love me" (one takes into account, of course, the nonappearance of the expected punishment for the child's vengeful feelings at not having been protected, and other such vicissitudes of aggression).

In terms of the drives and defenses, it appears to me that this identification with the consoler and the comforter, as with other forms of identification with the active mother, increases the child's capacity to bind its aggression and thus helps bring about the required reaction formations.

In reference to guilt and the superego, the point should be made that the behaviour described is a part of a relationship between the child and its parents, and probably not a part that, at the time, involves intersystemic conflicts. In the examples given, it is possible—though doubtful, in my opinion—that there is the feeling in the child of "I will never do that again." Even where there is such a feeling, I am sure it is quickly given up; if a structure or fixed pattern of response is present, it is certainly not independent of an object relationship. An important point in considering previous development in reference to the concern for the object, as noted, is that not only is there greater integrative capacity which results in a conflict between love and hate, but there has also been a diminution of the wholly narcissistic state of the need-satisfying object (toward object constancy).

In reference to the ego-ideal-superego, this *identification with the comforter* not only takes place on the basis of the value of power (Jacobson), but it is rather object-directed, motivated by the pre-existing factor of concern. I believe that in the "I am sorry" there are also elements that later become part of the moral portion of the total superego structure. Later disappointments in the parents' omnipotence may also play a part, and one sees revivals of the omnipotent comforter that may enter into pathological ego-ideal formation. I think it enters universally into the ego-ideal content of "the parent."

References

Jacobson, E. (1954). "The self and the object world." *Psychoanal. Study Child* 9:75–127.

Klein, M. (1933). "The early development of the conscience of the child." In: *Contributions to Psychoanalysis 1921-1945*. London: Hogarth, 1948.

Spitz, R. (1958). "On the genesis of superego components." *Psychoanal. Study Child* 13:375–404.

CHAPTER 18

The Development of a Preschool Symbiotic Psychotic Boy

(1964). *Psychoanalytic Study of the Child* 19:448–469

Supported by National Institute of Mental Health Research Grant M-3353 "Investigation of Symbiotic Child Psychosis," Principal Investigator, Margaret S. Mahler, M.D.; carried out at the Masters Children's Center, New York City.
Medical Director, Masters Children's Center

The purpose of this case report is to describe some of the processes by which a preschool-aged psychotic child reinvested the object world and the world of reality, and some of the consequences in his personality development.

REVIEW OF LITERATURE

The following brief review is concerned with theoretical conclusions about normal development in the earliest period of life which seemed to be helpful in understanding the case material. Margaret S. Mahler's clinical and theoretical contributions to the understanding of child psychosis are implicit throughout.

In Freud's original formulation, the ego evolves out of the id under the impact of reality. Instead of this formulation, Hartmann, Kris, and Loewenstein (1946) introduced the concept of an undifferentiated phase out of which both id and ego are gradually formed. According to them, this structural differentiation depends on the ability of the infant to distinguish between his self and the world around him. They point out that partial deprivation is probably an essential condition for this piece of development; on the other hand, this distinction does not seem to be possible unless a certain amount of gratification takes place. The theory states that an object in the external world is experienced in the beginning as part of the self; in economic terms, that the object partakes of the narcissistic cathexis of the infant. When the distinction has been made, the object, now experienced as independent of the self, has retained this cathexis, even though separated.

Jacobson, in her paper "The Self and the Object World" (1954), attempted to clarify some of these issues. In dealing with the distribution of psychic energy, she conceives of the state of primary narcissism and primary masochism as one in which there is both a continuous low-level discharge of energy toward the inside of the body through physiological channels and, at the same time, a discharge to the outside through feeding and excretory functions. She considers the latter as the precursor of object-related discharge. In psychosis, she points out, the semi stuporous states represent a regression to this inner discharge, except that in the psychotic there is a generally pervasive destructive quality which contrasts with the libidinal quality of normal sleep. She suggests that psychic energy is still in an undifferentiated state at the beginning of life and that it develops into two kinds of drives, partially under the influence of external stimulation (their potential form is predetermined.)

To solve the problem of secondary investment of the ego with psychic energy, Jacobson proposes, as had Hartmann (1950), the concept of a self representation as opposed to an object representation. Both result from memory traces of the infant's experiences, as distinct from the system ego, which is made up of certain functions. The self-image is, of course, first fused and confused with the object images, and consists of fluctuating memory traces of inner sensations and experiences.

Finally, Jacobson points out, the repeated unpleasurable experiences of frustration, deprivation, and separation from love object not only aid in the differentiation of the self, but also induce fantasies of incorporation of the gratifying object, thus expressing wishes to re-establish the original unity of self with pleasurable ministrations of the mother. These are the foundations upon which all future types of identification are built.

The infant progresses from wishes for total incorporation to fantasies of only partial oral, anal, visual, and respiratory incorporation of the love object. True ego identification, although ultimately derived from the early infantile wish to achieve oneness with the love object, partakes of a change of function, which she calls partial introjection. In this process, the self-image is modified through the assumption of certain characteristics of the object, becoming like that object, and no longer striving for union with the object *in toto*. In the transitional stage there are constant shifts of libidinal and aggressive energy from object to self and back again, reflected in introjective and projective mechanisms based on fantasies of oral incorporation and anal ejection of the love object.

Margaret S. Mahler has written extensively about the earliest formations of entity and identity (1958). She states that in early infancy the young organism is beset by potentially traumatic stimuli, both from without and from within. Protection against the stimuli from without is provided by the relative lack of cathexis of the perceptual conscious system, which sets up the stimulus barrier. Inner stimuli have no such barrier. Both outer and inner stimuli must be organized for the infant by the symbiotic partner's nursing care, in order to prevent organismic distress that might jeopardize the development within the ego of the distinction between the self and the object world. Primitive undifferentiated drive energy, she states, is vested mainly in the visceral abdominal organs. The buffering, protective action of the nursing mother is necessary for this energy to progress toward a gradual libidinal cathexis of the periphery of the self, as well as for the centrifugal direction of the primitive aggressive discharges away from the early body or self-image. In psychosis, one finds a defusion of drives and a preponderance of aggressive cathexis of the primitive self.

Winnicott, in his paper on transitional objects and transitional phenomena (1953), describes what he calls the intermediate area of experience, that is, the experience having to do with the infant's first awareness of an external world. In terms of behavior, it is the experience that occurs between the thumb- or fist-in-mouth activities (which constitute a psychically complete part of the reflex functioning of the body at birth) and the attachment to a teddy bear which is clearly a representative of the outside world. For example, the infant's babbling, especially the tuneful babbling before going to sleep, is part of this transitional experience. Winnicott claims that this area of existence is never challenged for the infant, because it represents a resting place for "the individual engaged in the perpetual human task of keeping inner and outer reality separate yet inter-related." In describing the self-comforting of the infant, he points out that thumb sucking is accompanied by other activities—the rubbing of an object with the other hand, the production of certain noises—and postulates that thinking and fantasy gradually become linked with these experiences. He states, in addition, that the transitional object (the first not-me object) may also stand for the infant's feces and that transitional objects may later develop into fetish objects, which occurred in the case to follow.

CASE STUDY

Evaluation

Malcolm was first seen at our Center when he was three years five months of age. His family had sought help because of the child's isolation from people, his extreme stubbornness, the retardation in his speech, his head banging, the breakdown of his toilet training, and his general inaccessibility.

The mother said that during the first half of his first year, he had been a friendly, happy, smiling baby, and she recalled playing peek-a-boo with him when he was about eight months old. When he was seven weeks old, a hernia was discovered in the left inguinal region. The physician decided to postpone surgery until Malcolm was half a year old. His mother was taught to reduce the hernia, but there were at least three occasions on which she was unable to do so and the baby screamed with pain until the mother could get him to the doctor, who then reduced it. He was operated on when he was five and a half months old. The mother stayed with him the first day, but was allowed to visit him only once in the subsequent five days he stayed at the hospital.

We have little information about his experience in the hospital; he did not appear overwhelmed, but was rather indiscriminately friendly to adults. The mother feels sure that at five months Malcolm recognized her and distinguished her face from others', and at that time was not particularly interested in his father.

In the second half of his first year, Malcolm became increasingly sluggish, to such an extent that at about eight months his pediatrician gave him thyroid. He sat quietly in his crib, engrossed for a long time in some tiny object he had happened to pick up; he would not reach for toys put in his crib.

During the second and especially the third year of Malcolm's life, his mother had difficulty in handling him, carrying him, and dressing him because she had severe low back pain. Consequently his father, who had a store in the building in which they lived, took over much of the physical care of the child. Gradually Malcolm developed an intense, demanding, clinging relationship to his father; he went into wild tantrums and banged his head whenever his father left him.

Malcolm had never seemed to want to walk (though he began at fourteen months) and had insisted on being wheeled in his carriage, even for short distances, until three years of age. His extreme stubbornness may have started as early as the second year of life; it was well established by the third year. When his mother asked him to go outdoors, he would accompany her; but as soon as he reached the outside, he would stop and refuse to move, and remained this way for periods of over an hour. When his mother forced him, he would have a tantrum and bang his head. This happened also in response to a changing street light; when the light changed, preventing him from continuing, he would stand still for many changes, refusing to move on.

The head banging had started when he was about two years of age, probably when the stubbornness became apparent, and was in general a response to frustration; it always occurred when his mother was

200

angry with him. In the third year of life, after his mother had started to worry about him, Malcolm apparently protected himself by putting his hand between his head and the cement sidewalk when he banged his head in the street.

Malcolm had been toilet trained, after several attempts, at two years ten months. In the summer prior to coming to us, there was a regression in his toilet habits, to which his mother responded angrily. When she reprimanded him for soiling, he banged his head on a windowpane, breaking it. It was this event that had brought her to seek treatment. By the time Malcolm came to us, he seemed indifferent to his bowel functioning, and was withholding and soiling without apparent awareness.

His mother did not recall any speech in this child until he was eighteen months of age, when he began to use single words to name objects. There seemed to be no progress in his speaking until the summer prior to admission, when his mother, now anxious, tried to teach him and he began to repeat and echo speech that he heard from her or his older brothers. It was with this type of echolalic speech that he appeared.

When Malcolm was first seen at the Center at the age of three years five months, he was withdrawn, lethargic, with an empty, lusterless expression. Most of the time he seemed preoccupied with his sensations—placing his eye almost against the edge of the arm of a chair, pulling at his eyelids, his head cocked to listen to the radiator, or rolling any object available back and forth with his hand. If directly approached, he became sullen and irritable and avoided one's glance. If he wanted something, however, he directed one's arm toward it, as if it were an extension of himself. He named object in a desultory manner and repeated what was said to him in an exact imitation, including the inflection. The first time he seemed to make overt contact, he climbed onto the window sill, threw a ball down and then fell down himself, perhaps with the expectation that the therapist would catch him, as she did. The therapist was a woman. His immediate reaction to the presence of the male supervising analyst in the therapy room was to form a bridge with his body, his back and head in the analyst's lap and his legs on his mother's lap, while he rubbed the analyst's tie and sucked his thumb.

Discussion

In the initial evaluation of preschool-age psychotic children, for the purpose of prognosis and of determining the therapeutic methods to be applied—or, rather, of determining where, along the line of object relationship, the therapist may start—many factors have to be taken into account. To begin at the pessimistic end of the spectrum of psychotic phenomenology, there are children among the group that are seen at the Center who almost completely avoid the outside world, primarily the human, animate outside world. Attempts to impinge upon the isolation of these children generally result in severe panic tantrums.

Even these children, however, will show some relationship to an inanimate object. We have come to call this object colloquially the "psychotic fetish." Whatever interest these children may have in anything outside their bodies seems to be directed toward such objects as a baby bottle, a jar, a piece of cloth, or the edges of furniture, boxes, etc., as in Malcolm's case. They may voice no words at all, or, if they do, it is in imitation and with no apparent communication intended. They show a great deal of random movement, which we have learned to recognize as a reaction to physical discomfort or slight, deep pain, and which seems to be a motor discharge in response to the internal stimulus, with little organization. In hospitals, I have seen more deeply regressed children whose entire waking day is spent in continuous auto aggressive or kinesthetic stimulating activity, such as whirling about or head banging, with no relationship to external objects at all, not even inanimate ones.

Malcolm belonged in the group of children who form a fleeting contact with animate objects; this contact is revealed in an altered expression when the eyes of such a child meet those of the observer. Usually there is also speech, in the form of echolalia, though among more disturbed children this echolalic repetition is usually speech heard from nonanimate sources, such as television or records. Among the less severely disturbed children who have a better prognosis, there seems to be some interposition of thought or fantasy between, for example, bodily distress and its external manifestations. In Malcolm's case, the hallmark of distress was a kind of back-and-forth movement of the hand; later he held a toy (a train car) at such times. In our observation this movement seemed to represent an awareness of the downward movement of feces. Later we learned that he feared the expulsion of feces and also had connected the word "broken" with it.

The conceptualization of these phenomena in terms of ego development and psychic structure can only be speculative. What we observe at the outset can be explained by a combination of a disordered development, a very deep regression or lack of development, and a very primitive defense organization.

Some of the phenomena suggest primitive levels of ego-id functioning; for example, what appears to be the immediate motor discharge in the entire body of any slight internal discomfort, or what would appear to be a somewhat more organized attempt to combat this discomfort by the production of other sensations as seen in the

203

whirling and head banging. It is difficult to find any thought content for this activity, although subsequently, when the child's ego development in general appears to be more advanced, these movements and activity become organized in symptoms such as tics or play activity, the psychic content of which we are able to understand. Another striking feature in this regard is that the mother, as well as other observers, find it very difficult to anticipate what the child will do when he approaches her—whether he will bite or kick, or press his lips against her (without any of the puckering or sucking involved in a kiss), which seems at least more affectionate. The observer's inability to understand the child's intentions may possibly be caused by the child's having regressed to a stage at which the drives lack differentiation. Moreover, at such times, one seems to be unable to empathize with the distress which the child appears to be in, whereas in a later period of treatment the mother and therapist both have the feeling that the child is pathetic and in need of them when he cries, and become quite sure of his intentions on approaching them. These changes, which appear to be in the children rather than in the observer, are among the most heartening events for the mothers.

The psychotic child suffers from extreme panic and anxiety, and at first cannot be comforted. The source for this anxiety is not always clear, though the frequency of self-stimulating and body-defining activities such as rubbing the body with sand, or head banging (see Greenacre, 1954), as well as the wild aggressive outbursts, have led many to speculate that such behavior has to do with the fear of loss of body boundaries and with the lack of capacity for binding aggression.

The most prominent defensive maneuvers are the withdrawal from reality, especially from the animate or human external world, or deanimation as Mahler (1958) has called it. Any awareness or involvement with a human object that is separate from the self seems to be beyond the capacity of the most severely disturbed children, and can be sustained for only short intervals by children like Malcolm. When a more sustained involvement with an external human object occurs, it appears to be in the form of a primitive identification in the sense of an omnipotent mother-child dual unity.

There are many indicators of what appears to be an incomplete separation of self from object: the echolalia; the use of the other person, especially parts of that person's body as extensions of himself; the expectation of the omniscience and omnipotence from the other person in response to the most minimal cues; and, as will be described, the imitation of inanimate objects. At the outset, one cannot find meaning, in the sense of communication, in the repetitive phrases or actions. However, the echolalic speech later begins to be used in an appropriate context; for example, "goodbye, Chet, and goodbye, Dave," imitating a portion of a TV newscast, is used at the time of leaving. Later on in the treatment, such phrases are integrated into more complex communications of feelings and thoughts.

Although the investment of actual human objects is in the most severe cases almost completely withdrawn, cathexis of the mental representations of these objects, merged with self representations, seems to be maintained in the children with better prognosis. I believe this is shown by the investment, often the intense investment, in the inanimate object, "the psychotic fetish." In our experience, the children who come to the Center with such a focused activity have a better prognosis. Other, more regressed children must first develop some awareness of the therapist and mother before such an organization and focusing of behavior occurs; when it does, it shows itself most often in an involvement with inanimate objects. In the course of treatment the child will make both destructive and loving gestures toward such a "fetish"; and, even more important, there will often be long periods in which the child plays the game of throwing the object away, with the expectation that the therapist will return it. Such activities are indicative of the growing differentiation between self and object and the attempt to master the fear of loss. Still later, when the investment returns to the mother and separation anxiety appears, this object can substitute for her, as one sees in normal development.

Malcolm arrived with a preoccupation with edges, that is, the edges of any object, whether a piece of furniture or a piece of wood or part of a toy; he had to be able to touch the edge with his finger, or with his body as a whole if it was large enough, as he did over the large apex of the roof of a doll house, and almost touched it with his eyes, as it were. From evidence in his later behavior, I am inclined to think that he was attempting to fuse his body or self-image with a form of object image; this fusion was probably represented physically by an act of incorporation through touch and vision, modalities which may not have been clearly differentiated in his mind.

This preoccupation with the inanimate object and, as it seems to me, with his own bodily sensations that accompany what he does with this object has a close relationship to the "intermediate area of experience," which Winnicott has labeled transitional; that is, though the object concerned is a "not-me object," it remains for the child a fused representation of experiences of his own body and of the external world. Most important, it seems to me, is the fact that this preoccupation with "the psychotic fetish" contains within it some residue of gratifying mothering experiences and thus allows for the possibility of reviving them or bringing them closer to consciousness. These cathected inanimate objects seem to me to represent the remnants of a tie to the maternal object; they are evidence that a mental representation of the maternal object has been cathected, that this cathexis has a predominantly libidinal quality, and that it has been preserved.

Malcolm's preoccupation with edges seemed to contain memories of the gratifying experiences of being carried by the mothering person, who in this case was his father. Later in his treatment, when his attachment shifted to his mother, he developed an insatiable demand to ride the subways with her. Also, as will be seen in what follows, during treatment there was a transition from these preoccupations with edges and riding trains, in which it appeared that self and object were not differentiated, to make-believe play with toy trains, when it appeared that this differentiation had been accomplished.

Early Phases of Treatment

The therapeutic procedures adopted in Malcolm's case cannot be described here in detail. Each child treated at Masters Children's Center is seen, together with the child's mother, for two to two and a half hours, three to four times a week. The child's therapist makes herself part of his experiences and of those dimly perceived, not-me forces which bring comfort to the child; for example, she joins him in his rocking or rocks him herself when it seems appropriate. The therapist thus becomes part of the symbiotic dual unit as a comforting agent. She is there when the child omnipotently expects her to be; for example, when he jumps or falls into her arms.

In another sense, she can be called his auxiliary ego; she performs certain ego functions that his own ego is not able to do. For example, she protects him in innumerable little ways from being hurt. The communication between them is essentially a signal communication; i.e., it takes place within the symbiotic dual unit. The child signals and the therapist is part of the result of that signal, not really a separate being. Whatever may be said by the therapist in helping the child understand his actions cannot at first have the same function as in work with a neurotic; to the psychotic child, it is a signal from another part of the dual unit. His initial capacity to withstand inner distress without being overwhelmed seems to come from the strength supplied by the therapist as part of the dual unity. She performs the reality testing of which the child is incapable and thus corrects his reality sense. The first interpretations supply a primitive education, simply giving the child words for his actions or moods.

The disintegration of Malcolm's functioning was extreme, especially in terms of his lack of awareness of his sensations and his emotional needs, and the connection between them. It is probably this disorganization that made empathy with him so difficult during the early part of his treatment.

Later, the organization of his experience by the therapist's intervention, especially by the therapist's supplying of words to which past and present similar experience could be connected, is also an important part of treatment. Later phases of therapy involve many aspects of mastery of anxiety through play as well as through the therapist communicating her understanding of the meaning of the child's behavior. The special importance and place of the mother in this treatment has been reported in a preliminary observation (Mahler and Furer, 1960), and will not be considered in this report.

The next steps had to do with the participation of the therapist and the mother in the focused "transitional world" in which the child had now begun to live and out of which his individuation would take place. In the period prior to that described in the next section, he spent a great deal of time fascinated with the edges of furniture, running his fingertips over them, putting his eyes almost in touch with them, and pulling at his eyelids, the latter seeming to distort his visual image of these edges which he later came to call train tracks.

The Discovery of "Self"

Malcolm's conscious discovery of the "I" as separate from the external world took place after one and a half years of treatment. This was a culmination of various trends in his therapy. At the time there were a number of interweaving developments: (1) a shift of the symbiotic relationship from father to therapist and mother, in which he had to be physically carried by the therapist and taken for endless rides on the subway by the mother; (2) at first there had been a total bodily imitation of inanimate objects; this was replaced by a shift of interest from the body to the toy; (3) an awareness of bowel functioning and a struggle over bowel retention.

The therapeutic team gradually became aware of the fact that much of Malcolm's behavior seemed to consist of a total body imitation of various inanimate objects. At this time the "symbiotic-like relationship" to the therapist (more as a whole being rather than as voice or arms) had been established; he rarely responded with complete withdrawal, and frequently behaved as though the therapist were a part of his actions. His body represented a train which he moved across the floor, setting up bridges for it to cross and tunnels for it to go through. He stopped, we learned from his mother, in response to various imagined lights. A peculiar waving movement of his body as he stood still turned out to be an imitation of the flag in the playground. A bizarre movement of his head as he ran represented the police cars that have a rotating red light on the roof. It should be made clear that this behavior was not a playful imitation, as seen in very young children;

this bodily activity occupied him continuously most of the day, and was often accompanied by a return to the lusterless expression seen on his first arrival. All of this greatly alarmed the mother because she felt, as she said, that at those times he had again withdrawn from her. He did not play with toys, that is, with toys as representations. Instead, there was a kind of externalization of body sensation via imitation; for example, he rolled the toy train car back and forth with increasing rapidity when he was in apparent distress, as his body tried to move his feces out and he tensed to retain them. At that time we could not yet make him consciously aware of his bowel sensations or of his conflict (as we later understood his behavior).

In the course of the treatment Malcolm seemed to develop a growing awareness of therapist and mother as separate whole persons who could supply his needs—and not simply as extensions of himself which he steered toward these supplies. In conjunction with this new awareness of separateness, Malcolm showed varying degrees of anxiety which he attempted to combat by having the therapist copy his activities or, even more reassuring to him, carry them out as though they had done them together. For example, another child who began to write, first numbers and then his name and his mother's at the age of five, would do it only if the therapist's hand were on top of his as he made the lines. Such observations are regularly made in the treatment of these children. The growing awareness of separateness is regularly accompanied by manifestations of anxiety, and the defenses against that anxiety include the attempt to regain a state of fusion with the object—an indication, at the same time, that the object is now perceived as separate from the self.

As Malcolm emerged from his shell a striking change was manifested in his intense, almost insatiable desire to ride the subways with his mother. When his father was home over week ends, Malcolm would leave his father only if he could take a subway ride with his mother. She felt both so guilty toward her son and so grateful for his loving interest that she spent many hours traveling the subway system with him. The other area of their closest interchange during this period was in the bathroom, where Malcolm agreed to defecate if his mother drew him pictures of trains or, later, told him about the rides they had already taken.

During the same period, if random motor activity did not appear during distressing bowel pressure, the child sometimes developed the same blank facial expression that had been an indication of his earlier autistic withdrawal. As treatment progressed, this expression occurred only when he had been frustrated and probably enraged.

Severe anxiety began to appear when he could no longer withhold and feces appeared in his pants. It should be mentioned that although the mother had been angry with him several times after he had begun to soil about a year before we saw him, the attempts to train him had not been accompanied by severe demands or threats. In the treatment, soon after the appearance of this anxiety a period began when he seemed preoccupied with his feces and the functioning of the toilet. He endlessly played a game with the therapist through the swinging Dutch door at the entrance to the bathroom. The therapist had to put her fingers under the door, he swung at her fingers, then she took her hand out and showed it to him; he would be delighted and the process would be repeated. On other occasions, he would emerge from under the door and return, and he made her do the same. Finally, he put his own hand into the toilet bowl, repeatedly flushing the toilet and taking his hand out to look at it. At one point he defecated on the ground and insisted by gesture upon his mother's touching the feces, after which he touched them. Direct libidinal and aggressive behavior toward mother and therapist had previously appeared in the form of spitting.

After a period of this repetitive game, a differentiation of the self image seemed to develop rapidly, and was accompanied by the appearance of more fully personal communicative speech and the use of toys as symbols. Instead of moving his body as a train, Malcolm began to push a chair around the room, refusing to allow his hat to be removed (we later learned that his hat indicated that he was the engineer); and soon thereafter he admitted the therapist into the game as a passenger.

The next step seemed to center around his imitation of the playground flag. His mother was always upset by his bodily imitation of objects, because she could then feel how withdrawn he was. She made toy flags out of paper and sticks and offered them to him again and again. Then, during a therapy session, he discovered a small cloth flag in the treatment building. He had acquired communicative speech, but from echolalic sources as described; that is, he used phrases imitatively but in an appropriate context; he now asked for what he wanted; on the other hand, he continued to mix his pronouns, using "you" for "I" and often using his name instead of "I." When he found the therapist's flag, he said "*I* have a flag." Later he said, "This is a real flag," and then, "This is mine." With great astonishment shortly thereafter, he discovered that the toy trains were not real trains such as he had seen near the treatment building; and finally he began to play with the toy train, that is, he used it as a representative symbol for the actual train he saw outside. He then became afraid that the cars of the train would be separated from one another and insisted that they be securely fastened together—a return, we thought, to his concern about the loss of body parts and his feces, now displaced into a true toy.

These expressions of self-awareness—although followed by a temporary state of anxiety and regression to a clinging, demanding attitude, wanting to be constantly in touch with mother and therapist—

212

represented a momentous step in his development and heralded a change which has remained intact to the present day, about four years later. He never again showed his particular kind of withdrawal and "autism" in relation to human objects, nor did he return to a state, previously so prominent, in which he apparently had lost his self in the environment. Also, from then on we were consistently able to empathize with him because of the change in his facial expression and the quality of his communications; finding it so difficult to feel along with her child or to console and comfort him had previously caused this mother great distress.

Discussion

When this child emerged from his autistic withdrawal, he lived in what I would like to call a "transitional world" and in a static state. By this I mean that in his waking life he behaved more or less continuously in a manner one might consider to be similar to that phase of early development where, though external objects are recognized, the psychic images of self and object are not adequately separated. His situation was also static as compared to normal development where this is, as Winnicott calls it, a transitional stage. In our experience, many psychotic children, either spontaneously or in treatment, seem to progress and regress back and forth from this state to that of autistic withdrawal, but rarely proceed further in development.

During this period his body did not seem to be fully separated from his inanimate environment. Either he imitated the inanimate object or, later on, was often found in a state of rapt fascination as he beheld it (trains and tracks as derived from edges). In this state of fascination, which recurred later during his period of fetishistic

213

behavior, it also seems likely that there are fluid boundaries between the mental images of the self and of the object observed (Bernfeld, 1928). One may speculate that this state provides the psychotic child with the "resting place" Winnicott describes for the infant.

In the case described here, the therapeutic efforts of mother and therapist seemed to set a progressive development in motion. This began with Malcolm's acceptance of the human object—what might be called a gratifying transitional object, and what may be a universally important form of a not-me object that carries and moves the child. The experiences Malcolm demanded were probably connected with memory traces of previous libidinally invested experiences which, as noted, had occurred after his first year, particularly with his father. The mental images are assumed to derive from the early gratifying interchanges taking place in a mothering person-child unity. In these interchanges the psychotic child is in an almost totally passive state, and often molds his body to fit that of the carrier. At a later time the child's behavior alternates between this passive molding and an active pushing away, which indicates the conflict over the beginning awareness of separateness. During the time of self-object unity I have hypothesized that the child experiences the therapist not as a whole person but only in terms of isolated qualities, such as the voice, or a feeling tone, or the supportive body.

In Malcolm's case, the anal sphere seemed to play a highly important role in the process of differentiation of self and object. The feces (also spit and urine) are parts of the body that make a complete transition to the external world, concrete representations of the experience that what may be inside can become outside. Moreover, the feces are a source of inner bodily sensations which, as noted previously, cause such distress in these children. In the course of their further development, connections are set up between these internal sensations, their concrete representations, i.e., the feces, and the self-and object-directed feelings once such representations of self and object are organized.

The struggle with the experience of bowel functioning seemed to reflect the process of self-differentiation. The role of the aggressive drive in this differentiation can be seen, I believe, in the withholding of feces and in the fear of losing the feces from the body. For these children, loss of a body part seems to be equivalent to destruction.

In our contacts with psychotic children we repeatedly observed that, as the child begins to emerge from his autistic shell and to make aggressive and libidinal investments in both therapist and mother, he regularly withholds feces. Once again one can see that in the child's mind feces have the characteristics of a transitional object; i.e., it is the focus of the libidinal and aggressive cathexis of poorly differentiated images of self and object and at the same time indicates the beginning formation of this differentiation. This image, and the feces representing it in reality, acquires importance to the child because of its increasing libidinal cathexis; the retention of this bodily product may then be explained as an attempt to prevent its loss by destruction; i.e., to protect it from a predominating and overwhelming aggressive cathexis which would cause the loss of the beginning representation of both self and object (to some degree separate from each other). We seem to be dealing here both with the fear of the loss of the object, that is, of the beginning cathexis of the object representation, described by many authors in relation to schizophrenia, and with the fear of extinction or dissolution which has been connected by others to the fear of loss of the self-representation. The narcissistic investment of the feces in psychosis was noted by Stärke (1919) and von Uphuijsen (1920). There may be a regular relationship in early normal development between awareness of bowel functioning, a clearer differentiation and increase in intensity of the aggressive drives, and the differentiation of self from object.

This material does not provide any explanation of the causation of the psychosis. The role of the early painful bodily experiences in what may be a constitutional predisposition is suggestive. The mother, we felt, could be included in the category of "ordinarily devoted mothers" and did not have a narcissistic or depressive illness.

In the process of recovery we see again the intimate and mutually dependent relationship between ego functioning and object relationship. As has been noted in previous studies on prognosis (Eisenberg and Kanner, 1956), the functioning of communicative speech is crucial for a development in the direction of recovery. In Malcolm's case we see that the appearance of communicative speech was part of the last steps in differentiation of self and object. This differentiation may also be facilitated by the neutralization or binding of the aggression so that separation-individuation was not equivalent to the destruction of both self and object. Words and meanings derived from and made possible by the developing object relationship now could be put in the service of reality testing. As Freud (1911) stated in discussing the reality principle, with the conversion of freely displaceable cathexes into "bound cathexes," a person's thinking becomes endowed with "further qualities, perceptible to consciousness [through connection] with verbal residues" (p. 221), which result in a vast expansion of his appreciation of both outer and inner reality.

Further Development

The foregoing covers the first year and a half of treatment. Malcolm has been at the Center for another year and a half, and will continue at least one further year. Some aspects of his later development are worth mentioning because they illustrate changes in his over-all functioning and in his self identity.

As noted, when he withheld his feces, his mother was able to obtain an evacuation first by promising another subway ride, then by drawing pictures of trains and signal lights. Later, he accepted his mother's verbal account of a previous experience on the subway. After his "self" discovery, he evacuated his feces in exchange for his mother's wiping his anus, revealing, it seemed to us, that the libidinal gratification from his mother had become predominant. In the subsequent year, except for transient regressive reactivations, the anal sphere seemed to become less invested, and he carried out the toileting on his own without any fixed ritual.

In the third year of treatment, the material centered on intense oedipal conflicts, showing manifestations of both feminine and masculine strivings, and, for a period of some months, of a fixation to exhibitionistic and fetishistic activities. He was now five and a half years old, was fully verbal, and had grown to be a tall, muscular boy. The sequence of events was roughly as follows. The manifestations of his oedipal conflict seemed to coincide with the loosening of his teeth, which he inspected with fascination in front of the mirror, and during this period of time several teeth fell out. He first became preoccupied with the problem of where babies come from. He then again retained his stool, which at that time seemed to be a masturbatory equivalent because he obviously became genitally excited by the sensation, and talked about having babies himself. He expressed fears that his body had come loose and that his head might come off. He gradually became jealous of his brothers, his father, and the analyst who interviewed his mother, and had fantasies of their death. In these, they usually dropped into a river and were washed away and drowned. Sometimes, however, he saved them by drawing them back, at the same time exhibiting his great power (as over his own feces). In contrast, his passivity was illustrated by a dream of this period: he is standing on the bank of a river and a strong wind churns up the waves which reach higher and higher, finally up to the boy, dragging him down into the river's depths. His mother comes after him and saves him. At a later date, he developed a fear of tornadoes.

This period was followed by one in which the overt sexual preoccupation disappeared and instead there came into prominence various delusions of grandeur. One, in which he could stare down the sun, alternated with the delusion of omniscience of his therapist, who should know everything, and if she did not, he was furious. He fantasied that when he had feces within him, he was bigger and a creature of great power, which was lost when he passed the feces.

At about this same time, seeing his mother on the toilet and in the shower, he said, "Mommy has a penis in her tushy," after which he made a bowel movement in his pants, a rare occurrence during that period. He then insisted that his mother take the "duty" out of his pants, put it on the floor, and then put it back into the pants. The feces here seemed to represent a penis for his mother as well as for himself.

Overt genital masturbation appeared while he was riding with his mother on the subway train, especially when the train moved into the station. A transient toilet ritual appeared in that he wanted stories about what he would be like when he was grown up and bigger. He shifted his interest from riding in trains to fans, and later, to the bathroom fans that he looked at with clear scoptophilic interest.

Finally, he arrived with a flag that he had asked for after having seen the flag outside of his brother's school. The following months were spent in preoccupation with this flag, preening it, building a flagpole for it outside the treatment building, constantly worrying about the effect of wind and rain upon it, and when he became acutely anxious, wrapping his body in it and seeming to fall asleep. At other times he took the flag and its flagpole out of the window and, holding it against the lower part of his body, marched back and forth in front of the mirror as he observed himself. Most of the time was spent in gazing in rapt fascination at the flag while he masturbated. Although he was obviously self-preoccupied at these times, none of the observers felt that the quality of his facial expression indicated the kind of withdrawal with which he had originally come to the Center.

At the end of the year a series of neurotic symptoms appeared: fear of the dark; fear of automobiles crashing, especially if his mother was driving; fear of airplanes crashing; fear of death and of being buried. He continues to show primitive functioning in his feeling of the great power of either himself or the people around him (at six years of age, when he is accidentally hurt, he still turns with rage upon his mother as though she had caused his injury, or he hits the offending piece of furniture); and he still insists that the therapist or mother knows everything, and becomes panicky and angry if they deny this. He also retains a concretistic kind of thinking, a vulnerability to narcissistic hurt, and a propensity for primitive defenses like denial. Recently, for example, when he was given a flag by a neighbor and brought it to his therapy session, he discovered that the flag he had brought was larger than the one he himself owned. He developed one of the typical panic tantrums until the therapist explained that even though an object may be smaller than another, it can still be stronger, such as the tugboat which pulls the ocean liner. For a month thereafter, he was preoccupied with strength rather than size.

Summary

In Malcolm's case, therapy was begun by bringing the child from his withdrawn state into a primitive relationship with the therapist as a need-satisfying object, chiefly through her communication to him of her empathy with his needs and their gratification. At the same time, she became a part of his omnipotent dual unity. Gradually she helped him to organize his experience and to explore reality, in this way fostering the libidinal cathexis of herself. A previously static state in his psychosis, liked to the resting place of Winnicott's transitional experience, and in the mother-child relationship which was reflected in the therapist-child relationship, was altered and progressive changes ensued. When we first saw him, he was already capable of delaying, of interposing thought and fantasy between instinctual pressure and discharge, and showed some organization of his psychic life, at least in the preoccupation with the "psychotic fetish," which in his case were the edges of inanimate objects. However, there appeared to be a profound disorganization in his instinctual and affective expressions. Gradually, however, his reactions became more differentiated and understandable to observers, when he began to show aggressive responses to frustration and libidinal responses to gratifications from the therapist and mother. There were indications that the human object had become invested, though self and object seemed not yet to be distinguished. Despite this lack of complete differentiation, a coalescence of memory traces of separate object images and a separate self image took place. In this period the child's previously chaotic behavior became better organized and we saw a flowering of life and interest in the "transitional world," which now included the human object, and the appearance of a variety of understandable symptomatic behavior.

It seemed that both the emerging self and object images were invested predominantly with aggressive energy. The child only gradually mastered the anxiety which seemed to be related to this aggressive investment, and which was eventually focused on his feces and anal functioning. His anxiety seemed to concern the loss not only of the image of a need-satisfying love object but also of the self representation. It was warded off by total incorporation which seemed to be represented by the bodily symptom of fecal retention.

Along with the progressive development in object relations, there occurred a differentiation of the self from both the inanimate and human objects, and the conscious discovery of "I" as a separate entity. There were also changes in the direction of greater organization and integration of his ego functions, an increased libidinization of his activities, and increased ego strength in such things as the control of his rage and the capacity to withstand frustration.

In the last year of Malcolm's treatment, oedipal conflicts appeared, which resulted in symptoms. These indicated that various levels of ego functioning and various levels of defensive functioning were present. On the one hand, there were periods in which there was an intensification of his feelings of omnipotence, sometimes delegated to others and sometimes to himself. On the other hand, a fetishistic interest in the flag seemed to arise from an attempt to resolve the castration fear associated with these conflicts. It is noteworthy that this fetishistic interest was centered upon an object, the flag, which had played a prominent role during the time when his behavior had been dominated by imitation of inanimate objects, and which was also involved in his experience of the discovery of "self."

Toward the end of the year, Malcolm became more sad than angry, often telling both mother and father to go away and leave him alone. He seemed to be increasingly aware of internal conflict. On close observations, some of his movements and sometimes his vocal inflections are strange; on the other hand, those who see Malcolm for the first time now are no longer impressed by his severe disturbance, which had previously been apparent even on cursory observation.

References

Abraham, K. (1924). *A Short Study of the Development of the Libido: Selected Papers on Psycho-Analysis*. London: Hogarth Press, 1927.

Bak, R. (1954). The Schizophrenic Defence against Aggression. *Int. J. Psychoanal.* 35:129–134.

Bernfeld, S. (1928). Über Faszination Imago 14:76–87.

Brodsky, B. (1959). Self-Representation, Anality, and the Fear of Dying. *J. Am. Psychoanal.* Assoc. 7:95–108

Eisenberg, L. & Kanner, L. (1956). Early Infantile Autism. *Amer. J. Orthopsychiat.* 26(3):556–566.

Freud, S. (1911). Formulations on the Two Principles of Mental Functioning. *Standard Edition* 12:213–226.

Greenacre, P. (1954). In: Problems of Infantile Neurosis: A Discussion *Psychoanal. Study Child* 9:16–71.

Hartmann, H. (1950). Comments on the Psychoanalytic Theory of the Ego, *Psychoanal. Study Child* 5:74–96.

——— Kris, E., & Loewenstein, R.M. (1946). Comments on the Formation of Psychic Structure *Psychoanal. Study Child* 2:11–38.

Jacobson, E. (1954). The Self and the Object World *Psychoanal. Study Child* 9:75–127.

Mahler, M.S. (1958). Autism and Symbiosis: Two Extreme Disturbances of Identity *Int. J. Psychoanal.* 39:77–82.

———. & Furer, M. (1960). Observations on Research Regarding the 'Symbiotic Syndrome' of Infantile Psychosis *Psychoanal. Q.* 29:317–327.

——— ——— & Settlage, C. (1959). Severe Emotional Disturbances in Childhood: Psychosis American Handbook Psychiatry New York: Basic Books.

Stärke, A. (1919). The Reversal of the Libido-Sign in Delusions of Persecution *Int. J. Psychoanal.* 1:231–234.

van Ophuijsen, J. H. (1920). On the Origin of the Feeling of Persecution *Int. J. Psychoanal.* 1:235–239.

Winnicott, D.W. (1953). Transitional Objects and Transitional Phenomena *Int. J. Psychoanal.* 34:89–97.

CHAPTER 19

Editor's Note

The Cathy Papers (Chapters 19-21)

In the following three papers, Dr. Furer uses one remarkable case history—that of a little girl named Cathy—for three different purposes:

- To describe the workings of the Masters Child Center Research programs;
- To illuminate Margaret Mahler's central concept of the Mother-Child Symbiotic Relationship;
- To demonstrate the development of an "As-If Personality" in the course of a child analysis.

The case history itself was not re-written but re-used, with resulting overlap and repetition in the three papers. However, studied separately, each paper is rewarding in its own way.

Herbert M Wyman MD
Editor

Observations on the Treatment of the Symbiotic Syndrome of Infantile Psychosis-Reality, Reconstruction, and Drive Maturation

These comments in honor of a beloved and highly esteemed teacher and collaborator derive from the work at the Masters Children's Center, from that part of the total program that has to do with the day care center for the intensive treatment of preschool psychotic children. The Center was established by Dr. Mahler and myself 1957, under the auspices of the Masters Nursery Inc.

This report is designed not so much to serve as a theoretical psychoanalytic contribution as it is to be a brief history of the Masters Children's Center, with some observations concerning the treatment design we employ there. As such, it should provide some evidence of Mahler's contribution both to the evolution of therapeutic techniques for the treatment of the psychotic child and to direct service to the community. Her theoretical contributions and her teaching in other settings have had a vast impact in many different fields and would require a separate study.

There is, of course, nothing in Mahler's influence that is not firmly rooted in psychoanalysis. Her contributions in the area of child psychosis have long been appreciated and have been presented in her book, *On Human Symbiosis and the Vicissitudes of Individuation*

(Mahler, 1968). The pioneering nature of her contributions and some evidence of how they have illuminated our work are also illustrated in the papers written for this volume by Bergman and by Kupfermann.

Historical Background

An unsuccessful attempt to introduce a psychotic child into an established therapeutic nursery school (1957–1959), which had until then been made up of severely disturbed but not psychotic children, led to the tripartite therapeutic design (Mahler and Furer, 1960). From 1959 to 1963, therapeutic action research into the natural history of symbiotic child psychosis was undertaken under the auspices of the National Institute of Mental Health. The results of this study have been incorporated into some seasons of Mahler's (1968) book, including an exposition of the therapeutic design.

From 1963 to 1965, the program for the treatment of psychotic children was continued under the auspices of the Masters Nursery.[1]

In 1965, the therapy section of the Masters Children's Center became a New York mental health clinic, servicing the community under the joint auspices of the Community Mental Health Board of the City of New York and the Masters Nursery. Beginning in September 1968, a classroom at the Center, supported by the Board of Education of the City of New York, was established to supply educational

---

1 Parallel with the therapeutic set-up for preschool, and later for school-age psychotic children, first a pilot study and then, continuing into the present, a formal research project on the normal separation-individuation process has been carried out at the Masters Children's Center, with Drs. Mahler and McDevitt as principal and co-principal investigators, respectively. This project has also been sponsored by the Board of Managers of the Masters Nursery (see Pine and Furer, 1963).

services for those psychotic children who became educable as a result of treatment, as well as for other disturbed children in the community.

Treatment Design

It was during the earliest years of the Masters Children's Center that the treatment design shifted from that of the conventional therapeutic nursery school to the tripartite setting of mother, child, and therapist, in which the mother not only observes but participates in the therapeutic work. Those years have been described in a previous paper (Mahler and Furer, 1960). The basic innovation in the design was not so much that the mother and child were treated together, but rather that it enabled us *to* aim directly at the basic treatment goal: altering the pathological equilibrium between mother and child so that the mother can regain her mothering function and thereby become, in a sense, an auxiliary therapist. According to Mahler, the mother must retain this latter role in critical situations, at least throughout the course of the patient's childhood.

An important element in the total psychopathology is the mother's adaptation to the child's psychosis, which includes: autistic withdrawal; the child's giving up of the usual requests for mothering-i.e., for protection, care, gratification-and his relinquishing of reality (i.e., the separate mother image). The mother is dealt with by the child as though she were not present, or as though, if present, she were part of his own delusional, omnipotent, dual unity. Under these circumstances, the mother either withdraws and gives up her mothering function, or else she is forced to function as an extension of the child's self.

Theoretical Orientation And Treatment Procedures

The initial goal of treatment, the "corrective symbiotic experience" (Mahler and Furer, 1960), requires that the therapist who lures the child from his autism take it as his purpose then to form a bridge, so that the child's emotional investment can be directed toward the mother. As can be appreciated, to do this requires an unusual degree of empathy, not only with the child but also with the mother (see Bergman 1971).

Various gifted therapists have been able to bring both mother and child, gradually and sometimes dramatically, to reunions and emotional reconciliations. Even though these are in many instances subsequently warded off by both mother and child, they do nevertheless become a groundwork for reconstituting a "mother-infant relationship." Bergman (1971) and Kupfermann (1971) have shown how the various phases of separation-individuation, as found in normal children, reappear in the treatment of psychotic children, along with the anxieties that stand in the way of the latter's development.

Subsequent steps are concerned with the development of a sense of identity in the child, and along with it, of awareness of a separate maternal person-a significant step in the developing sense of reality (Furer, 1964a). The further development of the child involves the appearance and psychotic elaboration of anal and oedipal conflicts. In the resolution of these conflicts, "the mother as therapist" once again supplies the "key" at crucial moments, conveying to the child not only understanding, but maternal comfort. Other crucial steps in development include the emergence of the child's ability to evoke or coerce the mother's response at a higher level, i.e., as a separate individual, and later to empathize with her and to return comfort and concern (Furer, 1967).

230

The children start in the treatment program at two, three, or four years of age, and in the "successful" group are able to enter the regular school program at the age of six or seven. From a psychotherapeutic point of view, the school situation allows us to add carefully dosed measures of external nonhuman and human reality, often of a frustrating nature. This acts, in a sense, as a half-way station to the age-appropriate external world away from the Center. In the case of the little girl described by Bergman (1971) , this correctly timed addition to the child's life, accompanied by interpretative work, resulted in a marked social advance.

Bergman's patient had formed a very dose attachment to both the teachers and children in the nursery group. A sort of "chasing and being chased" game was her favorite, and she played it with many children; but with one little girl, she showed a calm, tender, affectionate relationship. This could be maintained, however, only so long as the other child was willing to join in a ritualized play delineated by the patient-a displacement from the control exerted over her by her mother. As the other child tired of the game, the patient became openly aggressive toward her and the child turned away.

This experience was understood in terms of the current relationship to the mother, as well as of the transference, in which there was the usual rage at the mother's unintended failure to become part of her daughter's delusional fantasy of omnipotence. Now it was repeated by her friend's refusal to go on playing the game--a different aspect of reality in that the child and the teachers reacted with anger and emotional withdrawal (in contrast to the mother's reaction of tolerance and understanding). Persistent interpretation did not alter the behavior at school, and finally it was decided that she would have to be sent home.

231

When this happened, she was inconsolably unhappy; but the very next day she started to repeat the same behavior and was told that she would again have to leave. She then directed the teacher to sit down with her and to write her (the child's) name next to a drawing of a figure, and the name of her friend next to another drawing. Acting on her dictation, the teacher then went on to write: "If I bother_____, then you have to go home. If you are nice to _____, then she will play with you."2 The child then copied both the drawings and the words onto many, other sheets of paper. The beginning of internalization of prohibitions was in evidence.

Her obvious struggle brought forth the sympathy not only of the teacher, but of some of the other girls. That day our patient did not play with the other children, but imitated them, as she had done at an earlier time, and the next day she again covered successive sheets of paper with the admonitions noted above. On the third day, with the teacher's help, she rejoined the group and played with her friend. She indicated her memory of the experience to the teacher: When the latter said, "Now you can play," she added to the teacher's statement the verbal command she herself had previously been giving to her friend. She had mastered a segment of external reality in that she had learned to distinguish a world of experience that included only her mother and mother substitutes from one which included other separate objects, i.e., the children in the school. She subsequently accepted temporary separation from the children in the classroom as an aid in self-control.

The importance of autistic withdrawal as a secondary defensive formation has been emphasized repeatedly by Mahler. Her original (1952) clinical impression of two general categories of infantile

---

2 Bergman (1971) elaborates on the child's failure to distinguish between "I" and "You."

psychosis, the predominantly autistic and the predominantly symbiotic, has been confirmed many times. From a therapeutic standpoint, we have found that some psychotic children require, as exemplified in the case described by Kupfermann (1971), a long and arduous reconstitution of a nurturing "mothering," as well as a reliving of early phases of development.

There is a long drawn-out period of existence by the child in the "transitional world," during which inanimate objects come to take on the meaning of the "not me" environment, especially the "not me mother, and of the self or the omnipotent extension of the self (Mahler and Gosliner, 1955; Furer, 1964a). During this period, the treatment concern is with "plateaus" in the therapeutic process: the child remains at a certain level in development. His progress is impeded by anxiety aroused by the dangers arising out of the emerging sense of separateness and the loss of infantile omnipotence. The most crucial step for such children, as was emphasized early by Kanner and Eisenberg (195 5), is toward the initiation of speech and, from there, to spontaneous, verbal communication, as distinguished from imitative (at best, signal) language.

In those children with a better prognosis, there is a relatively rapid (usually within the first year) giving up of the autistic defense, with the appearance of elaborate psychotic symptomatology, including catatonic-like excitement and rages, and, in later stages, delusional formation. In a personal communication, Mahler suggested that those children in whom secondary autism seems to diminish rapidly may differ in regard to the integrative capacities of the ego from those children whose progress is slower. The more advanced and organized psychic phenomena may well have been covered over at first, rather than lacking because of a true defect or incapacity of the ego.

Finally, in these cases, as in adolescent and adult schizophrenia, we have the problem of the split within the ego. Alongside a correct awareness of reality there exist drive-propelled projections. The outcome depends ultimately upon the balance between these two factors and, as noted, a crucial element in that balance is the mother, who has been described by Mahler originally as a buffering love object, and at this point has to be considered also as a neutralizing, reality-conveying love object.

The problems of the later phases of treatment are illustrated by the case of a six-year-old girl who was preoccupied with the fairy tales of *Snow White* and *Sleeping Beauty*. (The mother was no longer in the room with the child, but in a room nearby.) At certain points in her re-enacting of these dramas, she would suddenly become convinced that the wicked witch was an actual person who meant to destroy her, that it was in fact her mother. The child would be taken at once to see the mother in the flesh. At such times the mother would be ferociously attacked by the little girl; yet she was able to reassure the child and to help explain her projective mechanisms to her. Often, there ensued an amazingly rapid diminution of the child's rage and anxiety.

These correct understandings of the child's fears, and earlier of her wishes, came to be referred to by this very intelligent and empathic mother as "keys," since with them she was able to unlock seemingly incomprehensible content. The important thing was that this content was accompanied by the child's strong affective reaction, and allowed the child rapidly to regain self-control. Interpretations to the child, for example, included simple explanations of displacements she had made from the mother to inanimate objects or to other people. On one occasion, while she was talking about her fantasies of the injury to the woman in sexual intercourse, and calling upon a memory (later confirmed) of having observed the primal scene at the age of two and a half, she started to blow her nose. Suddenly, she began to scream, and dashed out of the room to her mother who, upon hearing the story, explained that the child was probably also remembering some very frightening nosebleeds that she had had just prior to the age of two. The therapist then gave final verbal form *to* the child's hallucination that there was blood in the Kleenex, and interpreted that she feared she had had another nosebleed, which was also related to her wish and fear of replacing her mother in sexual intercourse, as well as to her current struggle about masturbation. As a result, there was a sudden dropping away of her panic.

I shall add here a very brief comment about the work done directly with the mother in the tripartite setting. A very complex transference relationship is established among the three participants in this setting—therapist, mother, and child. Our original expectation—that there would be an imitation of and identification with the therapist by the mother, as the child emerged from his autism—has been borne out.

It is not easy to evaluate the meaning of the changes that we observe in the mothers; the variations are great. For example, in some cases a change is noted as taking effect only with regard to the psychotic child in treatment with us, and not with his siblings. With other mothers, however, the change in emotional responses seems to be more far-reaching. Our social worker attempts to engage the mothers in as intensive psychotherapy as is acceptable to them. The greater the insight that can be gained, of course, the more solid the changes appear to be.

The case of Eric provides an example of the cooperative work that can be done with the mother in individual therapy and in tripartite sessions (Kupfermann, 1971). The mother's tendency was to overstimulate the child, sometimes in an obviously aggressive manner, such as hitting him with a pillow. An explanation for this was gradually brought forth from her: her purpose was to prevent her son from "tuning out," which she associated with dying.

Further investigation of this conflict in the mother was left to her individual therapy. The purpose in the tripartite setting is not only to give the mother a greater awareness of herself, but primarily to enhance her empathy with the child. In this particular instance, the child's response to the pillow play was to run to the mirror and to bite himself—presumably as a form of defensive hypercathexis of the body. The mother, going along with her denial of her own impulses, mistakenly took this to represent a pleasurable excitement. However, the therapist succeeded in calling her attention to the anxiety, with which she was then able to empathize, and pointed out the child's efforts to relieve his tension by himself. The therapist went on to indicate that mothering ministrations were needed and appropriate, and that they could be helpful in eliciting a response from the child.

I shall now present a brief case description of a child who changed relatively rapidly, in order to illustrate two interrelated clinical findings and recurring aspects of technique--namely, the deferred drive maturation that we have observed, and the role of the mother in the reconstruction of traumatic events from the child's past.[3]

Cathy, when first seen, at the age of four and a half years, had a repertoire of memorized songs and rhymes. While she was able to allow fleeting eye contact, if further relationship was pursued, she rapidly withdrew into an autistic state. The pathological equilibrium that is customary in such cases had become established between the child and her mother. The mother was able to explain many of the child's bizarre gestures to us, and to reconstruct for us the source of

---

3 See also Bergman's (1971) case about early experiences with skin stimulation.

her child's memorized phrases. She herself had given up any attempt to make use of this understanding because she had been unsuccessful in eliciting a positive response in the child, and was met instead with her further withdrawal. The mother's efforts, therefore, had gone into manipulating and controlling her daughter, because of her fear of embarrassment in public, her husband's feelings of hopelessness, and her own anger at her child.

During the first year of treatment, as this equilibrium came to be alerted, and as emotional awareness grew between therapist and child and between mother and child, more elaborately organized behavior and symptoms appeared. Most notably, there was a catatonic-like posing of ballet or ice-skating positions, which were copied from book illustrations. These poses served a number of different functions: they represented hypercathexis of the body and the residue of memories of events; they were symptoms, in the sense of being combinations of defense and wish-fulfillment; and they contained residues of ties to the maternal object in the form of imitative identifications. In a sense, the child's own body—that is to say, the entire body—had become a transitional object between her own self and the mother. (The mother had once aspired to be a ballet dancer and had many ballet books in the home; she was, of course, represented by the ice-skater. The mother's father composed music.)

Two years after treatment began, the child's basic psychotic structure was greatly altered, yet it still included the usual magic delusional fantasies of power and fusion. These were accompanied by uncontrollable rages and attacks upon the mother when frustrating reality intruded—for example, when a television program that fascinated the child came to an end and mother was unable to restore the images to the screen. Later on, as has been already noted, when Cathy became preoccupied with fairy tales involving wicked stepmothers and witches, she became delusional with regard to the mother.

With reference to reconstruction, which is essential to any psychoanalytic work, in our setting we have the great advantage of being able to draw directly on the mother's memory during the treatment session. One can well imagine that the memory of traumatic events—especially of those that involve both the mother and the child—would meet with resistance from both. In the child, however, there is also an upward surging movement, particularly when the memories take on new relevance because they have since become involved in higher levels of maturation and development, such as the oedipal phase.

For example, material about Cathy's hospitalization for diagnosis at age three emerged as follows: The child was building a road with blocks, and kept tripping and falling down; there were many symbolic references to what we inferred were her hospital experiences, such as being X-rayed. The atmosphere in the room at that moment was one of anger and fear, involving both mother and child. The mother then said, "Now I know what she is dramatizing! The day before we went to the hospital, Cathy ran out into the street; when I ran after her, I tripped and fell down on her, and she scraped her face." In response to these remarks, Cathy leveled another physical attack on the mother for "trying to kill me," and subsequently gave a full presentation of her fantasy at the, then, age of five and a half years regarding the hospital experience.

Another instance occurred during a period when Cathy had a transient fetishistic-like symptom (cf. Furer, 1964a). Again, there appeared to be an intimate connection between body-image formation and fetishistic-like phenomena. She had long been preoccupied with ballet shoes. Aside from its phallic-aggressive components, this

238

preoccupation, like the extended ballet poses, was part of the process by which she became aware of her body. For a time, she became very frightened whenever her mother went into the bathroom. Subsequently, Cathy indicated, chiefly by way of drawings, that her concern was with the shoes and the feet, which she drew repeatedly as being placed under the bathroom door.

In the therapy sessions, Cathy showed much concern over spotting her clothing. She covered the lower part of her body when she verbalized and dramatized fantasies of being a mermaid. After she had come very close to indicating that the specific memory had to do with blood, and the tension mounted, the mother finally recalled that she herself had been hospitalized two years previously, in her home town, for a uterine dilation and curettage. On the way back from the hospital, in an airplane, she had hemorrhaged spontaneously, and had rushed into the bathroom, taking her daughter with her.

After the interpretation and reconstruction of this event within the context of the child's intense oedipal conflicts (she was now close to seven years of age), the various related fears and fetishistic preoccupations dropped out of the clinical picture, only to reappear in connection with the effort to repress feelings of loss when memories of her therapist appeared during the year after the therapist had left.

This case presents a parallel to Freud's (1918) postulate about the deferred action of a trauma. For the Wolf Man, observation of the primal scene (probably at one and a half years of age) did not have a traumatic effect until his nightmare at the age of four, when phallic and oedipal development had taken precedence (see also Stewart, 1967). In our case, although the little girl was four and a half years of age when she observed the mother's hemorrhage, there was no evidence of phallic or oedipal phase derivatives. These did not appear until she had been in treatment for about three years—that is, when she was about six and a half years old. There were also no immediate effects of the trauma observable at age four-and-a-half.

In this case we have to postulate deferred reaction to a trauma, because of the delayed maturation and development of the drives and also of object relations. The latter postulate has been emphasized by Mahler, whereas the former is implicit—it has not received sufficient recognition. In order to explain the data, however, one has to consider many complex variables. Did the psychosis, with its concomitant withdrawal from reality, from human reality, and its consequent holdups and regressions in object relations, interfere with the maturation of the drives (Furer, 1964b)? Or was it that distortion and delay in ego development—for example, in the function of speech—did not allow for discharge patterns that were recognizable to us?

Similar questions emerge when one attempts to consider the reconstruction (the recovery of memory) with respect to ego functioning. On the one hand, there is, to some degree, a return of the repressed. On the other hand, the development of ego functions—such as the organization of thought and of speech—may be integrally necessary, or at least necessary for the communication of the memory. The one element that is most convincing in the treatment of psychotic children, as in normal development, is that object relations are the necessary condition for drive and ego development.

In considering the transient fetishistic-like preoccupation and related fears, it should be pointed out that these symptoms did not appear during the course of Cathy's treatment until she was clearly in the oedipal phase, with its concomitant castration fears, even though the crucial trauma had occurred at an earlier time, a time when a neurotic or normal child would already have experienced the oedipal conflicts. As has been noted, the child's posing led us to infer the existence of fears of object loss and body dissolution and of primitive defenses designed to deal with these fears. There was also direct evidence of faulty body-image formation.

Later, during periods of acute anxiety and disorganization, Cathy's extensive drawings showed a particular form of disruption. The body of the ballerina, which had previously been very well organized and full of detail (including the costume), seemed literally to fall to pieces before one's eyes. Eventually, what remained were distorted representations of the feet, which were associatively linked to a phallus, but then became a pointed "V," representing a biting tooth. There is collateral evidence in the anamnesis of intense oral sadism.

In conclusion, the point I wish to make is that among the multiple determinants of this transient fetishistic-like symptom there were predisposing factors to severe castration anxiety-namely, faulty body-image formation, accentuated oral sadism with concomitant introjective mechanisms, and a particularly relevant traumatic event, which contained visual perception of body mutilation. Another crucial factor was the girl's bisexual identification. A most cherished possession for her was a creche, acquired during her first years in another country and kept ever since. The origin of the attachment to the creche was, of course, related to experiences of closeness with her mother, having to do with Christmastime and the mother's love of decoration. During the child's phallic-oedipal development, this material was intertwined with that of the recovery of the traumatic incident, and represented a shifting identification with the baby Jesus as an admired asexual boy, and at the same time with the masochistically damaged woman of the primal scene, which she both longed and feared to be.

References

Bergman, A. (1971). "I and you": the separation-individuation process in the treatment of a symbiotic psychotic child. In: *Separation-Individuation: Essays in Honor of Margaret S. Mahler*. Lanham, MD: Jason Aronson, pp. 325–355.

Freud, S. (1918). History of an infantile neurosis. *Standard Edition* 17:3–104. London: Hogarth Press, 1955.

Furer, M. (1964a). The development of a symbiotic psychotic boy. *The Psychoanalytic Study of the Child* 19:448–469. New York: International Universities Press.

——— (1964b). Book review: *Infants in Institutions*, by S. Provence & R. C. Lipton (New York: International Universities Press, 1961). *Psychoanal. Quart.* 33:289–291.

——— (1967). Some developmental aspects of the superego. *International Journal of. Psycho-Anal.* 48:277–280.

Kanner, L. & Eisenberg, L. (1955). Notes on the follow-up studies of autistic children. In: *Psychopathology of Childhood,* ed. P. H. Hoch & J Zubin. New York: Grune & Stratton, 1955.

Kupfermann, K. (1971). The development and treatment of a psychotic child. In *Separation-Individuation: Essays in Honor of Margaret S. Mahler.* Lanham, MD: Jason Aronson, pp. 441–470.

Mahler, M. S. (1952). On child psychosis and schizophrenia: autistic and symbiotic infantile psychosis. *The Psychoanalytic Study of the Child* 7:286–305. New York: International Universities Press.

——— & Furer, M. (1960). Observations on research regarding the "symbiotic syndrome" of infantile psychosis. *Psychoanalytic Quarterly* 29:317–327.

———— in collaboration with Furer, M. (1968). *On Human Symbiosis and the Vicissitudes of Individuation. Vol. I.: Infantile Psychosis.* New York: International Universities Press.

———— & Gosliner, B. J. (1955). On symbiotic child psychosis: genetic, dynamic and restitutive aspects. *The Psychoanalytic Study of the Child* 10:215–240. New York: International Universities Press.

Pine, F., &; Furer, M. (1963). Studies of the separation-individuation phase: a methodological overview. *The Psychoanalytic Study of the Child* 18:325–342. New York: International Universities Press.

Stewart, A. (1967). *Psychoanalysis, The First Ten Years 1888-1898.* New York: Macmillan.

CHAPTER 21

Margaret S. Mahler Symposium Series: Reconstruction in Psychoanalysis: Its Relationship to Mahler's Concepts Construction and Reconstruction in the Tripartite Treatment of a Psychotic Girl

The focus of this communication returns to one of Dr. Mahler's most fundamental conceptual contributions, that of symbiosis of the dual unity of mother and child, as illustrated by its regressive manifestations in symbiotic child psychosis. The vicissitudes of the transformation of the pathological symbiosis is looked at from the point of view of the release of potential development as well as the therapeutic effect, particularly in regard to the change from catatonic posing during the height of the psychosis, to a modification of its form during the recovery from the psychosis to an as-if personality organization. From the technical side, the necessary and inevitable participation of the mother in the tripartite treatment design that arose from the fundamental concept of a dual unity, and the vicissitudes of this quasi-therapeutic mother-child relationship is also necessarily focused upon, though as we shall see, it was also transformed into a transference neurosis with the therapist during her recovery.

This is a long case history, five—a little over five years, to be exact—and in my study of it I have not yet attempted to integrate the material with the more complex subphases of separation-individuation, though

I think there is clear evidence on the one hand of the return of aspects of the differentiation. practicing, and rapprochement subphases, as well as what may be a new appearance of these during the treatment of this child. I hope the panel will help me in this regard. I think I see the forest and some of the trees, and would appreciate a brighter light on some of the trees that I have not yet been able to bring into sharper outline.

Cathy was treated from the ages of 5 through 10 years at the Masters Children's Center in the tripartite design that you all know about. Clinically, what was most interesting was the form her psychosis took when she emerged very rapidly after only two months of treatment from a state of secondary autism, namely a catatonic-like posing in which she used her body to copy and represent various pictures she had seen in books. This behavior was at its height while the child continued to ward off external human reality almost completely. At best, we were able to infer, with the mother's help, her perceptions from the particular content or the change in the content of chanted bits of songs and stories that she had heard, in her case, from both animate and inanimate sources.

To begin with, the poses were not communications but complex psychotic symptoms involving a regression to the stage of omnipotent symbiotic dual unity. What was most fruitful for therapeutic purposes, however, was that the poses contained memories which could be deciphered with the help of the mother, who, as you know, in our tripartite treatment design, was not only present but participated in the therapeutic hours. As you will hear, the constructions and reconstructions that could be made using the child's material and the mother's associations, was vital in this child's recovery. In the early phases, learning from her autism, in organizing and integrating her experience, and also in the resulting expressions.

246

In this I disagree with those who feel that reconstruction should not be done in the treatment of psychosis.

In this case, we had the advantage that the decathexis or deanimation of the object representation was not complete, if it ever is in psychosis, and that the memory islands of object cathexis could be built upon in, certain aspects, setting normal developmental processes in motion, and in others resulting in a kind of restitutional paranoid psychosis which gave way to a deviant personality organization, but with a greater investment in reality.

The posing and withdrawal from contact with the therapist and the mother was, at the beginning, the child's response to the impingement of human objects, particularly their emotional expressions. Gradually, however, we were able to communicate our understanding of the memory, the wish, the missing affects, and the connections which began to appear between the past memory in the pose and the present reality experience in the therapy room and at home .

One of the most frequent poses was a copy of the picture of Mary leaning over the Baby Jesus. For the mother, Christmas was a focal point of the year, but always awakened longings for closeness with her family, particularly her father, She cherished its rituals, most especially the setting out of the little figures of the nativity scene. Cathy, I must explain, had been conceived unexpectedly in the first year of the parents' marriage, in a foreign country where the father was on assignment for his company. Before relocating permanently in New York for the purpose of placing the child in treatment, the mother and child had returned to the States only twice: at age of 2-1/2 when the maternal grandfather was dying of cancer, and again at age 4-1/2 for the purpose of a full in-patient neurological and psychiatric evaluation. From the age of six months to 2-1/2 years, Cathy's care had been turned over to a 16-year-old native girl, and it was in the language of this nursemaid. that Cathy produced her first words and phrases. Development during this period was apparently normal or precocious. The visit to the States, upon the grandfather's illness, broke this connection, and Cathy never saw the nursemaid again. Cathy, as we first knew her, presented echolalic speech, bizarre darting and grimacing, flailing of her arms, panic rages, autistic refusal of contact, sudden inexplicable fears and flight, and an attachment to little pieces of black plastic. The mother had ceased to regard the child's behavior as comprehensible or as a communication, and she directed her efforts to controlling displays of bizarre behavior.

In the first months of treatment, as the mother was able associate to Cathy's poses, the child's feelings of loss, her yearnings and her rage related to the above events, became a meaningful exchange between the mother and the child. The content was confirmed by another strange pose, the copying of the figure of a boy on skates pushing a girl on a sled, taken from an illustration in a Mother Goose book. In this early period of the treatment, the crucial image was not in the pose but in the picture, namely surrounding snow. It was at the age of 2-1/2, upon the occasion of her grandfather's illness and death, that the child first saw snow and it was also the time that her mother because depressed and withdrawn. The pose of the happy children by the child, now age 5, denied again the painful experience of this emotional separation from the mother who so suddenly had become her sole caretaker.

By highlighting and selecting these particular moments and not detailing our procedures, one necessarily does violence to the case. I have to skip over the antecedent and concomitant reestablishment of the relationship between therapist, mother, and child, that required the correct timing of both anticipatory and participatory empathy with her behavior in general, once we were able to read this child's cues. Summarizing very briefly, by this kind of symbiotic union to which she had she had regressed, and to ward off the painful affects associated with her perception of separateness—that is, of self from object—which on a different psychic level was accentuated by her particular life history. The rage and subsequently sadness in response to our interventions were first expressed in a global fashion, then directed the mother and the therapist, and eventually integrated in the sense of being able to differentiate present reality from past, present self from past self, and to an increasingly greater degree, self from objects.

Instead of her placid withdrawal, the warded off new tended to flood her and her new defenses became an effort at omnipotent control by a fantasy of the mother's power which we had get from affects from her behavior. For example, when the mother was unable to make the sun go down or restore images on the television screen, the child was thrown into the panic rage and now in addition, viciously attacked her mother whom she had come to see as cruelly withholding this power.

After two years of treatment, her progress had been substantial. Poses appeared only in emergencies, having been replaced by renditions in play of the stories of ballets, particularly one taken from the fairy tale of *Sleeping Beauty*. The ballet dancer pose had also been one of the frequent early rigid postures. The mother had wished to be a ballet dancer and the ultimate source of the interest was again the maternal grandfather. In addition, as an indication of the shifting from deanimated or inanimate objects to the original human object, the cherished possessions ceased to be the pieces of black plastic and became the figures of the Nacimiento, or nativity scene .

As she was approaching her 7th birthday, the material of the oedipus complex burst upon the scene. She became aware of and preoccupied with the sexual differences with an intensity of anxiety that was still closely related to the earlier fear of total bodily destruction or disintegration. Dogs, cats, and finally people were classified as to whether or not they possessed a penis or whether or not they menstruated. Her apparent sexual identification in her actual behavior took on a masochistic character. It was at this point that she developed an already fetish-like symptom: her preoccupation with shoes, and in particular with shoes that could be glimpsed beneath the sill of a door. This preoccupation appeared particularly in what now came to be an almost endless series of drawings of the ballet dancer and of the ice-skater that we knew so well from her posing. The mother had once been able to abort a panic tantrum in reaction to her departure for an outing with her husband by giving the child a pair of toe slippers which, however, the child was not allowed to dance in. Gradually a phobia appeared of the mother going into the bathroom and, as on later occasions during such periods of focused anxiety, the flooding by her own affects was less of an issue. The fear of the bathroom emerged as a fear of what was going on in the parents' bedroom and a concern that her mother was damaged in sexual intercourse. The shoes visible under the sill of the bathroom door represented the maternal phallus and reassured her that the mother was intact. In the therapeutic process described above in relation to the posing the mother the memory of an experience on the flight home from the grandfather's funeral. She had hemorrhaged while in flight, having had a dilatation and curettage for intermittent bleeding a few days earlier. She had taken the child into the peculiar small bathroom on the airplane. The small bathroom was represented in Cathy's drawings, as were spots on her clothing. It appeared to me, as previously reported, that there had been a deferred effect of that trauma, as in the case of the Wolf Man, now operative with the child's phallic genital development and involvement in the oedipus complex. The reconstruction of the memory of the hemorrhage and of at least two periods of observation of the primal scene resulted in the disappearance of these fears and preoccupations.

The focus now became a conflict over her masochistic feminine wishes that overlaid an earlier bisexual identification with the baby boy, Jesus. In essence, as enacted in the ballet fairy tale, Sleeping Beauty, she participates in sexual activity, is damaged by pricking her finger on the spindle, and is punished by the mother, the wicked witch. On the other hand, she sleeps the quiet, peaceful sleep of the asexual baby boy Jesus, until the prince comes—a denial, but at the same time a return of the re pressed wishes as well as a memory of the parents' activity and of her own excitement. However, in the intensity of the play literally carried her out of reality, into a dramatic—though temporary—delusional state

That is, the conviction the persecutor in the grip of which she would violent physical attack on the mother, and forced to have the mother wait on another floor, raging. In the midst of one such *Sleeping Beauty* performance, when the mother was not in the room and the therapist grazed the child's cheek in passing, and Cathy said with full and fierce conviction, "Why did you slap me, mother?" She then returned to the play. In this same period, the child's earlier hospitalization for psychiatric evaluation at age 4-1/2, could be reconstructed from her play, including a particular instance prior to entering the hospital when the child had run out into the street, the mother ran after her and fell down on top of her.

This was interestingly presented to us by Cathy, who was trying to make a pathway with blocks but kept tripping and falling. In a delusional belief she amalgamated the girl on what she called the operating table for an EEG with the penetration and pinning down of Jesus on the cross, playing the mother as killer of Jesus and herself as the victim. Similarly, a gastrointestinal upset was proof that the mother, like the witch in *Snow White*, had poisoned her and the contents of all foods served her had to be checked and verified by the therapist.

At this point Cathy began to show evidence of the development of a cruel and all-encompassing superego. Now fear of injury from the persecutor varied erratically with the fear that she would be injured by her own impulses. Masturbatory activity and sexual excitation were predominant, and the drawings featured elongated fingers, elaborately costumed princesses and ballerinas which disintegrated in consecutive drawings into arms, legs and shoes. At this point the child returned once again to bodily re presentations of early preoccupations, but without the withdrawn, autistic, catatonic-like state. She concentrated on being the ballet dancer who was both good as a dancer and good as a child, holding her arms above her head, never touching herself. The child displayed a capacity to think in the analytic setting on a very high level. She became preoccupied with what is truth and what is a lie, namely the expression of the fear that mother would not return to her after a weekend off with the father—the lie—whereas, as she confessed, the wish and the truth was that she hoped only the father would return. At this point in the setting of her first experience with formal learning in school, exhibitionistic aspects of the ballet poses and an exaggerated narcissistic ego ideal shared by mother and child became evident. In entering school she had expected to be an instant success, and when this did not occur she reverted in the schoolroom to the earlier posing, expressing the wish for omnipotence without the intrusion of reality. At the same time material emerged revealing the child-idea that one had to be both good at what one does and good in moral terms, if one were to be like the mother that is, satisfy the latter's own exhibitionistic longings, hut also if one were to win the mother's love.

As is evident above, the child, at this point into the third year of her treatment, was now able to retain the separate object image during therapy despite temporary delusional episodes and transient regressions to earlier psychotic disguises, to distinguish fantasy from reality in the play and to move in and out of fantasy and reality with impressive ease. At the end of the third year of treatment, there appeared for the first time an as-if type of behavior used as a defense and a denial of feelings aroused by the impending separation from the therapist over the summer vacation. Her first reaction to this material was to say, "I do not like your voice. It is my voice," then to demand that the therapist change her own eyes and hair and look exactly like Cathy. The response to the interpretation that being the same would undo the pain of goodbye was the return of regressive and more instinctualized mechanisms such as the masochism described earlier, panic reactions to the loss of the shoe, and clear evidence of the return of the wish for fusion and of the fear of bodily disintegration. On the last day of the therapy that year, permitting for the first time since the above session, a discussion of the impending separation, she asked, "Will I be same Cathy Ruth J. when you are away?"

On her return the following fall, an enlarged school setting faced her with a conscious dilemma. She could no longer blot out the other children and their expression of emotions, and these particularly frightened her. She knew her own emotions were overwhelming, and as often expressed in the past, was never sure that any one feeling would ever stop. Her response was to imitate the voices, movements, and various other behaviors of her classmates with the idea that the imitation would be real, but as her own creation, manageable. And thus she could relate to the other children and control their responses as well as her own. Strikingly, instead of the stereotyped voice inflections and uncoordinated facial expressions and body movements other severely disturbed children adopt in response to potential affect, Cathy became apparently many different bodies, voices, and facial expressions. She practiced before the mirror, became dissatisfied, and ask both therapist and mother to demonstrate the appropriate facial expressions for various emotions and situations which she could then copy and use. At one point, she interrupted her practicing to paint her arms the color of the mother's favorite dress, and thus attired, resumed work. The result was a facade of strangely mannered but fairly accurate renditions of a variety of affects. However, although she became adept at matching affect with gesture and face, these creations were recognized by the child as failures, or in her own words "Why don't I have a real friend?" Nevertheless, this imitative, as-if personality was impervious to interpretations, and comments or references to the behavior were so vigorously fought off that efforts to understand, empathize, and interpret were postponed.

To summarize another portion of the therapy at this period, demonstrating that although the regression to the earliest dual unity had been overcome, the self- and object- differentiation was unstable, and the boundary permeable. The idealization of the maternal figures and the exhibitionism, the beautiful, talented, precocious child as the counterpart, could only be sparsely analyzed. Perhaps, we thought, because this had been a necessary and, for this particular child, a particularly intense portion of the corrective symbiotic experience, that we had fostered. In any case, the idealized self became another portion of the as-if state, and appeared in the transference during the fourth year of treatment.

At age 9 Cathy began the fourth year of treatment, still driven by her sexual conflicts. She asked endless questions about anatomy, mating, and birth, in an attempt to master her feelings. She remembered, as did the mother, several observations of parental sexual intercourse that had been the subject of previous reconstructions. The child drew these things in great detail. The questions to the therapist were, "Do you take your nightgown off? Do you keep the covers on?" bringing the voyeuristic, exhibitionistic focus to the forefront. "Do you do it every night?" she asked, indicating her nightly struggle with masturbation.

Her drawings again showed people with grossly elongated middle fingers, and people mutilated—the punishment for masturbation At home, what would start as a wish to be either physically or emotionally close to her father could not be contained, and she had fantasies of intercourse with him, during which she was injured, and the wish was quite conscious. Again, in the treatment situation, these wishes took on hallucinatory reality, as in a session when her excitement culminated in a sensory experience, namely that she was having a nosebleed. As expected, the was dealt with by the projection and the belief that the mother wanted her injured and killed. Via the mother's associations, we learned that the nosebleeds had in fact occurred during the time when Cathy was in care of the young nursemaid. The rage about the abandonment could be reconstructed as a substratum for the paranoid reaction. (See Velde's paper "The Structure of Paranoid Ideas.") Cathy's solution was again an aggressive demand to learn the forms of social behavior from the therapist, to acquire supplies, to become the same but also, we felt in some degree to de-differentiate the self.

She again became involved with differences between truth and falsehood, real appearances as opposed to the happy face. The latter a demand from distant past again, that the mother had made both of herself and the child. There was a defensive, as well as aggressive, aspect of this imitation of social convention, but curiously, at the same time the child made insistent demands for total truth and total empathy from the therapist, also regressive vestiges of old omnipotent fusion fantasies, warding off the anxieties of the ongoing oedipus complex, again both by the de-differentiation as well as the oral gratification. By now, however, the imitation varied between an as-if defense and a yearning for identification with a separate and admired individual—the therapist—perceived as a beautiful, golden-haired woman princess. In addition, the imitation of this period contained evidence of superego conflict, the copied happy face is false in the additional sense that the maternal figure in the transference was hated as well as admired.

In the final year of therapy, the child's anxiety was manifested in an effort to find out what she, Cathy, should be in order to elicit the therapist's admiration. She still presented a facade, the result of efforts of imitation and integration that was perceived as peculiar by us, exaggerated, and hollow. It was felt however, that Cathy had gained sufficient strength to deny her the borrowed personality, and to interpret the defense. In response to a tentative introduction of this approach, she reenacted those images that had previously brought her admiration—the imaginative child, the artist, the performer, the patient concerned with sexual problems, the polite and correct child. Her initial reaction to interpretation was terror and a return to catatonic posing, but this time of such grotesque form that it could only be understood as a depiction of an image of the destroyed and destructive self.

The as-if mechanism seemed to be Cathy's protection against impulses and emotions that, arising in ordinary situations, rapidly became extreme, fearfully unending, and finally, in fantasy, destructive. For instance, she expressed jealously of the therapist: "You won't tell me about your private life. You won't tell me what your furniture looks like. If you're a Mrs. _____, you must have a Mister _____. You don't understand because you always know where you are. Regression and primitive defenses followed rapidly, and the anger and betrayal were projected. In Cathy's fantasy, the therapist was to cut out her tongue so that the therapist alone would have the only beautiful voice. She, Cathy, would then attack, take out all the therapist's blood and drink it. But the blood would then hurt her. On, no, now she remembered, her tongue was cut out. Not only could she not have a beautiful voice, but she could not commit the destructive acts. Her face would show her emotions. Her tongue, being cut out, she is the voiceless replication of the therapist, and no one would be hurt.

This primitive ambivalence in the transference was also related on a higher level to her struggle over masturbation. The therapist, she said, was the good nurse who fed her, and then the bad nurse who spanked her and kept her in bed at night. Then Cathy decided that both she and the therapist were good and bad nurses and must sit imprisoned on a rock over water teeming with witches. If princes could vanquish the witches, both of them would live. If the witches won out, they would die. The two of them together, experiencing the same dangers, seemed to us to represent the lessening in the extreme cruelty of the superego, plus a basis for empathy and genuine identification. The importance of this good maternal figure and the capacity for maintaining a relationship to a love object was such that Cathy was willing not only to control her impulses but to give them up in order to keep the good, kind therapist. One solution, consequently, was to give up, as she said, men entirely. As she explained, the therapist must be bored with her stories about Chris—a boy in school—so they could now consider there were only two people in the world left to talk about: herself and the therapist.

However, as Cathy came to be fully aware of the actual relationship between the adult therapist trying to help her and the sick child driven by her wishes and fears, her relative helplessness became terrifying. The therapist, she said, was to play a devil. If the devil caught her, she, Cathy, would die; but if Cathy let go of the devil, she would also die. Her defenses in the fantasy play were identification with the powerful aggressor, her mother, and in transference the therapist, and the projection of the hostile impulses onto the therapist. In the effort to maintain what was the real image of the therapist, she would ask the latter to leave the therapy room and then ask for forgiveness. Occasionally and fleetingly, Cathy experienced her conflicts as fully internal, which again frightened her. Hollowly and without affect she said one time, "I'm sorry for you. You're such a good therapist and I don't try hard enough."

At this point in time the child told a story, expressing in a creative way, with a deliberate use of symbol and metaphor, her understanding of what had been happening in her life, past and present. She said that she was like Helen Keller who was loved by her parents like a little dog. Then Anne Sullivan came, a woman who understood Helen, since she herself was half blind, and had had a terrible childhood. Anne decided that the child had had too much pity, that she was intelligent and could learn. Before the teacher came, Cathy explained, Helen had been lonely. She had to feel the mouths of people talking. She thought, "Why won't they play with me?" But then, and it's no wonder, she had tantrums, and kicked and screamed, Still, if she could—and she did—make the same mouth movements, who would she be? The little dog? No one? Not herself, and no one's friend. In association, she said sometimes parents do cruel things to children without realizing it. Spankings aren't cruel. It is cruel when a child approaches a parent and the parent holds out her hand to stop you from touching her, and then she takes the child to her room.

The last of this final year of therapy brought external stress into the treatment of this child. The Masters Center was to close in June after a prolonged effort by parents and staff to retain public funding, an effort of which Cathy was aware. Soon after the new year, Cathy had to enter another school. She was terrified by the complex social situations, by the sheer volume of children, and their aggressive movements, and responded by standing in the stairway in rigid postures or by clinging tightly to adults. The failures all around her reactivated the wish and demand that the therapist be all-powerful, and save her like a princess in the tower, from the frightening prisons of home and school. However, the memories of her present and past realities flooded her, and she saw the therapist as well as herself as weak and worthless. Perhaps if the therapist curled her hair and she, Cathy, looked prettier, school and home would be more appreciative. Activating an old memory to bring the mother back and win her love by exhibiting herself. However, as these illusions were not sufficient, the demands became impossible and fantastic, that the therapist make her able to fly and to fly away, a disguised return of the shoe fetish was expressed in the only wish she had in the world, a wish for a pair of high-buttoned antique shoes of very particular design. When these could not be found, she raged, but then settled on having the therapist sew her a pair of high-buttoned shoes out of flannel. During these sessions, Cathy would sit silently reading one of her own books, occasionally glancing up to watch the therapist sew, and cutting off all comment with, "Don't talk." The shoes, as omnipotent phallus, were also clearly a bridge between her and the maternal figure, the good maternal figure whom she feared be lost in the destructive atmosphere. Only when the therapist tried a shoe on her foot for fit did Cathy relax briefly in the physical closeness; again we felt, not only a wish but a memory of the mother's physical care prior to the mother's leaving her with the nursemaid,

For Cathy to recognize that any of her problems were internal, or especially that her difficulties with her parents, who were now both depressed and demanding, were real, made her feel too unhappy, too helpless, vulnerable, and separate, disillusioned, and disappointed, and she withdrew, spending her sessions reading, often not in the same room with the therapist, often not hearing the bell when the mother came to pick her up, and refusing to open the door herself.

The therapist broke into this new and, we felt, disadvantageous situation at termination by a strong statement of the reality, namely that Cathy was trying to say that they had no relationship, and she, the therapist, could not continue to act as part of that belief. Cathy was living out a fantasy of despair, and using her parents' scolding to support it. She was playing that she was being abandoned by her mother rather than acknowledge her hurt and disappointment. She was warding this off by becoming cold and dead, and pretending that the parents were as well, which she did not wish them to be. The child responded by confirming the interpretation but revealing that the therapist had not recognized that an old kind of attempt at solution was present, the as-if state. She said, "I am not like other 10-year-olds. I am unordinary. I cannot feel, I can only copy. That is what I have been doing in my head. That is also part of it. I know my mother doesn't really know what to do next." Cathy was able, after a time to acknowledge the therapist s description of the realities of her position, as well as her responsibility for the defensive alterations in her personality.

The termination, it should be said, also meant for Cathy a change such as she had experienced many times in her life, namely, that the family would be moving a very great distance away. She produced a fantasy of a girl named Glass Slipper who loses the maid she loves because her mother, conceited and strict, does not want her to play with grownups. Her mother dies, and robbers come to kill Glass Slipper, as they stupidly think she is guilty for her mother's death. In punishment, the robbers are taken to a prison far away where they have clean air, a parental description of the future family home. Some of the latent content included the warding off of the pain of loss which could be connected with the previous reconstructions having to do with the nursemaid and the mother's emotional withdrawal. Her own destructive feelings are projected into the form of robbers who are taken away, but also taken home. Most crucial in her associations was Cathy's fear that in the absence of the therapist, her needs, wishes and emotions would again become overwhelming. However, the libidinal attachment to the mother was now much stronger, as it was to the therapist. The analysis proceeded and a painful mourning reaction took place. She was also realistic about herself and her parents, as she had not been before. She talked about yearning for a boy in her old school whom she would like to see again before leaving. However, she thought her mother would not want her to do that. As she described the closeness she wanted with this boy, the therapist was able to focus upon the feeling that she had expressed before of the mother who holds out her hand to prevent contact and then takes the child to its room. Cathy wept and said, "I have to work it out. I have felt pushed away and many times I have been pushed away. Some of it is my fault when I get so angry, but not being yourself doesn't help." In the very last weeks of the therapy, the fears of robbers and whirlwinds reappeared, behind which was the belief that the world was too dangerous, that the only safe place was with the therapist forever, whatever the therapist wished her to be she would be. However, in the main, they were able to think over the time they had spent together sadly, and yet with the feeling that the therapist had a real and separate existence that would continue, and that Cathy could thus remember her as the therapist would remember Cathy.

In summary, I have tried to present clinical picture of the recovery of this child from her psychosis. There are many interesting features, but I will point in particular to one: the as-if state, which seems to me to be on the line of development in this child from the original catatonic posing, from a more complete fusion of self and object, to a partial and more differentiated state of the self and object representation. In a general sense, this change was accompanied by a progression in the sense of reality, especially in regard to the human object, which was never fully lost during the period of the as-if personality organization, in contrast to the earlier period of posing, and toward the end of the therapy seemed, to a large degree, to have attained a state of secondary autonomy.

From the technical side, the reconstruction of the past and the integration of the past in the present seemed to me to have been a necessary prerequisite for the progression of the level of object relations, particularly the self-object differentiation as well as the interlocked progression in the sense of reality. Although at times, the resurrection of past feelings and fantasies produced disruptions and acute intensification of the psychotic symptoms, it is my belief that Cathy would not have attained as firm a hold on the present-day reality without her knowledge of the past.

In conclusion, I have a very short and inadequate follow-up letter from Cathy, six months after she left, to her therapist. In it, Cathy first gave her address, and then continued: "We don't know for sure what the zip code is. Some friends of ours have found a house and they described it to us. It has four bedrooms, two bathrooms, a recreation room, a big kitchen, a large living room, enough room for a wash room, a study, a basement, a back yard, and a covered patio. I think it's going to be a terrific house to live in. It will also be so much fun to have your own back yard. I'm going to stay at my grandmother's house while my parents unpack things. They'll stay at her house, too. But sometimes they'll go and run back. Someday I'll come to New York and cook stew with onions, noodles, and carrots, and also have a glass of wine. Dr. Furer reminds me of Mr. ____, who is a teacher at the school. He drove us home in his car, and it was midnight by the time we came home. I'm very glad you like the pink dress. It makes me feel happy to know that you like something I have given you. Love, Cathy.

P.S. I had to use plain typing paper to write because all the stationery I have is packed. Almost everything I want to look at out in the living room is packed."

I'm afraid we are left only with our own associations to the letter.

CHAPTER 22

Conference On Borderline States Personality Organization During The Recovery Of A Severely Disturbed Young Child

In this brief communication I hope to share with you what can be thought of either as a problem at the outcome or as an interesting development during the treatment of a psychotic girl, Cathy, from the ages of five through ten years. Essentially it was the appearance and consolidation of what we considered to be an as-if state of personality organization—an aspect of some borderline conditions—in the fourth and fifth year of treatment, although what we consider precursors of this state had been present earlier.

Of particular interest in this regard was the form her psychosis took when she emerged, very rapidly after only two months of treatment, from a state of secondary autism, namely, a catatonic-like posing in which she used her body to copy and represent various pictures she had seen in books. This behaviour was at its height while the child continued to ward off external human reality almost completely. At best, we were able to infer her perceptions from the particular content or the changes in the content of chanted bits of songs and stories that she had heard and was repeating.

To begin with, the poses were not communications but complex psychotic symptoms involving a regression to the stage of omnipotent symbiotic dual unity. However, what was most important for therapeutic purposes was that the poses contained memories which could be deciphered with the help of the mother, who in our tripartite treatment design, was not only present but participated In the therapeutic hours. The posing and withdrawal from contact with the therapist and the mother was in fact the child's response to the impingement of human objects, particularly of their emotional expressions. Gradually, however, we were able to communicate our understanding of the memory, the wish, the missing affects, and the connections which began to appear between the past memory and present reality experience in the therapy room and at home.

One of the most frequent poses was a copy of a picture of Mary leaning over the baby Jesus. For the mother, Christmas was a focal point of the year that always awakened longings for closeness with her family, particularly her father. She cherished its rituals, most especially the setting-out of the little figures of the Nativity Scene. Cathy, I must explain, had been conceived unexpectedly in the first year of the parents' marriage, in a foreign country where the father was on assignment for his company. Before relocating permanently to New York for the purpose of placing the child in treatment, mother and child had returned to the States only twice—at age two-and-a-half when the maternal grandfather was dying of cancer, and again at age four-and-a-half for the purpose of a full, in-patient neurological and psychiatric evaluation. From the age of six months to two- and-a-half years, Cathy's care had been turned over to a sixteen-year-old native girl, and it was in the language of this nursemaid that Cathy produced her first words and phrases,

Development during this period was apparently normal or precocious. The visit to States upon the grandfather's illness broke this connection, and Cathy never saw the nursemaid again. Cathy, as we first knew, her presented echolalic speech, bizarre darting and grimacing, flailing of her arms, panic rages, autistic refusal of contact, sudden inexplicable fears and flight, and an attachment to little pieces of black plastic. The mother had ceased to regard the child's behaviour as comprehensible or as a communication, and she directed her efforts to controlling displays of bizarre and hazardous behaviour.

In the first months of treatment, as the mother was able to associate to Cathy's poses, the child's feeling of loss, her yearning and her rage related to the above events, became a meaningful exchange between the mother and the child. The content was confirmed by another strange pose, the copying of the figure of a boy on skates pushing a girl on a sled, a scene taken from an illustration in a Mother Goose book. In this early period of the treatment, the crucial image was not in the pose, but in the picture, namely the surrounding snow. It was at the age of two-and-a-half, on the occasion of the grandfather's illness and death, that the child first saw snow, and it was also at that time that the mother became depressed and withdrawn. The pose of the happy children, by the child now age five, denied again the painful experience of this emotional separation from the mother who so suddenly had become her sole caretaker,

By highlighting and selecting these particular phenomena and not detailing our procedures, one necessarily does violence to the case as a whole. I have to skip over the antecedent and concomitant re-establishment of a relationship between therapist, mother and child, that required what we call the correct timing of both anticipatory and participatory empathy with her behaviour in general, once we were able to read this child's cues. Summarizing very briefly, by this kind of bodily representation, the child was able to live out the fantasy of omnipotent symbiotic union to which she had regressed, and to ward off the painful affects associated with her perception of separateness, that is of self from object, which on a different psychic level was accentuated by her particular life history. The rage, and subsequently the sadness in response to our interventions, were first expressed in global fashion, then directed at the mother and the therapist, and eventually integrated, in a sense of being able to differentiate present reality from the past, present self from past self, and to an increasingly greater degree, self from object

The warded-off affects tended to flood her, and her defense now became an effort at omnipotent control by a fantasy of the mother's power which was inferred from her behaviour and way of life. For example, when the mother was unable to make the sun go down or to restore images on the television screen, the child was thrown into the panic rage, and now in addition, viciously attacked her mother whom she had come to see as cruelly withholding her power.

After two years of treatment, progress had been substantial; poses appeared only in emergencies, having been replaced by renditions in play of the stories of ballets, particularly one taken from the fairy tale of *Sleeping Beauty*. The ballet-dancer pose had also been one of the frequent early rigid postures; the mother had wished to be a ballet dancer and the ultimate source of the interest was again the maternal grandfather. In addition, as an indication of a shifting from deanimated or inanimate objects to the original human object, the cherished possessions ceased to be the pieces of black plastic and became the figures of the *Naciemento* or Nativity Scene.

As she was approaching her seventh birthday, the material of the oedipus conflict burst upon the scene. She became aware of, and preoccupied with, sexual differences, with an intensity of anxiety that was still closely related to the earlier fear of total bodily destruction. Dogs, cats and finally people were classified as to whether or not they possessed a penis or whether or not they menstruated. Her apparent sexual identification and her actual behaviour took on a masochistic character. It was at this point that she developed an already described fetish-like symptom, a preoccupation with shoes, and in particular with shoes that could be glimpsed beneath the sill of a door. This preoccupation appeared particularly in what now came to be an almost endless series of drawings of the ballet dancer and of the ice skater that we knew so well from her posing. A phobia appeared of the mother going into the bathroom, and as on later occasions during such period of focused anxiety, the flooding by her own affects was less of an issue. The fear of the bathroom emerged as a fear of what was going on in the parents' bedroom and a concern that her mother was damaged in sexual intercourse. The shoes visible under the sill of the bathroom door represented the maternal phallus and reassured her that the mother was intact. In a therapeutic process described above in relation to the posing, the child's drawings and play behaviour brought from the mother the memory of an experience on the flight home from the grandfather's funeral; she had hemorrhaged while in flight, having had a dilatation and curettage (for intermittent bleeding) a few days earlier. She had taken the child into the peculiar small bathroom on the airplane and it was clear that the child had seen the blood. The small bathroom was represented in Cathy's drawing, as were spots on her clothing. It appeared to me, as previously reported, that there had been a deferred effect of that trauma, as in the case of the Wolf Man, now operative with the child's phallic genital development and involvement in the oedipus complex. The reconstruction of the memory of the hemorrhage, and of at least two periods of observation of the primal scene, resulted in the disappearance of these fears and preoccupations,

The focus now became a conflict over her masochistic feminine wishes that overlaid an earlier bisexual Identification with the baby boy Jesus. In essence, as enacted in the ballet fairy tale *Sleeping Beauty,* she participates in sexual activity, is damaged by pricking her finger on the spindle, and is punished by the mother, the wicked witch. On the other hand, she sleeps the quiet peaceful sleep of the asexual baby boy Jesus until the Prince comes, a denial but at the same time a return of the repressed wishes, as well as a memory of the parents' activity, and of her own excitement. However, in this child, the intensity of the play literally carried her out of reality into a dramatic although temporary delusional state—that is, the conviction that the mother was the persecutor—in the grip of which she would launch a sudden and violent physical attack on the mother, and later, when we were forced to have the latter wait on another floor, and seek her out there, raging. In the midst of one such *Sleeping Beauty* performance, when the mother was not the room, the therapist grazed the child's cheek in passing, and Cathy said, with full and fierce conviction, "Why did you slap me, mother?", but then returned to the play. In this same period the child's earlier hospitalization for psychiatric evaluation at age four-and-a-half emerged in play, but with a concomitant quasi-delusional belief, in which she amalgamated the girl on what she called the operating table (for an EEG) with the penetration and pinning down of Jesus on the Cross, playing the mother as killer of Jesus, and herself as the victim. Similarly, a gastrointestinal upset was proof that the mother, like the witch in *Snow White,* had poisoned her, and the contents of all food served to her had to be checked and verified by the therapist.

At this point, Cathy began to show evidence of the development of a cruel and all-encompassing superego. Now, fear of injury from the persecutor varied erratically with the fear of self-inflicted injury; masturbatory activity and sexual excitation were predominant, and the drawings featured elongated fingers, elaborately costumed princesses and ballerinas, all disintegrating, in consecutive drawings, into arms, legs. and shoes. Cathy now concentrated on being the ballet dancer who was both good as a dancer and "good" as a child, holding her arms above her head, and never touching herself. At the same time, the child also displayed a capacity to think, in the analytic setting, on a very high level. She became preoccupied with what is truth and what is a lie—the lie consisting of her articulating the fear that her mother would not return to her after a weekend off with the father; the truth, as she confessed, consisting of her wish that only her father would return. At this point in the setting of her first experiences with formal learning in school, exhibitionistic aspects of the ballet poses, and an exaggerated narcissistic ego ideal shared by mother and child, became evident. In entering school, she had expected to be an instant success, and when this did not occur, she reverted in the schoolroom only, to the early catatonic-like posing, expressing the wish for omnipotence without the intrusion of reality. At the same time material emerged revealing the child's idea that one had to be both good at what one does and "good" in moral terms, If one were to be like the mother— that is, to satisfy the latter's own exhibitionistic longings, but also if one were to win the mother's love.

As is evident from the above, the child, now into the third year of her treatment, was, at this point, able to retain the separate object image during therapy despite temporary delusional episodes and transient regressions to earlier psychotic disguises; to distinguish fantasy from reality in the play; and to move in and out of fantasy and reality with impressive ease. At the end of the third year of treatment, there appeared, for the first time, an as-if type of behaviour used as a defense and denial of feelings aroused by the impending separation from the therapist over the summer vacation. Her first reaction to this material was to say, "I do not like your voice, it is not my voice," and then to demand that the therapist change her dark eyes and hair, and look exactly like Cathy. The response to the interpretation that being "the same" would undo the pain of "good-bye," included the resurgence of regressive and more instinctualized mechanisms, such as the masochism described earlier, panic reactions to the loss of a shoe, and clear evidence of a return of the wish for fusion and of the fear of bodily disintegration. On the last day of the therapy that year, permitting for the first time since the above session, a discussion of the impending separation, she asked "Will I be the same Cathy Ruth J. when you are away?"

On her return the following fall, an enlarged school setting faced her with a conscious dilemma. She could no longer blot out the other children and their expression of emotions, and these particularly frightened her. She knew her own emotions were overwhelming, and as often expressed in the past, was never sure that any one feeling would ever stop. Her response was to imitate the voice, movements, and various other behaviours of her classmates, with the idea that the imitation would be real but as her own creation, manageable, and thus she could relate to the other children and control their responses as well as her own, Strikingly, instead of the stereotyped voice inflections and uncoordinated facial expressions and body movements other severely disturbed children adopt in response to potential affect, Cathy became apparently many different bodies, voices, and facial expressions. She practiced before the mirror, became dissatisfied, and then asked both therapist and mother to demonstrate the appropriate facial expressions for various emotions and situations, which she could then copy and use. At one point, she interrupted her practicing to paint her arms the color of the mother's favorite dress, and thus attired, resumed work. The result was a facade of strangely mannered but fairly accurate renditions of a variety of affects. However, although she became adept at matching affect with gesture and "face," these creations were recognized by the child as failures—or, in her own words, "Why don't I have a real friend?" Nonetheless, this imitative, as-if personality was impervious to interpretation, and comments or references to the behaviour were so vigorously fought off that efforts to understand, empathize, and interpret were postponed.

To summarize another portion of the therapy of this period, in bringing the child to a relationship with mother and therapist, certain aspects of the transference, particularly the idealization of the maternal figures and the exhibitionism, the beautiful, talented precocious child, were only sparsely analyzed. The idealized self became another portion of the as-if state, and appeared in the transference during the fourth year of treatment.

At age nine, Cathy began her fourth year of treatment, still driven by her sexual conflicts. She asked endless questions about anatomy, mating, and birth in an attempt to master her feelings. She remembered, as did the mother, several observations of parental sexual intercourse, and drew these scenes in great detail. The questions to the therapist were: Do you take your nightgown off?" "Do you keep the covers on?"—bringing the voyeuristic exhibitionistic focus in the forefront. "Do you do it every night?" she asked, indicating her nightly struggle with masturbation. Her drawings again showed people with grossly elongated middle fingers, and people mutilated, the punishment for masturbation. At home, what would start as a wish to be either physically or emotionally close to her father could not be contained; she had fantasies of intercourse with him during which she was injured, and the wish was quite conscious. Again, in the treatment situation, these wishes took on hallucinatory reality, as in a session when her excitement culminated in the belief in a sensory experience, namely that she was having a nosebleed. As expected, this was dealt with by projection and the belief that the mother wanted her injured and killed. In the midst of these preoccupations, she once again demanded to learn the forms of social behaviour from the therapist. She again became involved with the differences between truth and falsehood, real appearances as opposed to the "happy face"—the latter a demand from the distant past that the mother had made both of herself and the child. By now, however, the imitation varied between an as-if defense and a yearning for identification with a separate and admired individual, the therapist, perceived as a beautiful golden-haired woman. In addition, the imitation of this period contained evidence of superego conflict—the copied happy face is false in the additional sense that the maternal figure in the transference is hated as well as admired.

In the final year of therapy, the child's anxiety was manifested in an effort to find out what she, Cathy, should be in order to elicit the therapist's admiration. She still presented a facade, the result of efforts of imitation and integration, that was perceived as peculiar, exaggerated, and hollow—to us—an as-if personality. It was felt, however, that Cathy had gained sufficient strength to deny her the borrowed personality and to interpret the defense. In response to a tentative introduction of this approach, she reenacted those images that had previously brought her admiration: the imaginative child, the artist, the performer, the patient concerned with sexual problems, the polite and correct child. Her initial reaction to interpretation was terror, and a return to catatonic posing, but this time of such grotesque form that it could only be understood as a depiction of an image of the destroyed and destructive self.

The as-if mechanism seemed to be Cathy's protection against impulses and emotions that, arising in ordinary situations, rapidly became extreme, fearfully unending, and finally—in fantasy—destructive. For instance, she finally expressed jealousy of the therapist:

"You won't tell me about your private life. You won't tell me what your house and furniture look like. If you're Mrs. Blank, you must have a Mr. Blank. You don't understand because you always know where you are." Regression and primitive defenses followed rapidly, and the anger and betrayal were projected. In Cathy's fantasy, the therapist alone would have the only beautiful voice. She, Cathy, would then attack, take out all the therapist's blood and drink it, but the blood would then hurt her. Oh no, now she remembered, her tongue was cut out. Not only could she not have a beautiful voice, but she could not commit the destructive acts. Her face would show her emotions; with her tongue cut out, she is the voiceless replication of the therapist and no one would be hurt.

This ambivalence in the transference was related to her struggle over masturbation. The therapist was the good nurse who fed her, and then the bad nurse who spanked her and kept her in bed at night. Then Cathy decided that both she and the therapist—the latter as both good and bad nurses—must sit imprisoned on a rock over water teaming with witches. If princes could vanquish the witches, the two of them would live. If the witches won out, they would die. The two of them together, experiencing the same dangers, seemed to us to represent a lessening in the extreme cruelty of her superego, plus a basis for empathy and genuine identification. The importance of this good maternal figure and the capacity for maintaining a relationship to a love object was such that Cathy was willing not only to control her impulses but to give them up in order to keep the good kind therapist. One solution consequently, was to give up men entirely, or as she explained, the therapist must be bored by her stories about Chris, a boy in school, so that they now could consider that there were only two people left to talk about, herself and the therapist.

However, as Cathy came to be fully aware of the actual relationship between the adult therapist trying to help her and the sick child driven by her wishes and fears, her relative helplessness became terrifying. The therapist was to play a devil; if the devil caught her, she, Cathy, would die, but if Cathy let go of the devil, she would also die. Occasionally and fleetingly, Cathy experienced her conflicts as fully internal, which again frightened her., Hollowly and without affect, she said one time, "I'm sorry for you. You're such a good therapist and I don't try hard enough."

At this point in time, the child told a story, expressing in a creative way, with a deliberate use of symbol and metaphor, her understanding of what had been happening in her life, past and present, She said that she was "like Helen Keller, who was loved by her parents like a little dog. Then Anne Sullivan came, a woman who understood Helen since she herself was half-blind and had had a terrible childhood. Ann decided that the child had had too much pity, that she was intelligent, and could learn. "Before the teacher came," Cathy explained, "Helen had been lonely. She had to feel the mouths of people talking. She thought, 'Why won't they play with me?' But then, and it's no wonder, she had tantrums and kicked and screamed. Still, if she could and she did, make the same mouth movements, who would she be? The little dog? No one? Not herself and no one's friend." In association, Cathy said, "Sometimes parents do cruel things to children without realizing it. Spankings aren't cruel. It is cruel when a child approaches a parent and the parent holds out her hand to stop you from touching her, and then she takes the child to its room."

The last half of this final year of therapy brought external stress into the treatment of this child. The Masters' Center was to close in June after a prolonged effort by parents and staff to retain public funding—an effort of which Cathy was aware. Soon after the New

Year. Cathy had to enter another new school. She was terrified by the complex social situations, by the sheer volume of children and their aggressive movements, and responded by standing in the stairway in rigid postures or by clinging tightly to adults. The failures all around her reactivated the wish and demand that the therapist be all-powerful and save her like a princess in a tower from the frightening prisons of home and school. However, the memories of her realities flooded her, and she saw the therapist as well as herself as weak and worthless. Perhaps, if the therapist curled her hair and she, Cathy, looked prettier, school and home would be more appreciative. However, as these illusions were not sufficient, the demands became impossible and fantastic, that the therapist make her able to fly and to fly away. A disguised return of the shoe fetish was expressed in the only wish she had in the world: a wish for a pair of high-buttoned antique shoes of very particular design. When these could not be found, she raged, but then settled on having the therapist sew her a pair of high buttoned shoes out of flannel. During these sessions, Cathy would sit silently, reading one of her own book, occasionally glancing up to watch the therapist sew, and cutting off all comments with, "Don't talk." The shoes, as omnipotent phallus, were also clearly a bridge between her and the maternal figure, the good maternal figure whom she feared would be lost in the destructive atmosphere. Only when the therapist tried a shoe on her foot for fit did Cathy relax briefly in the physical closeness. To recognize that any of her problems were internal, or especially that her difficulties with her parents, who were now both depressed and demanding, were real, made her feel too unhappy, too helpless, vulnerable, separate, disillusioned, and disappointed, and she withdrew, spending her sessions reading, often not in the same room with the therapist, often not hearing the bell ring when the mother came to pick her up, and refusing to open the door herself.

The therapist broke into this new—and we felt disadvantageous—situation at termination, by a strong statement of the reality: namely, that Cathy was trying to say that they had no relationship and that she, the therapist, could not continue to act as part of that belief. Cathy was living out a fantasy of despair and using her parents' scolding to support it. She was playing that she as being abandoned by her real mother rather than acknowledge her hurt and disappointment, She was warding this off by becoming cold and dead, more cold and dead than she wished those on the outside to be. The child responded by confirming the interpretation, but then revealed that the therapist had not recognized that an old kind of attempted solution was present, the as-if personality. She said, "I am not like other 10-year-olds. I am unordinary. I cannot feel. I can only copy. That is what I have been doing in my head. That is also part of it. My mother doesn't know what to do next."

The termination, it should be said, also meant for Cathy a change such as she had experienced many times in her life, namely that the family would be moving a very great distance away. She produced a fantasy of a girl named Glass Slipper who loses the maid she loves because her mother, conceited and strict, does not want her to play with grown-ups. Her mother dies, and robbers come to kill Glass Slipper as they stupidly think *she* is guilty of her mother's death. In punishment, the robbers are taken to prison far away where they have clean air—a parental description of the future family home, Some of the latent content included the warding off of the pain of loss. Her own destructive feelings are projected into the form of robbers who are taken away, but also taken home. The libidinal attachment to the mother was now much stronger, as it was to the therapist. The analysis proceeded and a painful mourning reaction took place Also, she was realistic about herself and her parents as she had not been before, She talked about yearning for a boy in her old school whom she would like to see again before leaving. However, she thought her mother would not want her to do that. As she described the closeness she wanted with this boy, the analyst was able to focus upon the feeling that she had expressed before of the mother who holds out her hand to prevent contact, and then takes the child to its room, Cathy wept and said, "1 have to work it out. I have felt pushed away, and many times I have been pushed away. Some of it is my fault, when I get so angry, But not being yourself doesn't help." In the very last weeks of the therapy, the fears of robbers and whirlwinds reappeared, behind which was the belief that the world was too dangerous, that the only safe place was with the therapist forever, whatever the therapist wished her to be she would be. However, in the main, they were able to think over the time they had spent together, sadly, and yet with the feeling that the therapist had a real and separate existence that would continue, and that Cathy could thus remember her, as the therapist would remember Cathy.

Very briefly, as I understand this case, the as-if state not a deficiency or defect In the ego of this child, but rather a defense against overwhelming stimuli, and was on a line of development from the posing, in that it is a partial return to a lack of differentiation of the self from the object via incorporation—an attempt to blur the differences. However, in contrast to the earlier period of posing, the sense of reality in regard to the human object was never fully lost in this personality organization. Although the as-if mechanism was used as a defense, it was also an important part of a primitive mode of learning, evolving, perhaps, into a higher level of functioning, but never fully integrated in this child, as the capacity to empathize with another human being.

In conclusion, I hope I have illustrated the emergence of this child from the chaos of psychosis, and the pain and fright some children experience in becoming separate individuals.

CHAPTER 23

Observations on Research Regarding the Symbiotic Syndrome of Infantile Psychosis

With Margaret Mahler M.D.
(1960). *Psychoanalytic Quarterly* (29):317-327

Presented at the Pan American Medical Congress, Section on Child Psychiatry, Mexico City, Mexico, in May 1960.

This research is supported by a grant from the United States Public Health Service and is conducted at the Masters Children's Center, New York City.

Our previous work has resulted in the hypotheses that children pass through a 'normal-autistic', a symbiotic, and a 'separation-individuation' phase of development. We postulate that in the normal autistic phase, the infant has not yet become aware of anything beyond his own body. In the symbiotic phase, the infant seems to become vaguely aware of need-satisfaction from the outside, but the mother is still a part of his own self-representation: the infant's mental image is fused with that of his mother. In the third phase, the infant gradually becomes aware of his separateness; first, the separateness of his body, then gradually the identity of his self. He subsequently establishes the boundaries of his self.[1] We have postulated in previous papers that the primarily autistic-psychotic child has never developed beyond the autistic phase, whereas the symbiotic-psychotic child has regressed from the challenge of separate functioning at the onset or during the separation-individuation phase into a symbiotic-parasitic, panic-ridden state. As states of panic are unbearable for any organism, the child's very survival requires further defensive regression. We therefore find that many, if not all, primarily symbiotic children secondarily resort to autistic mechanisms.

Our first therapeutic endeavor in both types of infantile psychosis is to engage the child in a 'corrective symbiotic experience'.[2] This most essential step requires a long period of time to achieve and to consolidate, and a still longer interval elapses before the higher levels of personality development, beginning with the separation-individuation phase, are attained.

To achieve this goal we had at our disposal, and at first could not help but use, the existing methods of approach to the treatment of psychotic children within conventional institutions, all of which routinely entail exposure of the preschool psychotic child to group situations. Our experience with these facilities convinced us that premature efforts to expose such children to group situations which interfered with or diluted the corrective symbiotic experience by subjecting them to any kind of social situations, even in the most

---

1 In another research project, supported by a grant from the Field Foundation, we are engaged in studying the individuation phase of normal twelve- to thirty-six-month-old infants in the presence of their mothers.

2 'Corrective' is not used by us to indicate a manipulative kind of intervention. By promoting the re-experiencing of early stages of development, the child should be enabled to reach a higher level of object relationship. We arrived at calling this approach 'corrective symbiotic experience' by comparing it with Dr. Augusta Alpert's research on 'corrective object relationship', conducted at the Child Development Center.

carefully planned therapeutic nursery, were harmful. Not only was progress impeded but in many instances there were detrimental traumatic effects.

One boy, for example, who was referred for private treatment at the age of four and a half as a case of infantile psychosis, promptly developed a symbiotic attachment to the therapist. This child, S, was given a thorough preliminary examination as an inpatient in an academic center. During the psychological testing it was readily observed that he responded best to bodily affection. In fact, in the course of treatment his need for bodily contact, which he could provide for himself either only very passively or very violently, was continually in evidence. Before referral the psychologist noted: 'It may be of interest that S's highest level of success occurred when he was being caressed by patting or stroking on the head and shoulders; he was given this demonstration of affection because he seemed to be entirely impervious to vocal expressions of praise and encouragement'. His selective awareness of emotional situations was demonstrated by his correctly noting in a picture of the test that a child depicted with his mother was crying.

S responded rather unspecifically but very well to any exclusive relationship with an adult. In fact he loved to have two or more adults concentrate on him simultaneously. However, he clearly showed anger or proneness to tantrums if the adults excluded him by talking with each other. When his mother talked on the telephone, he would deliberately take apart one of his toys and yell, 'Fix it, fix it!'. He was fascinated by his baby cousin and imitated the baby talk, thus showing us the way he wanted to be treated.

This child's mother was, unfortunately, a very rigid and proper lady who, though loving her child very much in her own way and consciously ready to make any sacrifice for him, could not provide the warmth he needed. The child's father had abandoned them on S's first birthday. The mother could not tolerate her child's bizarre behavior, particularly in public. She talked with him almost exclusively on a rather adult level, despite her awareness that what she said had very limited meaning for him. She could not give him any tender physical affection. She was probably not capable of it. Gravely deficient in adequate self-esteem herself, the child was for her a conspicuous proof of her worthlessness and social inacceptability.

After a few months of treatment it became apparent that four hours weekly therapy in the office was not adequate for the child or the mother. The concentrated, partly symbiotic-parasitic, partly autistic atmosphere of an exclusive living arrangement of mother and child in a small furnished room needed to be counterbalanced; furthermore, the mother felt keenly that some more formal learning situation with other children should be provided for her child. We succeeded in having S accepted in a small nursery school. He behaved there as we had expected; not as a participant in the group but as a tangential appendage. Even this was possible only because his mother remained passively by and the school staff was most patient and helpfully understanding. He did not profit either socially or intellectually during the months he was patiently tolerated there, despite the fact that in the therapeutic relationship he made definite progress.

At the end of the school year the teacher's report stated: 'S does not participate in most of the activities of the class. He seldom talks to children or adults, but frequently communicates by sound and action rather than words. When he does talk, and this is when *one* teacher has time to be with him, he shows particular interest in trains and book illustrations, etc.'

S grew especially tall for his age and as it was impossible to keep him in the nursery, he was transferred to a kindergarten when he was five-and-a-half years old. In kindergarten his panic and tantrums instantly recurred. He had catastrophic reactions to the situation, especially as his mother was not permitted to remain with him. She was asked within a few days to withdraw him. This failure upset her more than all the other signs and proofs which should have made her aware of the gravity of the child's mental illness.

A few weeks later special tutoring was provided for S. Again, in this exclusive one-to-one relationship he made progress in a characteristic, peculiarly unspecific symbiotic experience, just as he had in the therapeutic relationship. With the help of the tutor and of the therapist, his tendency to autistic withdrawal diminished. His courage to test reality increased, as did his vocabulary and his perception of the outside world. For the first time in his life this child displayed fondness for such soft, transitional objects as pillows and toy animals. These now served—as they had not before—to allay his anxieties and tensions. He surrounded himself with these transitional objects, particularly at night, and relived early stages of babyhood in a more normal way.

Again we made the mistake of enrolling him in a group, this time in our pilot project, in what we thought was a particularly sheltered learning situation in a special therapeutic nursery group. S was bewildered but made, we thought, an initial adaptation because he shared the teacher with only one other child. His distress soon became apparent when a few more children joined the group. We were still inclined to attribute a rapid regression in his speech and in other areas of his functioning to measles he had contracted near the end of the school year. But when after a fairly good summer at the seashore he rejoined the group, his ego threatened rapidly to disintegrate. In uncontrollable panic and rage he violently attacked his mother and teachers. His speech became unintelligible, and he seemed to hallucinate.

This much of S's case is presented to demonstrate that in all situations this child desperately craved and violently demanded exclusive symbiotic possession of an adult. He repeatedly retreated after severe tantrums into lethargic states of hallucinatory withdrawal whenever he could not be given the exclusive attention of an adult to the extent that his fragmented ego craved and needed.

The last of numerous similar experiences which led us to abandon the therapeutic nursery design for psychotic preschool children was the case of a four-year-old psychotic child who had been placed in a smoothly organized group of five disturbed but not psychotic children with two teachers. When P arrived at the therapeutic nursery school, she appeared to be a serenely beautiful child. She quickly became extremely restless, sought constantly to find her mother, and then roamed through the building, followed by the teacher who had to leave the other children and go after her. The teacher learned that by rocking her and other devices she could induce P to remain in the room with the other children, to whom the child paid absolutely no attention. In her relationship to the adult, for P there were only two alternatives: either in a phase of autistic withdrawal she used the teacher as an extension of her own body in order to control the environment with this executive external ego, or there was a clinging, burrowing type of behavior during which the teacher had to focus her attention completely on P, lest she have a panic-tantrum. It became apparent that to keep the child at this higher level of relationship, the teacher had to abandon her duties to the other children. The child's behavior demanded an exclusive relationship with the teacher; any demand for the teacher's attention by the group was increasingly deleterious to her.

For a while we continued to believe that the deleterious effect of the group on P was due primarily to the fact that she was a case of early infantile autism, particularly vulnerable as she began to attain a symbiotic relationship. When we saw the process occurring with still another, a symbiotic-psychotic child, we realized that a revised research had to be designed for all cases of infantile psychosis. Our hypotheses about psychosis had already indicated this from a theoretical point of view.

That there was a conflict in P's mind about her growing attachment to the teacher and her relationship to her mother was apparent, for example, whenever she was hurt. She would run to and from the door leading to her mother, and then back to the teacher until finally she rubbed the injured part against the teacher's body. What was most amazing was that as the child's conflict mounted and she ran to seek her mother, the mother was increasingly difficult to find in the building. The mother was, in fact, almost consciously trying to avoid her child as the child became more demanding and expressive. These changes in P made the mother so anxious that she became angry with the child's therapist.

From this case we recognized another important factor in revising therapy and research. The revised design would not involve the child with other children in a group situation before he is ready for it. The two cases described and many others like them made it clear that to provide the psychotic child's need for protection within the corrective symbiotic experience must be the basis for treatment. The child's development from autistic withdrawal toward primitive, unspecific clinging to the therapist as well as to the mother gave us another significant clue for the revision of our research design. We had repeatedly observed that the presence of the mother within the therapeutic situation was not only very well tolerated but that it was a sign of progress when a mother was sought by her psychotic child. The mother's presence proved, furthermore, to be most helpful to our understanding of the child's 'signal communications' throughout treatment. In our experience, even though the mothers were not able to fulfil these children's needs, they understood their own child's nonverbal communications to a surprising degree.

It was evident that these considerations were not only of theoretical importance but that they indicated the direction which must be taken for the immediate treatment and for optimal future planning for the psychotic child's mental health. We evolved from this a method of research in which the mother, the child, and the worker are present in the room during the sessions, which extend from two to three hours, the mother and worker collaborating in the rehabilitation of the psychotic child.

The advantages of this design are manifold. Our initial understanding of the child comes not only through observations but also through information and explanations given by the mother. By this method there can be mutual exchanges of information and understanding between the child's therapist, the supervising psychiatrist, and the mother, as the child's behavior is being observed by all three. The mother is first gratified by our interest, and then heartened by the feeling she gradually acquires that someone believes her child can be helped. There also appears to be a great sense of relief produced by the understanding, initially intellectual, which the mother gains. She may, and often does use it defensively, but it gives her the feeling that some possible control can be exerted over what previously had been to her a desperate, hopeless, and uncontrollable problem.

The information the mother gives us enables the therapist to institute those procedures which seem to foster the development of the need-satisfying symbiotic relationship between the child and the worker. In the beginning, for example, a signal type of communication has to be fostered between the child and the worker, which can later be used by the worker in a corrective manner. A four-year-old boy, M, frequently rolled a toy car to and fro. The mother explained to us that this indicated he had to urinate. We had discovered from our observations that he also meant by this action that there was something wrong with the car; that it was broken. We learned, moreover, that this activity, which we took as a signal of his bodily need, occurred after many hours of withholding his urine, to the point where he was in pain and probably afraid that he could no longer withhold. We then understood these signals to mean that he was afraid of being overwhelmed by these inner bodily stimuli. Our therapeutic procedure was to respond to this signal as a mother would to an infant, that is, as an auxiliary ego which we hope the child can add to his own ego, thereby overcoming otherwise overwhelming anxieties. Instead, therefore, of interpreting the displacement and anxiety, the therapist tells the boy that he will feel very good when he goes to the toilet and that she will help him. She takes him with her to the toilet, encouraging him to urinate, and expressing her pleasure and admiration when he does. In this way we believe we have begun to liberate the child from the feeling of being the passive victim of bodily discomforts and discharges, and with this help he may proceed to independently active functioning.

In general the new design allows for the development of a more and more specific relationship with the therapist without interference from other children. The development of the child's relationship to the worker, which always brings with it changes in the relationship with the mother, can be observed directly, and the frequently occurring defeatist attitudes of the family counteracted. With the emergence from autism, and the achievement of a higher level of behavior, the patience of these children's families is often greatly taxed. The endlessly repetitive banging of doors, throwing of objects, switching off and on of lights, often generate uncontrollable hostility within the family, and sometimes lead to ill-considered placement of the child away from home.

After M became better able to comply when he was encouraged to urinate, he began to spit in an uncontrollable way. He first spat at his therapist, and soon at his mother. His mother reprimanded him for it, and he withdrew into his autistic shell. We had learned that the child's disturbance of urinary functioning had occurred as a consequence of the mother's disgust at finding that he urinated into the bathtub instead of the toilet. Had the spitting happened at home as an extension of the child's behavior in the therapeutic situation, this mother might well have reacted, as had P's mother, with hostility. But M's mother had been made a member of the 'therapeutic alliance', and the simple explanation she was given of the beneficial value of M's transient regressive behavior made sense to her. She had, in fact, previously reported in the course of the therapy that M had begun at home to invite her to exchange babbling and cooing sounds with him. The mother spontaneously expressed her opinion that he seemed belatedly to be permitting himself indulgences of babyhood which—in contrast to his brothers—he had missed completely. Observing the way the therapist handled the situation gave the mother a security of feeling, a way of understanding, a model for helping her child.

Such experiences with the example and help of the child's therapist, the supervising psychiatrist, and the social worker become assimilated in time if the mother herself is capable of learning and of providing the additional and essential corrective symbiotic experience for the child. Why the spitting developed in the case of M could be directly explained to the boy's mother by the worker, by the psychiatrist, and subsequently more fully gone into by the social worker. Whatever deeper fears and defenses might be involved in her reaction, the mother's immediate response to the child—and this is always partly dictated by unconscious forces—is opposed by her conscious determination, aided by her understanding and the example given to her by the team. This kind of therapeutic help for the mother of the psychotic child is consistent with our theory that the treatment of the child must extend over many years of the child's life and that his development must be re-experienced and relived, not only with the therapist but with the primary love object. The mother, therefore, must be trained to assume and maintain the corrective symbiotic experience developed by the therapist. This emotional-intellectual learning is stabilized by the mother's individual sessions with the supervising psychiatrist and the social worker.

In this method we believe we have evolved a mother-child-therapist unit, supervised by a male child psychiatrist, which can result in the development of the personality instead of in fixation at the stage of the psychosis. It is interesting and disquieting that it took us so many years to arrive at these inevitable conclusions and to apply their logical requirements in therapeutic research. They were inherent from the start in our theoretical hypotheses of autistic and symbiotic psychosis. Gradually, tardily, and retrospectively we came to these conclusions from clinical data which abundantly demonstrated that failures ensued whenever the corrective symbiotic relationship was threatened by disruption—as it too frequently was when we adhered to traditional methods.

The crucial therapeutic problem in psychosis remains the same. The psychotic child must be kept from retreating into the autistic defensive position. He must be enticed into and be encouraged to relive a more fully gratifying—albeit still regressive—exclusively symbiotic-parasitic relationship with a substitute mother. This relationship is made liberally available to the child for whom it becomes a buffer in the process of dissolution of the vicious cycle of the distorted relationship with the mother. Gradually and cautiously the child is then helped to develop some autonomous substitutes for the pathological primitive regressive demands exacted from the pathologically defensive and ambivalent mother. In this manner the child is led to discover the boundaries of his self, and to experience a sense of himself as a separate entity in his environment.

In the treatment of primarily symbiotic or primarily autistic children, a contradiction sometimes confuses workers in the field. Although these infants seem insatiable in their need for the passively available symbiotic partner, their symbiotic claim is at first not at all specific. Several adults are well tolerated and often simultaneously enjoyed. But at first, and for a long time, they are utterly intolerant of any type of group relationship involving other children, even the most carefully devised ones. Only the most important symbiotic partner who seals herself off as completely as possible with the child can form for him that insulating layer against the give-and-take aspects of social group situations for which he has no capacity or tolerance during the period described. Only after a prolonged period of corrective symbiotic experience should the psychotic child be given carefully graduated dosages of rhythmic play—preferably to the accompaniment of soothing music—in which the symbiotic partner is right at the side of the child. In the course of the therapeutic research, we carefully watch the preferences of these children as they slowly evolve interest and reach out for association with the other children treated at the Center. They show us unmistakably when they are ready for such social learning; also how much of it they can take.

CHAPTER 24

Studies of the Separation-Individuation Phase
A Methodological Overview

(1963). *Psychoanalytic Study of the Child*, (18):325–342.

Fred Pine Ph.D.

This work is being conducted at the Masters Children's Center, 75 Horatio Street, New York, NY 10014. The work with the symbiotic psychotic children has been supported by a grant from the National Institute of Mental Health, USPHS (Project M-3353, Margaret S. Mahler, M.D. and Manuel Furer, M.D., Principal Investigators). Funds making possible the study of normal children, and their comparison with the psychotic children, were generously provided by the Psychoanalytic Research and Development Fund, the Taconic Foundation, the National Association for Mental Health, and, earlier, by the Field Foundation.

Dr. Pine is, since September 1962, at the Psychology Laboratory, Department of Psychiatry, State University of New York, Downstate Medical Center, Brooklyn, NY.
Dr. Furer is Medical Director, Masters Children's Center.

Some time ago, Mahler (1952) advanced the hypothesis that in certain predisposed children the maturational spurt of locomotion and other autonomous ego functions, with a concomitant lag in emotional readiness for functioning separately from the mother, causes organismic panic. This panic is followed by arrest in ego development and fragmentation of the ego and eventuates in the clinical picture of symbiotic child psychosis. In later writings, Mahler (1957), (1958); (Mahler, Furer, and Settlage, 1959) has suggested that there is a *normal* and *universal* separation-individuation phase in childhood that confronts every child with certain potential crises. But, in contrast to the symbiotic psychotic child, the normal toddler has an amazing capacity "to extract contact supplies and participation from mother" (Mahler, 1963) while growing away from the symbiosis with her, and thus usually to deal with these crises effectively.

Earlier studies of separation of infant from mother (e.g., Spitz, 1945), (1946a), (1946b) had indicated the traumatic force of certain separation experiences and their disturbing effects on personality development. This work had focused primarily on a particular kind of separation experience: the infant was physically separated from the mother, often for long periods, for reasons beyond the infant's control. The child was passive in relation to the separation. The present study, in contrast, attempts to define a separation process in which the child plays a more active role, a process that is a prerequisite for normal development. The normal separation individuation process involves *the child's achievement* of separate functioning *in the presence of the mother* while the child is continually confronted with *minimal* threats of object loss. In contrast to situations of traumatic separation, this normal separation-individuation process takes place in the setting of a developmental readiness for and pleasure in independent functioning made possible by the continual libidinal availability of the mother (Mahler, 1963). Separation and individuation are conceived of as two complementary developments—the one consisting of the child's emergence from a symbiotic fusion with the mother (cf. Mahler, 1952) and the other consisting of those achievements marking the child's assumption of his own individual characteristics.

We currently have two interrelated research projects in process at the Masters Children's Center in New York City, each bearing on the separation individuation phase. The first is a study of the natural history of symbiotic child psychosis. Mahler has attempted to illustrate the failure of these children to meet the developmental crises of the separation-individuation phase (e.g., 1952), (1961). The second project is a study of normal toddlers from six months of age through the third year, the general age period of the separation individuation phase. Thus, the over-all research is set up so that we can study two groups of children: (1) toddlers who are presumably going through the separation-individuation phase normally, and (2) symbiotic psychotic children (from three to five years of age) in whom something presumably went awry during this same phase. The present paper will describe the general methodology of the study in relation to the issues under investigation.

Historically, the work began with studies of symbiotic psychotic children and led to hypotheses about events presumed to have taken place during the separation-individuation phase. It then seemed wise to take a firsthand look at these events as they occur normally. This led into the study of the normal toddlers. One of the broad issues that we were interested in investigating was the relation between the separation individuation process, the development of ego functions in the setting of particular mother-child relationships, and the psychosexual stages of early development.

While, historically, the psychotic children were studied first, at present the work with the two groups of children shows a good deal of interchange back and forth. For example, at an earlier period we became interested in the preferred modalities of communication between the individuating child and his mother. In the study of symbiotic psychosis, gaps in the communication process wherein mother and child could not respond to each other's signals and cues —a "communicative mismatching"—were a recurrent phenomenon. This led us to turn to intensive observation of the process of signaling and cueing between mother and child in the normal toddlers. The richly varied material that we gathered in that study brought into focus the crucial importance of mother child intercommunication for the *successful achievement* of normal individuation. This in turn highlighted the possible importance of communication failures in the development of the psychosis as well as in the symptom picture.

As we conceive of it now, the cues and signals between mother and child are particularly important for the resolution of the normal crises of the separation individuation phase. The very young child can sustain some degree of separation from his mother only if he is able to come into contact and communication with her when he needs it. This requires an increasingly complex and finely differentiated set of interactions between mother and child so that they can keep in close communication with each other even while the child becomes more and more of a separate individual.

We are now in a position to observe the normal limits of the misperception of cues in our normal mother-toddler group and the more extreme distortions in the psychotic group. It is certainly true that the normal mothers can more readily "read" their children than can the mothers of the symbiotic psychotic children, and that the normal children are easier to read. But there are similarities, some perhaps even more important, between the psychotic children and normal toddlers as well—for example, prior to speech development in the normal toddlers, communication in both is of course nonverbal.

And it is also true that there is some communicative mismatching even in these normal mother-child pairs, though it does not reach such proportions or such rigidity that mother and child cannot adapt to each other's mode of signaling and responding. The limits of the normal range of such communication failures requires a good deal of further study.

Setting and General Method

At present, in our therapeutic work with the symbiotic psychotic children, each child is seen together with his mother by a therapist, the three together in the same room. Each child-mother pair is seen from three to five days a week in sessions that range from one and a half to two hours. The purpose of our seeing mother and child together was indicated in a general way by Mahler and Furer in an earlier paper (1960). While the overwhelming symbiotic needs of these children make it necessary for them to have an intimate and personal tie with a single adult, this tie must ultimately be to the mother with whom, in contrast to the therapist, they must sustain a lifelong relationship. But the tie to the mother is often best effected through the therapist. There are phases in the treatment when the child's symbiotic demands are heightened to a degree not readily accepted by most mothers, especially from these children who are no longer infants, and the therapist must absorb some of these demands, help the child to relive (and to develop beyond) the symbiotic phase, and to form an attachment to the mother to which she can respond. While the children are, as noted, typically seen together with mother and therapist in a single room, this is not always the case. Certain clinical considerations supervene from time to time so that we must see the child without the mother. These include the emotional readiness of the mother to receive and respond to emerging demands for contact from the child and her capacity to understand and integrate interpretations that have to be given to the child.

Our material on the symbiotic psychotic children derives from the following sources: (a) daily reports of the therapists; (b) reports of the supervising psychiatrists (including reports of weekly interviews with the mother, observations of the child, and weekly conferences with the therapist); (c) reports of the social worker about her weekly or twice weekly interviews with the mother, and with the father in special instances when changing intrafamilial dynamics requires that he be seen; (d) monthly summaries concerning the therapeutic progress of the mother-child pair as well as the parents' progress; (e) minutes of the weekly clinical conferences. In addition, we have nonparticipant observations and psychological test reports of the children and their mothers. At weekly research meetings this material is evaluated and areas for further investigation are sorted out.

The work with the normal toddlers takes place in a playroom setting where a group of babies and their mothers are free to talk, play, and interact as they please. We want, and have apparently succeeded in creating, a situation where the spontaneous day-to-day relationship of mother to child can be observed in a natural setting. The playroom has a smaller area reserved as a sitting room for the mothers, in which they chat, sip coffee or read—and from which they have a full view of and free access to the children. There is another large area that has many attractive and colorful toys, and the children tend to move back and forth freely between the toy area, the section where the mothers generally sit, and all other parts of the room. The mother-child separation is by no means complete in the physical arrangements of the room; it is quite unlike the school situation, e.g., where the mother gives over charge of her child to the teacher for a period. It is more like an outdoor playground setting where the children play where they please while the mothers sit on benches and talk—with their children in full view and with the opportunity to attend to whatever mothering is required of them.

While there is no doubt that these mothers, who are aware that they are part of a research project, must, to some extent, be influenced in their behavior by such awareness, nonetheless we have been impressed by the great variety of seemingly quite natural behaviors that we have been able to observe. Indeed, with mothers and children seen for four mornings a week over a period of years and often with second (and even third) children, it would be hard to maintain that they show only a pose and an unrepresentative sample of their behavior with their children in the periods during which we observe them.

Our task in setting up the study of the normal toddlers was to obtain material comparable to that already obtained from the therapeutic action research program with the psychotic group. We therefore have psychoanalytically trained workers (each of whom participates now or has participated in the past in the therapy project) interview the mother of a normal toddler each week and observe the mother-toddler interaction. We have found that this procedure gives us valuable material even from these normal mothers who are not explicitly motivated by a need for treatment. As the material from these interviews has been studied in our research conferences, we have been able to focus our investigation on areas that are most comparable to the material from the treatment group.

We have material available from the notes of participant observers (the two toddler-group leaders) and from nonparticipant observers, from the interviews described above and from repeated testing of the children. This material, too, is discussed and assessed at out weekly research conferences and set in relationship to the material from the psychotic group.

Some Research Strategies

How to deal with the mass of data available? We have employed a variety of research strategies, attempting to explore in whatever way possible the issues under study. We have neither committed ourselves to the (soon apparent) impossibility of systematically treating all of the clinical data, nor have we limited ourselves to any too-discrete single mode of study that might blind us too much to that which may be of interest. We have used clinical approaches where seemingly appropriate—quantifiable approaches where workable—in each case varying and modifying our strategies where the phenomena or methodological difficulties required it.

Clinical Work

By far our greatest expenditure of time and effort has been in the observation of both the normal and the symbiotic psychotic children and their mothers, in attempts to formulate the dynamics of the mother's and the child's functioning and of their relationship to each other, and in minute and regular observations of developmental and therapeutic changes. The clinical observations, and the clinical research conferences based upon them, have been our major source thus far of new formulations. Through them we have come to learn of a pathological equilibrium of the symbiotic psychotic child and his mother (abandonment by the mother of her maternal commitment to the symbiotic demands of the child complemented by secondary autistic withdrawal by the child who then makes only minimal demands); and we have come to see, as described earlier, the communicative mismatching between the symbiotic psychotic child and his mother with each unable to respond to the other's cues, and the parallel misperception of cues within normal limits in the normal mother-toddler pairs; and we have come to see the significance for the normal mother of the increasing individuation of her child, an event requiring a developmental step in mother-hood wherein the mother must prepare herself for the coming separation of the child from his symbiotic tie to her (cf. Mahler, 1963); (Mahler and Furer, 1963).

The clinical explorations have thus far been highly productive of new, though untested hypotheses. Many of our formulations stem from observations that we did not anticipate in advance and that impressed themselves on us with particular clarity and force. We have tried to balance our approach to the data with more focused research strategies (see below), and the early clinical observations and discussions have provided a basis for developing some trial attempts at this in both the clinical and the quantitative work.

The clinical work confronts us with so many data on each child and each child/mother pair that we can barely cover the material in conferences, pin it down, and work with it, before new ideas are thrust forward by new clinical observations. And yet, at the same time, there are constant gaps in our information that prevent our following through more fully on specific hunches, and that require us continually to seek new modes of access to new information. One reason for the gaps in our information about the children is clear: we work in a research setting and not an analytic situation. While we are doing a good deal more than straightforward observation of natural life events, we do not get the kind of data in depth that are produced in psychoanalysis. Our research setting offers us certain distinct advantages, however. It permits us to see phenomena that are not ordinarily observable during analysis. We do not here get unconscious fantasies of the mother, but we do have a chance to see the mother-child relationship in actual process. This special situation of clinical observation leads us to special kinds of data and hypotheses. In addition, the fact that at least our normal mother-baby pairs are not in any formal treatment at the research project has the advantage that we do not essentially change the phenomena we are studying in the very act of studying them—at least not to the same extent that observation through psychoanalysis does this. These mothers are certainly a special group, but, so far as we can determine, their patterns of mothering do not basically change through their contact with us during the period that we study them, although certain developments and changes in their attitudes during the subphases of their infant-toddler's progress in the course of separation-individuation must be taken into account (Mahler, 1963); (Coleman, Kris, and Provence, 1953).

Because of the potential bias in the more open and impressionistic kinds of clinical work, and because of the presence both of floods of data and of gaps in what we do have, we are currently attempting more systematic modes of data collection within the general setting of the clinical work. We drew from our clinical notes and impressions a set of areas that seemed to us important to pursue further. Each interviewer and observer was then asked to amass data in these areas for each child and mother seen in both the normal and psychotic groups. Our hope is that the collection of these data in specified areas will simultaneously limit the clinical data at hand and give more complete coverage in these few areas.

The areas cover certain general points: (1) significant family events; (2) conspicuous aspects of the mother's behavior; (3) the child's relationship to his father—something that we do not ordinarily have the opportunity to see in process at the research center; (4) typical and exaggerated behavior of the child; and (5) differences between the child's behavior at home and at the research center. They also cover specific central aspects of the very young child's life: (6) feeding behavior; (7) toilet training; (8) discovery of the anatomical sexual difference; (9) separation anxiety and stranger anxiety; (10) imitative behavior; (11) speech development; and (12) the sleep pattern. Lastly, two additional areas of particular interest have emerged from our present and past work: (13) the child's and the mother's reaction to significant locomotor advances in the child; and (14) the mother's self-preparation for her child's separation from her as he grows older.

Our aim was to arrive from these data at formulations concerning the role in the separation-individuation process of certain commonly observed phenomena in very young children. Mahler's (1952) work on the role of locomotor advance in precipitating crises at this phase, and our comments earlier in this paper on the function of cueing and communication in maintaining mother-child contact while separation increases, are examples of this approach.

In the treatment of the symbiotic psychotic children some of our important advances in understanding have come where difficulties arose in the communication process between the child and his mother on the one hand and the research group on the other. Thus, it was a difficulty in making interpretations to certain of the psychotic children in the presence of their mothers that led us to see the need to keep the mother out of the therapy room at critical points in spite of our general conviction that her presence is necessary. And again, it was the withdrawal of certain children from treatment by the mothers that led us to see the pathological equilibrium of the mother child relationship described above; as the therapy freed the child to some extent from his secondary autistic withdrawal, and as he subsequently made renewed symbiotic demands upon the mother, the mother terminated the treatment.[1]

The problems which arise in the work with the normal mother-toddler pairs are somewhat different from those arising in the research with the symbiotic psychotic group. Here we have to tread a cautious line between having the mothers withdraw from the project in disinterest or fear (since they are volunteers, not coming for therapy, with no explicitly sought therapeutic gain in coming) and having them get too involved with the group leaders or with their interviewers, making demands that cannot be met in the nontherapy research setting. In actual fact, recently we have found the mothers to be quite committed to the group, deriving certain satisfactions from it (in terms of social contact in pleasant surroundings), and yet quite reticent and at times reluctant to give information in certain sensitive areas—a reticence that, in these persons who are not coming for treatment, we must learn to live with.

Behavior Ratings

As noted, the clinical observations and discussions provided a basis for some initial attempts at quantifiable approaches to the data. In our initial broad approach, all of the normal toddlers and their mothers as well as all of the symbiotic children and their mothers were at first observed and rated on a set of fifty-eight variables by nonparticipant

---

1 We can well understand the mother's plight when a child, now perhaps four or five years of age, makes the symbiotic demands for intimate physical contact and all absorbing attention more characteristic of infants, and ordinarily characteristic of only brief periods in the infant's day at that. It becomes imperative for the therapist to absorb some of this symbiotic claim so that the mother will not be overwhelmed by it.

observers working together in pairs. The variables were culled from earlier clinical notes. A series of three half-hour observations was made by a pair of raters on each child before they made a final rating of the child on each variable. The series of three observations was repeated at a later point when the child was several months older to make possible the assessment of developmental changes. Preliminary scanning of these ratings has shown excellent interrater reliability, and the preliminary analyses of the data suggest that the ratings pick up significant aspects of the individual mother-child interaction. Similar observations and ratings were initially being carried out with both groups of children so that comparisons would be possible, though this has since changed (see below).

What are the variables? One set has bearing on the development of object relationship: the child's reaction to his mother, to other adults, to other children, and to inanimate objects. This includes time spent with the mother, spatial position in relation to her, and preferred sensory modalities of communication between mother and child. We also study the amount and the quality of the mother's comforting and the child's receptiveness to it; the range of comforting behaviors available to the mother in her contacts with the child, and the degree of manipulativeness of her comforting. We study also the nature of the child's appeal to the mother for comforting, and the degree to which he can sustain this appeal in the face of delay by mother in providing it. In general, we are studying a variety of modes of approach and contact between mother and child for their bearing on the separation-individuation process. A second set of variables culled from our participant and nonparticipant observational notes and impressions relates to the development of ego functions which have for us some indicator value about the course of the separation-individuation process. This includes signaling-communication and motor functions.

The first of these bears on the communication processes necessary for maintaining contact between mother and child even as the child becomes increasingly separate from the mother. Our interest in the second (motor development) stems initially from Mahler's hypothesis about the rapid development of locomotion which, outpacing the child's emotional readiness for separation, may be the trigger that sets off the symbiotic psychotic fragmentation of the ego. Variables related to communicative activity include the development from autoerotic to communicative use of the mouth, and some developments in language. In the latter, we examine, for example, the specificity of the child's communications and the ways in which such communication is used to appeal to the mother. Motor behavior, too, is under study; and patterns of motility (in relation to separation from the mother), to mastery of the environment, to motor grace) are assessed.

All of these issues—in mother-child interaction and in the child's development—have been translated into specific descriptive categories that are currently being rated. For example, one item is entitled "focus in motor behavior." The rater is asked to decide whether a child's motor behavior is (1) typically wandering and rarely goal-directed, (2) slightly more wandering than goal-directed, (3) slightly more goal-directed than wandering, or (4) typically goal-directed and rarely wandering. Or, in another category, entitled "success in evoking maternal response," when the child wants or needs some response or satisfactory substitute from the mother, and when the mother does not seem instantly aware of the need, the rater is asked to decide whether the child (1) ably evokes a response every time, (2) can generally though not always evoke a response, (3) can rarely evoke a response, or (4) is unable to evoke a response and seems at a loss. The general plan in the analyses of these data is to assess individual patterns of mother-child relationships and to correlate these with particular patterns of the emergence of ego functions and of their integration in the child. To *illustrate* the nature of these data:[2] in preliminary analyses of the data for the normal mother-child pairs we find that those mothers who typically get no pleasure out of comforting their child tend, not surprisingly, to be manipulative in their efforts with the child; they also tend to respond only to the child's more explicit demands for comforting, ignoring the more subtle appeals that the child sends out. A second set of relationships in the rated variables suggests the following pattern: mothers who comfort in many different ways tend to use these diverse modes of comforting in ways that are related to *specific* needs of the child and when *the child* seems to need comforting. On the other side of the coin is a pattern where the mothers who have fewer kinds of comforting in their repertoire (*only* picking up, or *only* feeding, or *only* speaking, etc.) seem to comfort when *they* (not the child) feel the need for it, and in ways unrelated to the child's needs. A next step in the analysis of the data would be to study the relations of such patterns of mothering to the ego development of the child in the language, motor, and other rated areas. This will be done when all the data have been collected.

While this plan of study is being followed in general, a variety of complications have developed which bear consideration. This research strategy suffers from providing both too much and too little of the very specification and concreteness that the rating categories were designed to provide.

When we were initially faced with the problem of deciding how to collect comparable observations and descriptions on all of the children, we considered recording descriptions of certain kinds of

---

2 It should be emphasized that the relationships described here are illustrative only. They were suggested by analyses of data for the first few normal babies and mothers, but we do not yet know if they hold up for the total group.

behavior as they occurred, and then quantifying them in some way for comparative purposes. But it quickly became apparent that we needed more concrete specification of the "certain kinds" of behavior to be observed. And we ran into the problem of defining what were the units of a behavior sequence—when did it begin and end? Practically, collecting extensive descriptions that would later have to be codified and rated would have run us into time and financial demands not easily met. Hence we decided on the system described above—with *a priori* descriptions of behavior possibilities (drawn from our past observations and clinical experiences) and with direct rating of a child by a rater (by having the rater simply check off one of the *a priori* descriptions rather than record observed behavior in detail). We planned that the more descriptive material, lacking here, would come from the clinical work. But such *a priori* descriptions as were used in the categories at times did not quite fit any one child in the groups studied later. Raters would then force their ratings, often into the more innocuous categories, with the result that the categories did not always differentiate adequately among the children. In addition, some ratings within categories were simply too broad and included all of the cases, allowing no ratings of the other three positions in the scales.

On the other hand, the category descriptions were often not specific enough so that each rater would consider slightly different behaviors in making his ratings of a particular child. It has certainly become clear that, the more the rating categories are spelled out in terms of observable behaviors, the more rater consensus will there be. Thus, we found it considerably easier to work with descriptions of motor patterns than with inferences about the child's reaction to internal body processes or with the development of body image. Other more subtle and more tentative research approaches have to be developed for the study of the latter.

Midway through the collection of data we eliminated those categories which did not permit the raters to differentiate among the children and in which interrater reliability was low (i.e., when raters could not agree on what a child was like). Eliminating the poorest categories on these counts meant dropping out about one fourth of the original fifty-eight categories. We are currently working with the remainder.

The elimination of the poorer categories by no means solved all of our problems. The rapid developmental changes taking place in the normal toddlers created other problems for the behavior ratings with that group. We cannot take a picture of a child if he won't hold still. And hold still he won't. New developments are constantly taking place, and the variations from moment to moment even within the course of a day (say, with fatigue or hunger) are great. Moving pictures, yes; but a photograph, no. And yet the rating procedure is relatively static. It cannot show all of these moment-to-moment variations or the dynamics of change. We initiated more frequent observations and ratings (bimonthly, within the limits of our staff facilities), but even these give no more than a series of relatively static descriptions of the child, and we replaced them with continuing observations of specific behavior of interest to us.

If, in the clinical work, the processes of information-gathering and of discovery are temporally closely linked for the researcher, in these behavior ratings and subsequent correlational analyses the two are far apart. When ratings are collected for even a dozen children over a year or two, there is a long delay between any specific rating and the final correlational analyses carried out when all of the data are in. While, in some research settings, this delay need not be a problem, we have found it to be a major problem here because it makes it difficult to compare the quantitative findings with the clinical events at any specific moment. Our research, based, we had hoped, on a cross-fertilization between more clinical and more quantitative procedures, has not always had such cross-fertilization because of the delay required to carry through the formal research design. It is true that the clinical and quantitative data may mutually enrich each other at a later date, when all analyses are completed; but for the present we have been trying to bring the clinical and quantitative work closer together—through use of ratings in conjunction with clinical case studies, and currently through written descriptions of the observed phenomena on which ratings are based—with greater degrees of success.

Once again, as in the clinical work, some of our early findings with the behavior ratings were made where there was a break in the information-gathering process. Take, for example, the ratings of the several categories having to do with the child's appeals to his mother for aid and the mother's comforting of her child; the raters often found themselves unable to rate these categories as the babies in the normal group grew older because the relevant behaviors just were not observed—an indication of the not-surprising fact that at least the child's gross appeals to the mother (in a playgroup setting) and her comforting of him became less frequent as the child grows from late in the first year of life to late in the second year.

A considerably more problematic rating difficulty arose with the symbiotic psychotic children. Here, the rater (like the mothers in many instances) could not tell when (and if) the child was appealing to the mother or the therapist. How to interpret some of the stereotyped behavior patterns of the psychotic children? When as appeals? When as discharge phenomena? When as magical restitutive behavior? Or what? We have gradually come to see more clearly the need to decode specific behaviors in the psychotic children before relying on specific rating procedures for them. Problems such as these have made it necessary for us to go back to the clinical phenomena to refine the rating categories for these psychotic children, making them more fitting to the observed behaviors. We are no longer rating the psychotic children on the variables described above, but are instead attempting to discover just what variables can be rated.

Comparative Observations of the Children in the Mothers' Presence and Absence

Another avenue of study involved an experimental and observational procedure. The level of functioning of children in both groups was observed and evaluated when their mothers were present and when they were absent. We were interested in the extent to which certain achievements are maintained by the child in the mother's absence. In which children is ego functioning not impaired in the mother's absence, and in which areas? Here, with brief separations of the child from the mother, we hoped to study the dependence of the child's functioning on the physical presence of the mother.

We assessed six areas: play, attention span, understanding and use of language, and gross and fine motor skills. Raters were asked to judge whether the level of functioning in each of these areas is higher or lower in the mother's presence than in her absence, according to criteria that were spelled out in a rating manual. If such changes in functioning are found in the mother's absence, it still remains for us to draw on our clinical material to explain them. Developmental tests of the children in the toddler group were matched with these six areas so that we could explore the question whether those functions which the child has developed to a higher level are retained better in the mother's absence than are less fully mastered ego functions.

This work was initially set up in an attempt to create a relatively compact, and yet meaningful, experimental situation—varying only the presence of the mother and gauging changes in the child's reaction (presumably referable to the mother's presence or absence). The problem with young toddlers, however, is that no sooner is the mother out of the room than the mothers of other children and the two toddler-group leaders markedly change in their handling of the child. They become more watchful and nurturant; in short, they assume the maternal function. In the symbiotic psychotic children, when the mother is absent, the relationship of the therapist to the child also changes markedly at times—the therapist becoming more closely engaged with the child. Thus, more than the mother's presence varies, and it is difficult to refer specific changes in the child solely to the presence or absence of the mother. But in spite of this, the method gives some interesting observations which are relatively comparable for all of the children.

In the normal toddlers, for example, the children not only worsen but also improve in certain kinds of functioning in the mother's absence, and also change in the quality of their functioning. In any of these cases there is a suggestion that the child's functioning is not yet autonomous but draws in some way upon the mother for its enhancement or impairment. Thus, one child—a child whose gross motor (locomotor) behavior is highly developed for his age, and whose mother has always nurtured and valued that behavior—falls off in the level of his gross motor behavior when the mother is absent. This child has always obliged the mother by performing well, in the way that she wanted, but such performance still seems dependent on the mother's presence to some extent. At what point will motor excellence become autonomous (Hartmann, 1939) in the sense that it is maintained even in the mother's absence?[3]

Another child, in sharp contrast, had a motor pattern that was typically aimless and wandering; he fell often, and hard, without a whimper. His mother had a hand's-off policy in many aspects of her son's care, refusing to frustrate him, neglecting to support bowel and bladder control, ignoring his many hard falls. His aimless motor behavior seemed to lack in internal direction what he lacked in direction from his mother. But this behavior, too, seemed to be associated with the physical presence of his mother; in her absence he improved in his gross motor behavior—falling less, for example, and becoming somewhat more goal-directed. This close link between his motor functioning and his relationship to his mother perhaps foreshadowed the later improvement in motor functioning that came when the mother-child relationship changed. When verbalization developed in the child, and the mother was able to use this medium of communication to provide a more focused and organizing care, the child showed a developmental gain not only in the verbal area but also in the motor area.

In the symbiotic psychotic children, other phenomena were observed. As has been pointed out previously (Mahler, Furer, Settlage, 1959), these children often show a secondary regression to autistic mechanisms. In our observations, a psychotic child in whom autistic mechanisms currently predominated showed almost no reaction to the mother's absence. It was extremely difficult for observers to make differential descriptions of the child's level of functioning when mother

---

3 The motor apparatus has a certain primary autonomy, yet can be, to some extent, drawn into conflict and into motive patterns. The final achievement of secondary autonomy seems to be to some degree dependent upon the mother-child relationship and the child's endowment (Hartmann, 1939).

was present or absent; she behaved at both times according to certain stereotyped autistic patterns. Another psychotic child by contrast, one in whom symbiotic mechanisms were currently strong, showed a marked reaction to the mother's absence—his behavior in the two situations (mother present, mother absent) being markedly different. Thus, in the psychotic children, the reaction to the experimental variation of the mother's presence may itself be an indicator of the degree to which autistic or symbiotic mechanisms predominate. (Similar phenomena are seen in the normal babies. At certain subphases of the separation-individuation phase there is normally a quite intense reaction to the mother's absence, whereas in other subphases the pleasure in exercising the function then ascendant seems to render the child relatively oblivious to the mother's temporary absence.)

Conclusion

We have described an interconnected group of studies bearing upon the separation-individuation process. The settings that we have evolved for observing children—a specially planned playroom for normal toddlers and a therapeutic situation for psychotic children—were described. While we are convinced that these observational settings offer rich possibilities for research, our experience is that a changing array of research strategies best allows us to take advantage of these possibilities. We have presented here some of our research strategies, some problems that they presented, some incidental findings that grew out of these very problems, and some illustrative findings.

References

Coleman, R.W., Kris, E., & Provence, S. (1953). The Study of Variations of Early Parental Attitudes *Psychoanal. Study Child* 8:20–47.

Hartmann, H. (1939). Ego Psychology and the Problem of Adaptation New York: International Universities Press, 1958.

Mahler, M.S. (1952). On Child Psychosis and Schizophrenia: Autistic and Symbiotic Infantile Psychoses *Psychoanal. Study Child* 7: 286–305.

——— (1957). On Two Crucial Phases of Integration Concerning Problems of Identity: Separation-Individuation and Bisexual Identification Paper read at American Psychoanalytic Association.

——— (1958). Autism and Symbiosis, Two Extreme Disturbances of Identity *Int. J. Psychoanal.* 39:77–82.

——— (1961). On Sadness and Grief in Infancy and Childhood: Loss and Restoration of the Symbiotic Love Object *Psychoanal. Study Child* 16:332–351.

——— (1963). Thoughts about Development and Individuation *Psychoanal. Study Child* 18:307–324.

——— & Furer, M. (1960). Observations on Research Regarding the "Symbiotic Syndrome" of Infantile Psychosis *Psychoanal. Quart.* 9:317–327. [Also in this volume.].

———& ——— (1963). Certain Aspects of the Separation-Individuation Phase *Psychoanal. Q.* 32:1–14. [Also in this volume.].

———& ——— & Settlage, C.F. (1959). Severe Emotional Disturbances in Childhood: Psychosis In: American Handbook of Psychiatry ed. S. Arieti. New York: Basic Books.

Spitz, R.A. (1945). Hospitalism *Psychoanal. Study Child* 1:53–74.

——— (1946). Hospitalism: A Follow-up Report *Psychoanal. Study Child* 2:113–117.

CHAPTER 25

Certain Aspects of the Separation-Individuation Phase

With **Margaret Mahler M.D**
(1963). *Psychoanal. Q., (32):1-14.*

This study is supported by a grant from the Psychoanalytic Research and Development Fund. It is being carried on at the Masters Children's Center, New York, in collaboration with David L. Mayer, M.D., Fred Pine, Ph.D., and Herman Roiphe, M.D., and with the assistance of Anni Bergman and Edith Atkin.

Study of the normal development in the separation-individuation phase (from the end of the first year through the second and third years of life) was suggested by the cardinal hypothesis concerning symbiotic child psychosis derived from Mahler's studies. This hypothesis states that in symbiotic child psychosis the biologically predetermined maturation of ego apparatuses, together with a concomitant lag in development toward emotional separation individuation, is experienced as a catastrophic threat by the child in the symbiotic phase of development. There is a cessation of further ego development and fragmentation of the ego seems to ensue from the panic which the potentially psychotic child experiences when confronted with the task of separation-individuation.

Our study of normal infants, ranging in age from six to ten months to three years, has as its focus the elucidation of various aspects of the separation individuation process. Most studies to date, based on reconstruction and direct observation, have emphasized the child's passive experience of being physically separated from the mother, and have correctly indicated the traumatic effect of this passive experience and its disturbing effect on personality development. From our experience, however, it would appear that the separation process of the child from the mother is the prerequisite for normal individuation. Normal separation-individuation makes possible the child's achievement of separate functioning in the presence of the mother while continually confronting the child with minimal threats of object loss. However, in contrast to situations of traumatic separation, normal individuation-separation takes place in the setting of a developmental readiness for, and pleasure in, independent functioning. The predominance of pleasure in separate functioning in the atmosphere of libidinal availability of the mother enables the child to overcome that measure of separation anxiety that seems to obtain with each new step of separate functioning. This is illustrated with particular clarity in the development of motor skills since these allow for active experimentation with separation and return.

Several aspects of the separation-individuation process have especially impressed us. First, in the symbiotic phase which precedes separation-individuation there does not appear to be a clear awareness of the body-self boundaries as separate from the mother. Toward the end of the first year there occurs tentative experimentation at separation-individuation, such as self-feeding, feeding of mother, and, later, peek-a-boo games. After many intermediate steps, toward the end of the third year this process culminates in a relatively stable differentiation of self-nonself, self-object, inside-outside, animate-inanimate. Second, the separation-individuation process parallels the maturation and integration of such autonomous functions of the ego as motility and language. Characteristic individual patterns of integrated functioning emerge from the circular interaction between the child's innate patterns involving these primary autonomous functions in such areas as signaling of needs and the mother's selective perception of and response to these needs.

METHODOLOGY

Our aim in setting up this study of normal infants was to obtain material comparable to that already acquired from a therapeutic-action-research program of preschool-aged symbiotic psychotic children. We set up procedures in which each psychoanalytically trained worker, who also participates in the therapy project, observes the mother-infant interaction and interviews the mother. This procedure elicits valuable material even from these normal mothers who are not motivated by a need for treatment. Evaluation of the material from these interviews in our research conferences has enabled us to focus our investigation on those areas that are most comparable to the material from the treatment group.

In addition to these interviews, the infants and their mothers are seen in a specially designed large playroom divided into the mothers' and the children's sections only by a waist-high partition. The mother's presence and interplay with her infant allows an optimal position for observing the normal separation individuation process as it evolves. The infants and their mothers attend the group for several hours four mornings a week. Each week the mother is interviewed alone and also with her child present. The interviews with the mother alone permit us to assess her personality; the interviews with her infant present make it possible to evaluate various aspects of the mother-child relationship. Further, each research associate observes the particular mother and child he interviews as they participate in the group. Two participant observers collect clinical material of a general nature and also focus on specific behavior in the mother and child that the interview data has shown us to be particularly relevant to the separation-individuation at that time.

As our study progressed, we found that from the middle of the first year into the second year of life there was some evidence of an increased differentiation of the body-self in general and striking individual differences in the timing, quality, and hierarchy of the constellation of emerging ego functions in the infants. Among the many elements of the mother-child relationship in the early period of infancy we were especially impressed with the 'selection of cues' which appears to be important in the genesis and later development of the differentiated body-image and of individual characteristics. As illustrated in the clinical material which follows, we observed that infants present a large variety of cues to indicate needs, tension, and pleasure, and that, in a complex manner, the mother selectively responds to only certain of these cues. The infant gradually alters his behavior in relation to this selective response in a characteristic way— the result of his innate endowment and the mother-child relationship. From this circular interaction, patterns of behavior, functioning, and certain over-all qualities of the personality of the child emerge. We seem to see here the beginning of the child as an individual, separate from his mother.

I

Sara, a particularly out-going, well-endowed baby, and her mother, Mrs. Y, entered the group when the infant was in the second half of her first year. When tested at eleven months, Sara performed two months beyond her chronological age level in 'personal-social' development on the Gesell scales. Her communications[1] and signals were easily understood and similarly interpreted by all observers. The mother, however, although particularly devoted and closely attending, showed a peculiar inability to understand and respond in a natural and simple way to the baby's signals and to meet Sara's needs as her individuation progressed. If the child asked for something that the mother had not anticipated, Mrs. Y became confused. For example, one of the first things the mother recognized as a communication from the child was Sara's 'honking': Sara honked once and the mother swept her into her arms, explaining that she wanted to be picked up; when Sara repeated the same sound the mother explained that she wanted a cracker and gave her one; when Sara honked a third time, the mother appeared perplexed and asked an observer what Sara could want now.

A reaching gesture interpreted by the mother, according to her own state of mind, as a wish on Sara's part to be picked up one day, on the next day would be explained by the mother as Sara's wish to hold her hand as she learned to walk. The mother's interpretation of signals was modified depending on whether the child impressed her as a continuation of herself or as a separate individual. This mother, we predict, will continue to resist separation and yet maintain it as highly valuable, turning intermittently and suddenly to Sara for the

---

1 We are grateful to Sally Provence, M.D. of the Child Development Center at Yale University for her testing of these children.

direction of the baby's own care, always expecting Sara to function at a distance and yet as an extension of herself.

II

Danny, just under thirteen months, had developed considerable ability to function independently, particularly in the motor sphere. This quality appeared to be fostered by the mother's striving for her children's independence,[2] her defense against impulses to hold and cuddle him, and her preference for communication through distance receptors—hearing and sight. During the weeks preceding the events to be described, however, Danny's expressed need for his mother had occurred more frequently and vociferously. He crawled scramblingly in the direction in which she disappeared, refused substitute gratifications in her absence, and bellowed in grief-stricken fashion on her return from brief absences. The mother continued to strive to have the little boy function independently despite his increasing frustration. She often refused contact, holding her hands above her head as he pulled at her skirt.

At age thirteen months, it was noted that Danny seemed more 'grown-up' and more boy-like in that his relations to adults, other than his mother, and to children changed abruptly from transient, rather blank, eye engagements to long smiles of pleasure and seeming recognition. When this was brought to the mother's attention, she expressed no surprise but stated that he was 'grown-up now' as he had walked for the first time two days before. Subsequently, Danny showed much less separation anxiety.

---

2 *We had the older sister of this child in our group for two years.*

In this case apparently the demand for separate functioning had exceeded Danny's capacity to function separately in the mother's presence—that is to say, exceeded his capacity to control his degree of separateness by his own motor efforts. Learning to walk, therefore, brought a marked relief from separation anxiety; he was able to gratify a chronically frustrated wish toward the mother—to initiate physical contact—and the external and perhaps internal wish to comply with the mother's high values. Concomitantly the quality of Danny's relatedness seemed to imply that a new level of individuation had been achieved.

III

Cathie, eighteen months of age, and her mother, Mrs. A, entered the group when the child was a year old. The mother's narcissistic pride in her child was of such a nature that she seemed to regard the little girl as an extension of her own self and, at the same time, as a wonderful semianimate doll. Within the limits of this type of relationship, Cathie was capable of a great deal of precocious, seemingly independent activity which, however, appeared to be somewhat skewed in the direction of achievement and performance rather than in pleasure in her activity. To an unusual degree this child was ready to approach any adult and elicit a strong, admiring response which seemed to serve the mother's narcissistic need. It was our impression that the precocious development of Cathie's ego functioning was perhaps enhanced and promoted by the mother's too exclusive preoccupation with her child (the father was serving in the United States Army abroad). We wonder about many aspects of Cathie's development, which we predict will continue to show precocity for a relatively long period; will the more mature object-related aspects of her ego functioning (the capacity for empathy and for reciprocity, for giving as well as receiving) catch up with this child's advanced autonomy or will it lag as a result of the relative exclusiveness of the mother-child interaction? We feel, on the other hand, that in this unusually well-endowed child, other aspects of her personality may develop and the mother's narcissistic pride may change its form. The result could be a shift in the balance toward object-relatedness and a particularly rich personality development in Cathie.

IV

Carl and his mother, Mrs. H, were first seen by us when the baby was four months old. Mrs. H is a vigorous, masculine woman, with a gruff, pal-like manner. As a child her physical activity had to be restrained because she was in the care of an elderly woman. She emphasized the fact that her husband is an athletically built man who has a great deal of enthusiasm. They were both very pleased that their first child was a boy although the mother recalled that for a few days she was concerned because the boy had inherited her own weak chin.

When Carl first entered the group at four months of age he had just been weaned. Whenever he was near his mother he tried to suck at any part of her body or clothing that he could reach. She grimly ignored these signals and did not remember his behavior a week later when it had ceased. However, when his sucking seemed to become very intense, his need was responded to by the mother moving him in a vertical position up and down on her lap. She told the interviewer that this activity always made Carl feel better. Four months later at eight months, when Carl was able to stand by himself, we saw him repeat the same up-and-down movements of his body at times when he appeared to be fatigued or was frustrated and particularly whenever he became aware that his mother had left the room. He thereby actively repeated alone the behavior which had been initiated by his mother with him to lessen his tension. When his mother returned to him after an absence, she repeated these movements with him in her arms although she was not consciously aware of her actions. When this bodily activity of Carl's was brought to her attention, she pointed to the fact that this was how he showed his pleasure, especially when he became excited on his father's homecoming in the evening.

Starting at about five or six months of age his parents played their particular form of the peek-a-boo game with Carl by covering his face with his blanket, removing it, and saying, 'There he is'. Later the child occasionally repeated the game himself with the blanket, but the mother stated that an ecstatic peek-a-boo activity began at about eleven months of age when he was able to run behind the couch. He hid and then stood up expecting his parents to say, 'There he is', again actively using his body. At fourteen months of age he greeted newcomers to the house with this same game, insisting by grunts and groans that they do as his parents had done. This behavior illustrates Carl's effort to master the anxiety of separate functioning by repeating himself the highly libidinally cathected activity that had taken place between him and his mother. The selection of a motor activity from among many other kinds is consistent with his general motor orientation that probably has an innate predisposition but also reflects both parents' preferred modality of interplay with Carl. He integrated into his own rendition of the peek-a-boo game the earlier, passively experienced, and then actively used, behavior of moving his body up and down. We believe that doing this for himself, as his mother had done for him at four months, was his first pattern and preferred form of mastering anxiety in her absence.

At fourteen months Carl displayed certain over-all qualities in his behavior and personality that are very similar to those of his mother. This development seems to have come partly as a result of their interrelationship and by complex means that we have yet to define. However, it appears that it is in large measure based on the particular form of the sending and responding to cues between mother and child. For instance, at four months, as described above, the mother grimly denied Carl's reaction to weaning and his insistent demand to continue sucking at her body, determinedly substituting another form of tension reduction.

At about six months of age when Carl appeared to be distressed, he made various noises, all of which appeared to the observers to indicate this distress. However, the mother chose to interpret one of the noises as his wish to be picked up and he gradually limited his expression to this sound. When questioned about this Mrs. H said she always knew when Carl wanted her.

In many other areas of her interaction with Carl, this mother's character traits of determined persistence and directedness were expressed. When Carl started to walk he made a very striking contrast to some of the other children. The latter seemed to wander about happily pleased with their newly found ability of independent locomotion. Carl, on the other hand, always seemed to be going after something and if it was hard to get, he kept after it again and again. It was very impressive to see him return repeatedly to an object that he had not been able to reach a few weeks before because his balance had not been good enough, until he finally was able to get at it. Mrs. H has often remarked that Carl will have to become stubborn if he wants to deal with her.

Carl's experimentation with differentiating his own body from his mother's probably started as early as the fourth month, but was much re-enforced at the time of that further step in reality testing in differentiating the image of his mother from that of strangers.

When he was four months of age we observed very little exploration of his mother's body by Carl. The mother said that he occasionally seemed to look in her mouth at that age but it was at about six to seven months of age that he became very interested in exploring the inside of her mouth and nostrils with his finger. He also began to pat her on the face sometimes rather forcefully. At this age we frequently observed his offering a cracker from his mouth to his mother. It was at about seven to eight months of age when he showed the onset of anxiety with strange adults.

V

A mother-child pair in which the mother and baby appeared to be diametrically different in temperament were Mrs. B and Heather, forty-one weeks old when first seen. The mother was efficient, abrupt, impatient, impulsive, and loudly articulate. Though cultured and intelligent, she was rough in her behavior and almost crudely so with Heather, her small, puny baby. She gave little consistent, predictable, or tender mothering to the infant, and set goals and 'deadlines' for her baby's developmental achievements; from the beginning she imposed her own rhythm and needs on the child.

At fourteen months, Heather did not show any of her mother's vigor and abruptness. The mother's seemingly unmotivated bursts of attentiveness, unpredictable overstimulation, and rough, if playful, handling, alternating with long periods of inattentiveness, did not seem to be incorporated in the form of the separation-individuation pattern of this child.

As early as the second interview with Mrs. B, it was noticed that a constant, uneven struggle was going on between this mother and her barely ten-month-old 'lap baby'. The mother was most eager to 'discuss' her observations and 'opinions'. Heather seemed to be regarded as a kind of accessory by the mother. Mrs. B never failed to gather a few toys and bring them along with Heather to the interviewing office, clearly as a substitute for her own attention. She would place the baby on the floor near her chair, take the child on her lap for a few minutes when she began to fret, and then 'plop' her down again. On one occasion, in her impatient, abrupt, and ridding gesture, the mother jammed the chair leg on the baby's foot, bruising it. There were many other evidences of Mrs. B's efforts to extricate herself and offer transitional objects to Heather in place of tender mothering.

When the child was eleven months of age, Mrs. B was so intent on Heather's learning to walk that, holding her by one hand, she walked with the baby at her pace, not the child's, so that Heather was dragged along. The mother was disappointed at the child's 'late' walking. But long before she walked, Heather exercised and practiced in a patient, persistent, and competent way all kinds of preliminary well-coordinated motor patterns. At nine months she would propel herself to her goal with a belly crawl; later, when she could pull herself up, she would climb from chair to table, keeping perfect balance, and then examine the mirror surface of the observation booth. By eleven months, she seemed to fret less frequently to be taken on the lap but instead would pull herself up at her mother's feet and stand there. Even before she learned to walk she showed amazing innate resourcefulness and unusual endowment for manipulating toys and occupying herself with her own body skills. If she were in danger of losing her balance, she would slide into a safe sitting position.

By age one year, Heather had accepted separate functioning, or individuation, on the level demanded by her mother. It seemed that she complied emotionally even before her autonomous ego was mature enough in the locomotor area to function on the level of the walking toddler. In this way she complied with and complemented, rather than imitated or identified with, the mother. A few weeks later, she could occupy herself contentedly for a half hour with various toys, looking at her mother occasionally but not crawling to her. All this was done with hardly a sound and only rare appeals to her mother or other adults.

This placid, patient little girl was amazingly resourceful and self-sufficient, and showed remarkable readiness to accept substitute satisfactions as well as substitute objects, in marked contrast to her mother.

It is interesting to note, however, that in some of her behavior during separation-individuation, Heather did take over patterns of the mother. For instance, in her self-comforting devices she seemed to play mother to herself with patterns in many ways reminiscent of the mother's handling of her in the symbiotic phase. In her solitary occupation at the beginning of the separation individuation phase one could see in her self-comforting peek-a-boo pattern, the derivatives of earlier peek-a-boo games with the mother. Also, Heather showed increasing interest in gathering, holding, and manipulating toys, acting out what her mother had done for her.

When she began to walk she turned to transitional inanimate objects and appealed less and less to her mother. Instead of toddling to her mother—usually engrossed in conversation with other mothers in the group, often with her back turned to Heather—she would quietly toddle to a rocking boat and rock herself as vigorously as possible, in a way reminiscent of the mother's handling of her. Heather also used the same vigor when riding the hobby-horse or when working the seesaw. Elements in her active individuation patterns were obviously those of the rough handling she had passively experienced and visibly enjoyed in her first year of life with mother.

CONCLUSIONS

Certain postulations are possible from the material thus far available from our study of separation-individuation in normal children.

One generally assumes that a normal mother reacts to cues sent out by her child depending upon the needs of the child for her. We do not know whether these changes in behavior and expressions of the infant, apprehended as cues by the mother, are only discharge phenomena or whether they are also active communications. In general, however, we have observed a shift from discharge to signaling, as well as the mother's accurate, selective, or distorted responses to these cues which indicate the child's need for her. It is also apparent that mothers vary in their interpretation of the degree of independence or new developmental gain indicated by certain cues and respond in accordance with their own interpretations. Although many cues are misinterpreted, or even read into the child by the mother, normal infants have an amazing capacity to adapt to the needs, emotions, and demands of the mother.

In addition to the separation-individuation process in the infant, it appears that there is a concomitant and similar process of separation in every mother from her child. This can be observed in the mother's various misreadings of cues, especially in terms of whether a need is indicated and of what type. It is believed that the change of the infant from a 'babe in arms' to a toddler who can physically separate from his mother also marks a developmental step in motherhood, one that produces many conflicts in the mother. In our investigation it became increasingly evident that the normal mother anticipates the separation individuation of her baby and that this anticipation is one of the determinants of her behavior toward her 'babe in arms' long before the infant is ready for separation-individuation.

The clinical material describes many instances in which the mother reads cues correctly, others in which they are misread, and still others where cues are selectively neglected. The mother's selections often indicate conflicts in her and are not simply errors of perception of the child's needs. However, the result in the child's pattern of individuation in our experience has proven to be determined in large part by the mother's attempts to adapt to the maturation of her child, as well as the child's own active efforts to adapt to his mother's conscious and unconscious fantasies.

There appears to be a wide range of response in normal mothers in dealing with the anticipated separation from their children. In some cases we have seen reactions that appear close to mourning; in others an attempt is made to precipitate actively the independent functioning of the child; in other instances subtle combinations of or alternations between ridding herself of and clinging to the infant are evinced.

During the process of separation-individuation we suspect that there are particular developments of the unconscious meaning that her infant has for the mother. Very likely the infant has certain fixed meanings for the mother, but it also seems to be true that these meanings change with the maturation of the infant, and that the mother changes her behavior accordingly. For example, it appears that the infant, with varying degrees of intensity of cathexis, represents a body part for the mother, usually her illusory phallus. The mother's behavior toward her infant is molded by this fantasy but is modified by the infant's innate equipment and maturation. For instance, when the child develops the capacity for separate locomotor functioning, the mother will project her fantasy into different patterns of expected behavior from the child.

Beyond the mother's specific reactions to cues which indicate the child's maturation and consequent readiness to function separately, the mother's general character is a major determinant in her reactions to the child, and the child must adapt to her reactions in some way. The clinical material illustrates some of the child's adaptations to characteristics of the mother as was seen in the directedness that developed in Carl which paralleled a similar directedness in his mother, and the self-sufficiency and patient independent functioning and placidity of Heather was an effort to comply with and complement her mother's attitudes. The alternation between symbiotic needs and ridding reactions found in Mrs. Y generated an ambitendency on the part of Sara which resulted in a constant back-and-forth movement between them.

In general, as the child grows older and his personality unfolds and shows increasing complexity, we continue to find as its central core, and pervading it throughout, the residue of the earliest infant-mother relationship.

Bibliography
Manuel Furer MD

Principal Papers

Manuel Furer (1950): Reaction to pain as determined by the galvanic skin reflex. *Proceedings of the Association of Research in Nervous and Menial Disease.*

Manuel Furer (1959): Severe emotional disturbances in childhood. In: *American Handbook of Psychiatry,* New York: Basic Books.

Manuel Furer (1964): The development of a pre-school symbiotic child: Description of the treatment. *Psychoanal. St. Child,* 19:448–469. New York: International Universities Press.

Manuel Furer (1967): Some developmental aspects of the super-ego; the origin of empathy in childhood. *Int. J. Psycho-Anal.,* 48:277–289.

Manuel Furer (1971): Observations on the treatment of the symbiotic syndrome of infantile psychosis: Reality reconstruction, and drive maturation. In: *Essays in Honor of Margaret S. Mahler,* ed. J. McDevitt & C. Settlage. New York: International Universities Press, pp. 473–485.

Manuel Furer (1972): The history of the superego concept in psychoanalysis: A review of the literature. In: *Moral Values and the Superego Concept in Psychoanalysis,* ed. S. C. Post. New York: International Universities Press, pp. 11–63.

Manuel Furer (1974): The Psychoanalytic Process, the Therapeutic Alliance, and Child Observation. Paper presented at the Mid-Winter Meeting of the American Psychoanalytic Association December (1974). Unpublished.

Manuel Furer (1976): Construction and reconstruction in the tripartite treatment of a psychotic girl. *J. Phila Assn. Psychoanal.*, 3, No. 4.

Manuel Furer (1977): Psychoanalytic dialogue: Kleinian theory today. *J. Amer. Psychoanal. Assn.*, 25:371–386.

Manuel Furer (1977): Personality organization during the recovery of a severely disturbed girl; the origin of an as-if personality. In: *The Borderline Personalities: The Concept, The Syndrome, The Patient*, ed. P. Hartocollis. New York: International Universities Press, pp. 457–473.

Manuel Furer (1985): Transference Terminable and Interminable; A Fifteen Year Study of the Training Analysis and its Impact on Future Analytic Work. A.A. Brill Memorial Lecture of the New York Psychoanalytic Society. Unpublished.

Manuel Furer (1988): On the reorganization of compromise formations, from self defeat to success. In: *How Does Treatment Help? On the Modes of Therapeutic Action of Psychoanalytic Therapy*, ed. A. Rothstein. New York: International Universities Press, pp. 31–39.

Manuel Furer (1998): Changes in psychoanalytic technique: Progressive or retrogressive. *Journal of Clinical Psychoanalysis*, 7:209–235.

Co-Authored Papers and Books

Manuel Furer (1957): (with M. Horowitz, L. Tec, and J. Toolan) Internalized objects in children. *Am. J. Orthopsychiat.*, 27:88–95.

Manuel Furer (1960): (with M. Mahler) Research on the symbiotic syndrome of infantile psychosis. *Psychoanal. Q.*, 29:317–327.

Manuel Furer (1963): (with F. Pine) Studies of the separation-individuation phase: A methodical overview. *Psychoanal. St. Child*, 18:325–342, New York: International Universities Press.

Manuel Furer (1963): (with M. Mahler) Certain aspects of the separation-individuation phase. *Psychoanal. Q.*, 32:1–14.

Manuel Furer (1966): (with M. Mahler) Symbiosis: Reply to Welland. *Int. J. Psycho-Anal.*, 47:559–560.

Manuel Furer (1968): (with M. Mahler) *On Human Symbiosis and the Vicissitudes of Individuation. Infantile Psychosis, Vol. 1*. New York: International Universities Press.

Manuel Furer (1972): (with M. Mahler) Child psychosis: A theoretical statement and its implications. *J. Autism & Childhood Schizophrenia* 2:(3).

Panels and Discussions

Manuel Furer (1962): Psychic development and the prevention of mental illness. *J. Amer. Psychoanal. Assn.*, 10:606–626.

Manuel Furer (1970): re: A follow up investigation of schizophrenic children treated in residence. *Psychosocial Process*, 1:19–71.

Manuel Furer (1971): re: The effects of object loss on the body image of schizophrenic girls. *Bull. Assn. Psychoanal. Med.*, 10:31–35.

Manuel Furer (1971): To cast away: A vestibular forerunner of the superego. *Psychoanal. Q.*, 40:544–545.

Manuel Furer (1977): re: Nonverbal aspects of child and adult psychoanalysis. *Panel.* J. Amer. Psychoanal. Assn., 25:693–705.

Manuel Furer (1979): re: Reconstruction of an accident experienced during the rapprochement subphase; a paper presented by Muriel Chaves Winestine to the New York Psychoanalytic Society, September 25, (1979). *Psychoanal. Q.*, 51:(1) (1981).

Manuel Furer (1997): re: Modes of influence in psychoanalysis. *J. Amer. Psychoanal. Assn.* 45:217–229.

Manuel Furer (1998): re: Renik, O.: Beyond subjectivity and objectivity: Current issues in psychoanalytic technique. *Journal of Clinical Psychoanalysis*, 7:209–235.

Manuel Furer (1999): Regression: Essential clinical condition or iatrogenic phenomenon. *J. Amer. Psychoanal. Assn.*, 47:1169–1179.

Manuel Furer (1999): Discussion of panel on enactment. *Journal of Clinical Psychoanalysis*, 8:62–93.

Manuel Furer (2000): Modern defense analysis: Three perspectives on the same hours. *J. Amer. Psychoanal. Assn.*, 48:29–40.

Reviews and Introductions

Manuel Furer (1964): Infants in Institutions: Comparison of Their Development with Family Reared Infants During the First Year. Review. *Psychoanal. Q.*, 33: 291.

Manuel Furer (1965): Modern Perspectives in Child Development (Essays in Honor of Milton J. Senn. Review. *Psychoanal. Q.*, 34:289–291.

Manuel Furer (1965): Problems of Sleep and Dreams in Children. Review. *Psychoanal. Q.*, 34:120–121.

Manuel Furer (1965): The Bender Gestalt Test for Young Children. Review. Psychoanal. Q., 34:123–124.

Manuel Furer (1968): The Hampstead Psychoanalytic Index: A Study of the Psychoanalytic Material of a Two Year Old Child. Review. *Psychoanal. Q.*, 37: *439–440*.

Manuel Furer (1969): Discussions of the Vienna Psychoanalytic Society on Suicide in (1910). Review. *Psychoanal. Q.*, 38:*130–132*.

Manuel Furer (1970): Phobias, their nature and control. *Review. Psychoanal Quart.*, 39:*130–132*.

Manuel Furer (1998): Controversies in Contemporary Psychoanalysis. Lectures from the Faculty of the New York Psychoanalytic Institute, ed. Finer, Nersessian, Perri. Introduction. New York: International Universities Press.

Manuel Furer (1998): Consciousness Redux: Papers of Martin Stein, ed. B. Stimmel. Northvale, NJ & London: Jason Aronson. Introduction to the paper "The Unobjectionable Part of the Transference," pp. *119–122*.

Manuel Furer (2000): Passion's risk: A review of Love and Hate in the Analytic Setting by Glenn Gabbard. *J. Contemp. Psychoanal.*, 36:*148–155*.

www.ingramcontent.com/pod-product-compliance
Lightning Source LLC
Chambersburg PA
CBHW062115020426
42335CB00013B/971